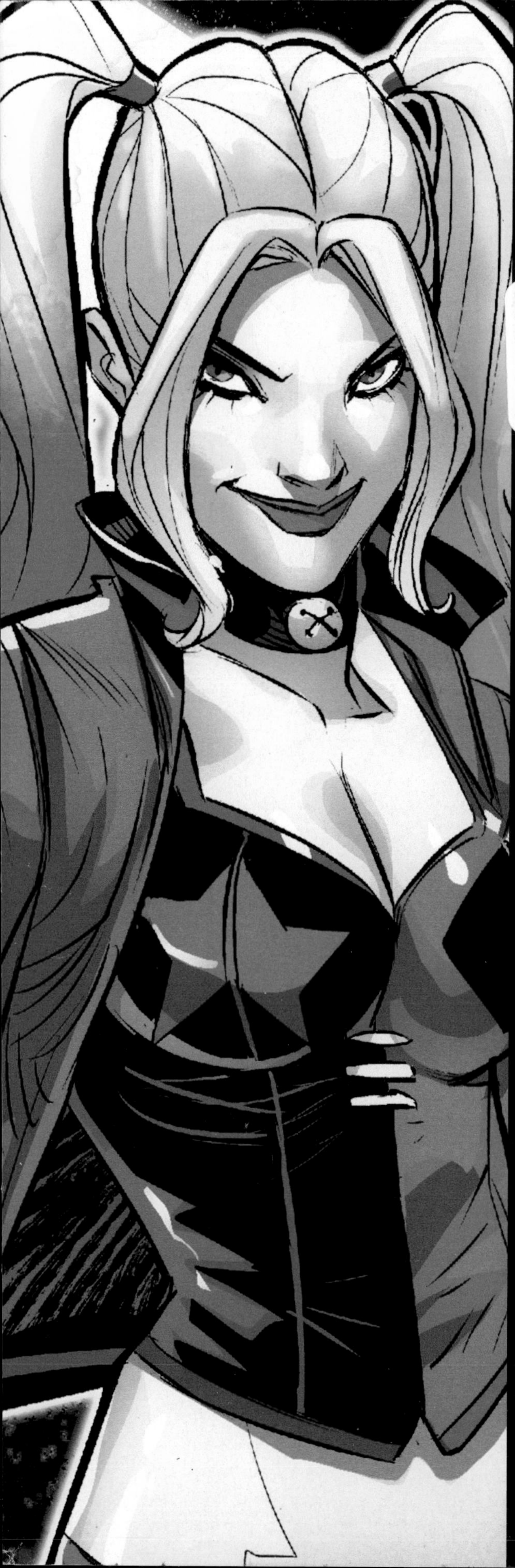

VOLUME 6

BLACK, WHITE AND RED ALL OVER

HARLEY QUINN

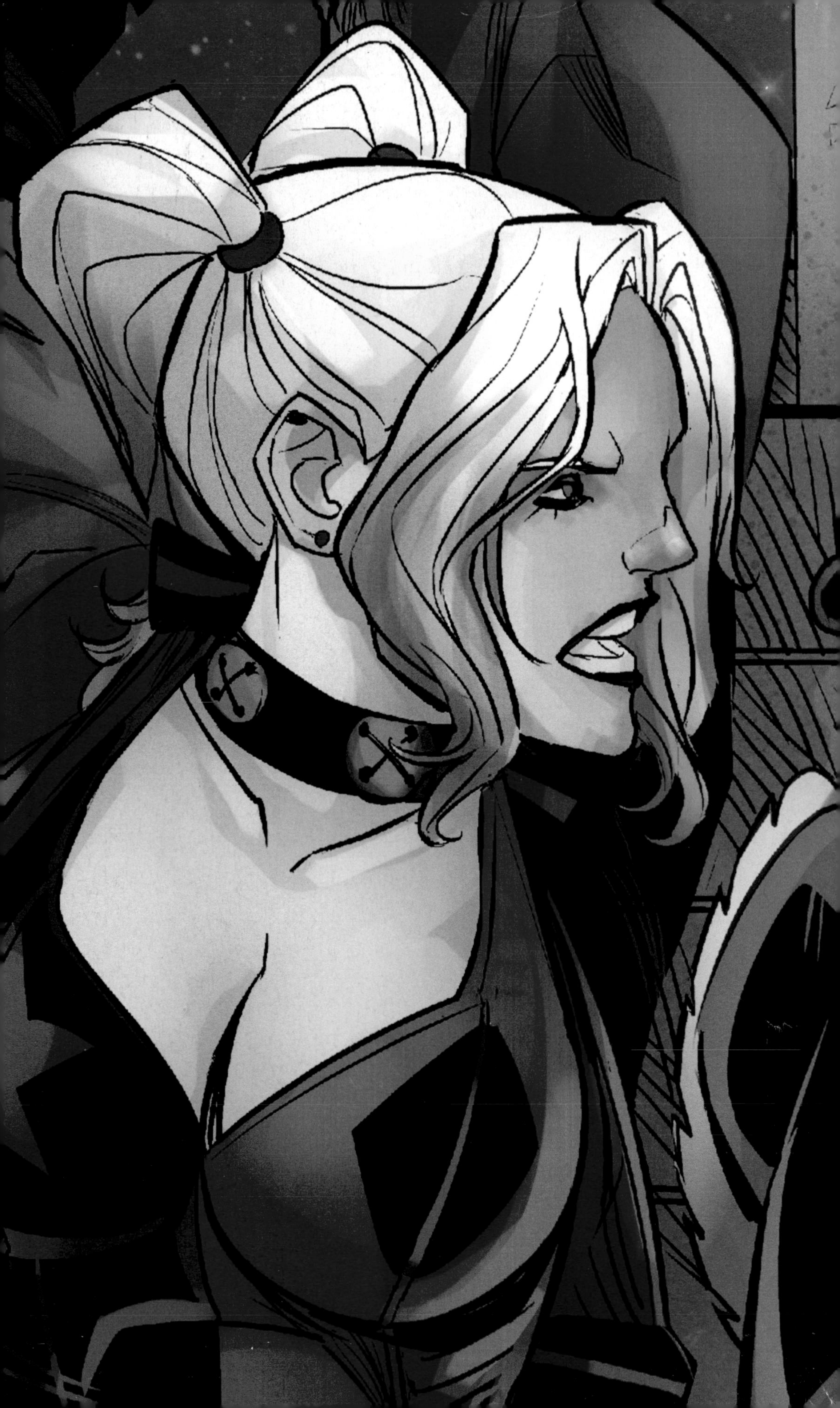

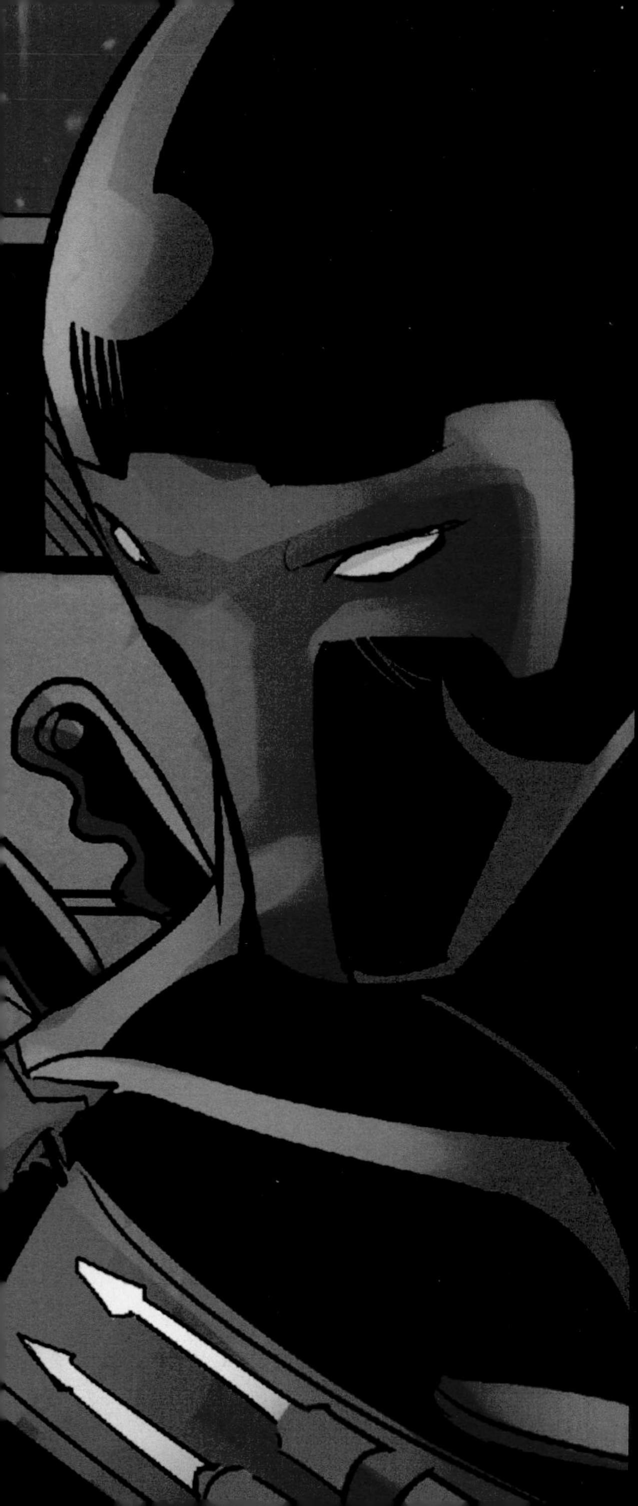

HARLEY QUINN

VOLUME 6
BLACK, WHITE AND RED ALL OVER

WRITTEN BY
AMANDA CONNER
JIMMY PALMIOTTI

ART BY
JOHN TIMMS
CHAD HARDIN
ELSA CHARRETIER
MORITAT

COLOR BY
ALEX SINCLAIR
HI-FI

LETTERS BY

CHRIS CONROY Editor – Original Series
DAVE WIELGOSZ Assistant Editor – Original Series
JEB WOODARD Group Editor – Collected Editions
ROBIN WILDMAN Editor – Collected Edition
STEVE COOK Design Director – Books
DAMIAN RYLAND Publication Design

BOB HARRAS Senior VP – Editor-in-Chief, DC Comics

DIANE NELSON President
DAN DiDIO Publisher
JIM LEE Publisher
GEOFF JOHNS President & Chief Creative Officer
AMIT DESAI Executive VP – Business & Marketing Strategy, Direct to Consumer & Global Franchise Management
SAM ADES Senior VP – Direct to Consumer
BOBBIE CHASE VP – Talent Development
MARK CHIARELLO Senior VP – Art, Design & Collected Editions
JOHN CUNNINGHAM Senior VP – Sales & Trade Marketing
ANNE DePIES Senior VP – Business Strategy, Finance & Administration
DON FALLETTI VP – Manufacturing Operations
LAWRENCE GANEM VP – Editorial Administration & Talent Relations
ALISON GILL Senior VP – Manufacturing & Operations
HANK KANALZ Senior VP – Editorial Strategy & Administration
JAY KOGAN VP – Legal Affairs
THOMAS LOFTUS VP – Business Affairs
JACK MAHAN VP – Business Affairs
NICK J. NAPOLITANO VP – Manufacturing Administration
EDDIE SCANNELL VP – Consumer Marketing
COURTNEY SIMMONS Senior VP – Publicity & Communications
JIM (SKI) SOKOLOWSKI VP – Comic Book Specialty Sales & Trade Marketing
NANCY SPEARS VP – Mass, Book, Digital Sales & Trade Marketing

HARLEY QUINN VOLUME 6: BLACK, WHITE AND RED ALL OVER

DC Comics, 2900 West Alameda Ave., Burbank, CA 91505
Printed by LSC Communications, Salem, VA, USA. 4/28/17. First Printing.
ISBN: 978-1-4012-7259-3

Library of Congress Cataloging-in-Publication Data is available.

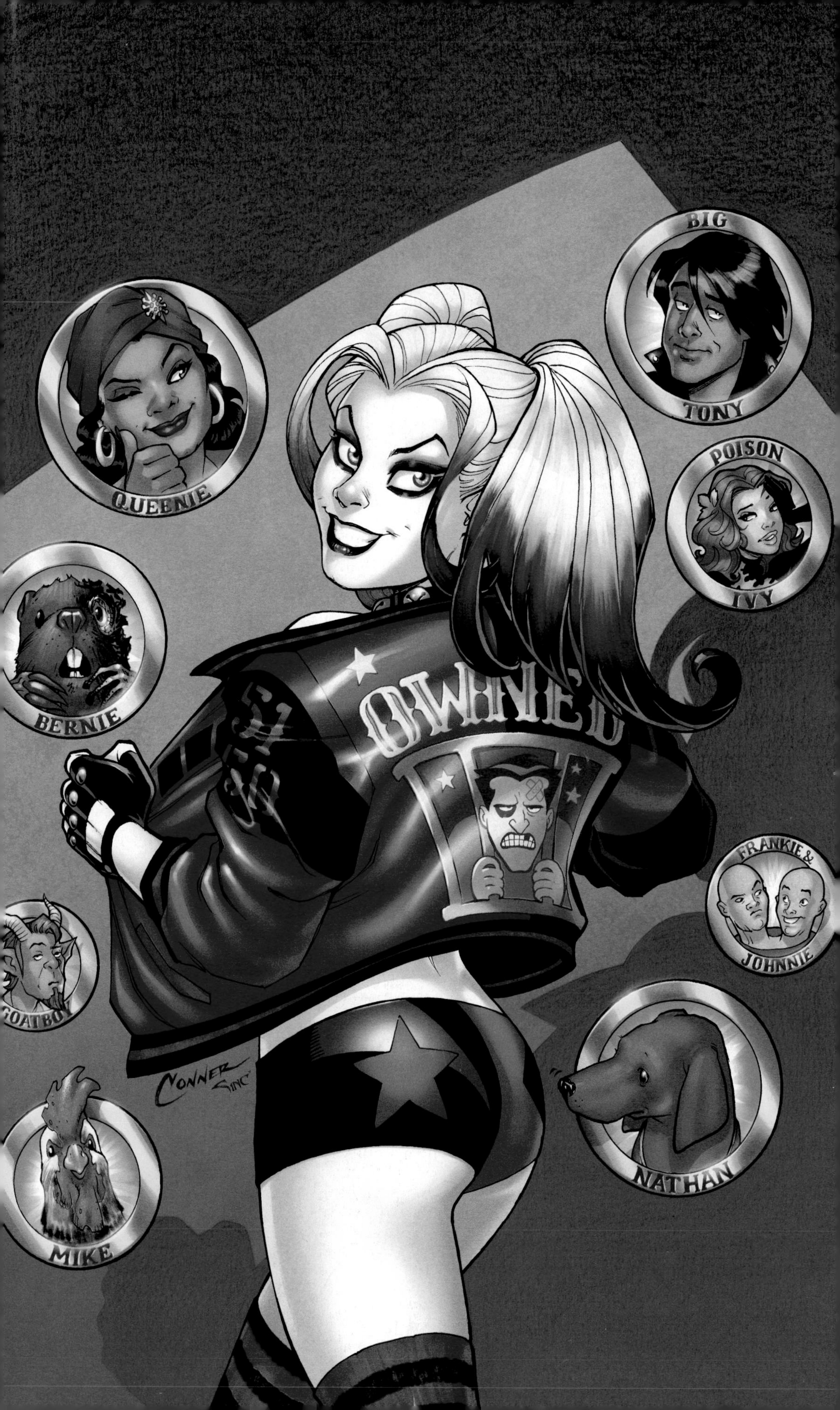

BIG
TONY
QUEENIE
POISON
IVY
BERNIE
OWNED
FRANKIE &
JOHNNIE
NATHAN
MIKE
CONNER

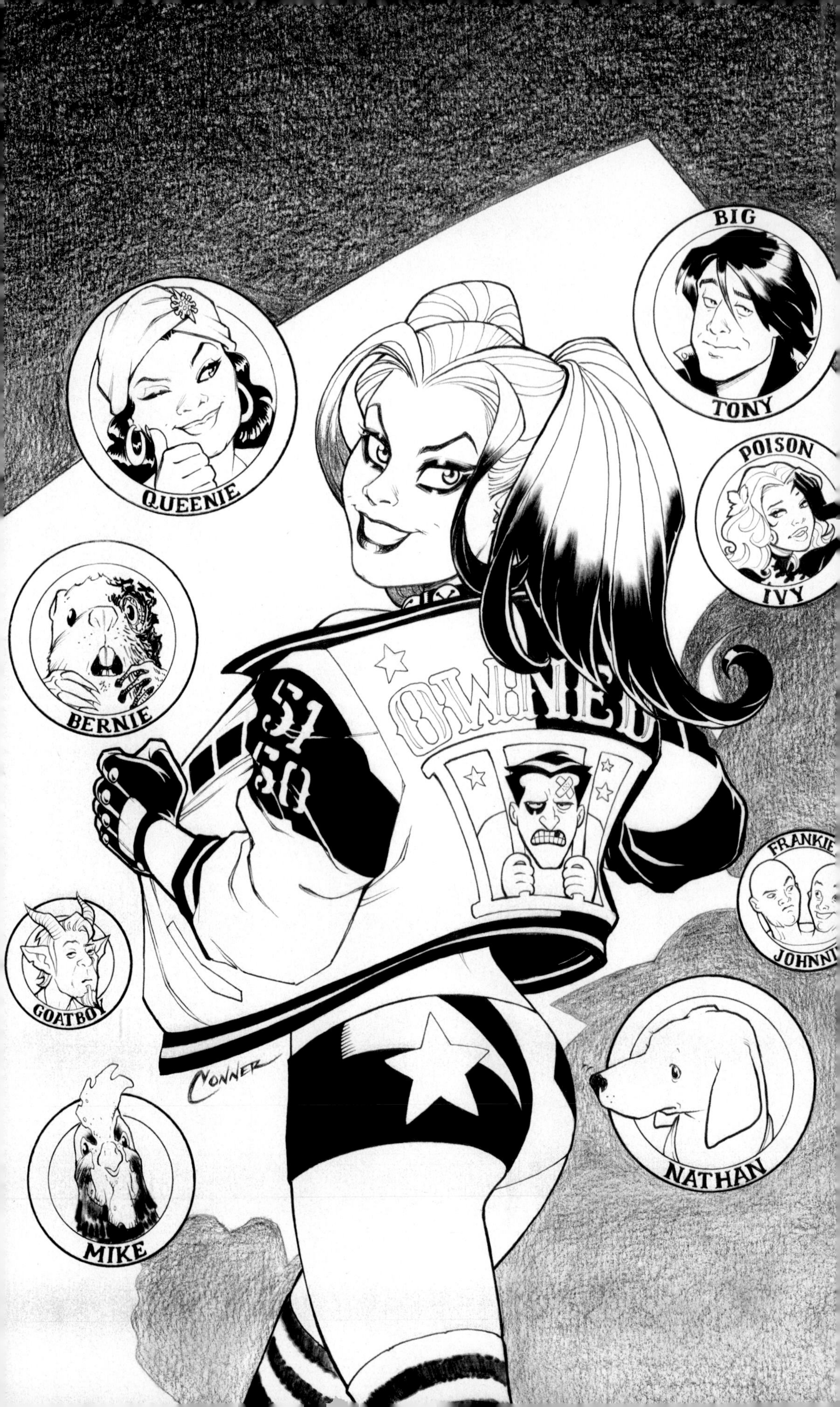

BIG
TONY
QUEENIE
POISON
IVY
BERNIE
OWNED
5150
FRANKIE
JOHNNY
GOATBOY
CONNER
NATHAN
MIKE

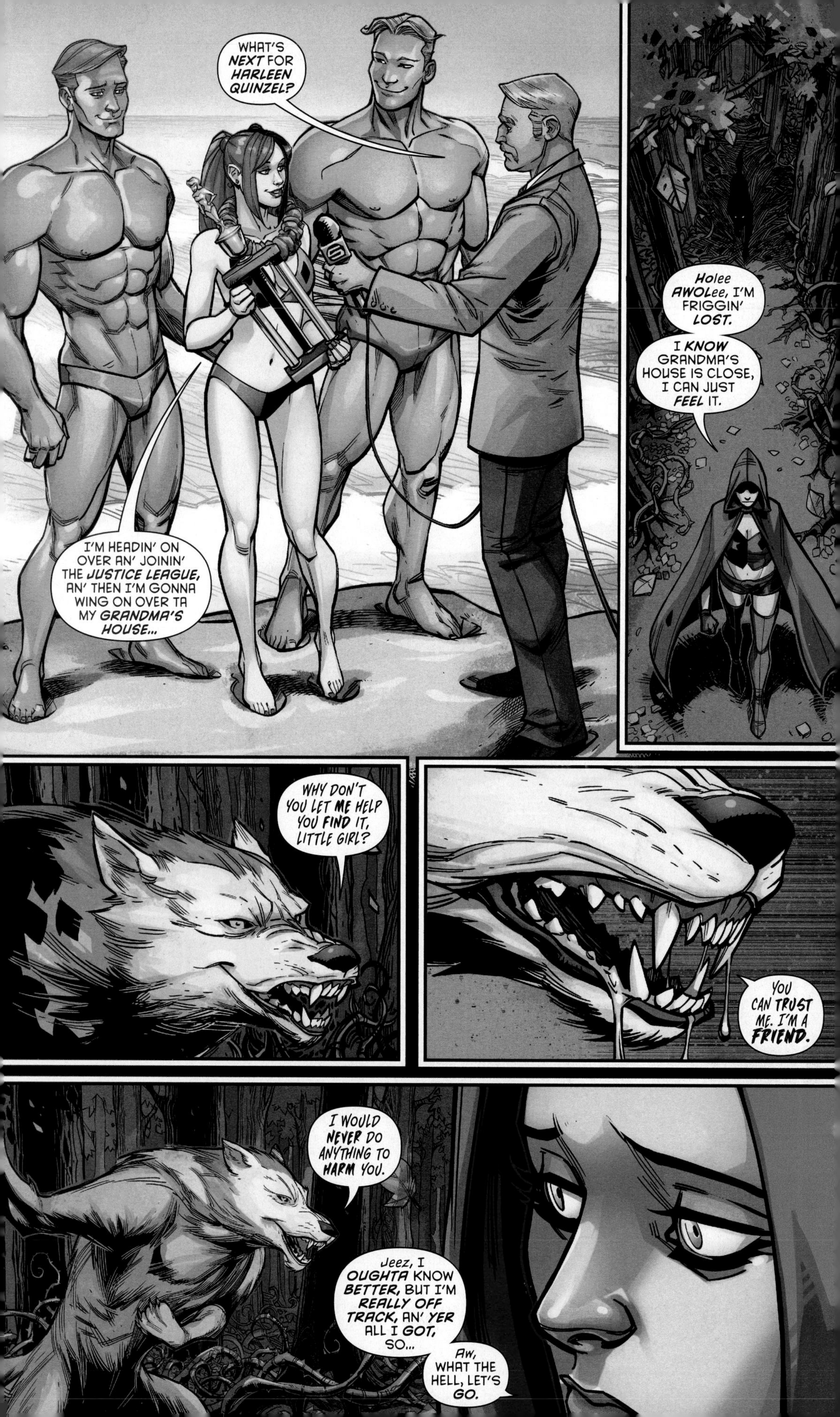
WHAT'S NEXT FOR HARLEEN QUINZEL?
I'M HEADIN' ON OVER AN' JOININ' THE JUSTICE LEAGUE, AN' THEN I'M GONNA WING ON OVER TA MY GRANDMA'S HOUSE...
Holee AWOLee, I'M FRIGGIN' LOST.
I KNOW GRANDMA'S HOUSE IS CLOSE, I CAN JUST FEEL IT.
WHY DON'T YOU LET ME HELP YOU FIND IT, LITTLE GIRL?
YOU CAN TRUST ME. I'M A FRIEND.
I WOULD NEVER DO ANYTHING TO HARM YOU.
Jeez, I OUGHTA KNOW BETTER, BUT I'M REALLY OFF TRACK, AN' YER ALL I GOT, SO...
AW, WHAT THE HELL, LET'S GO.

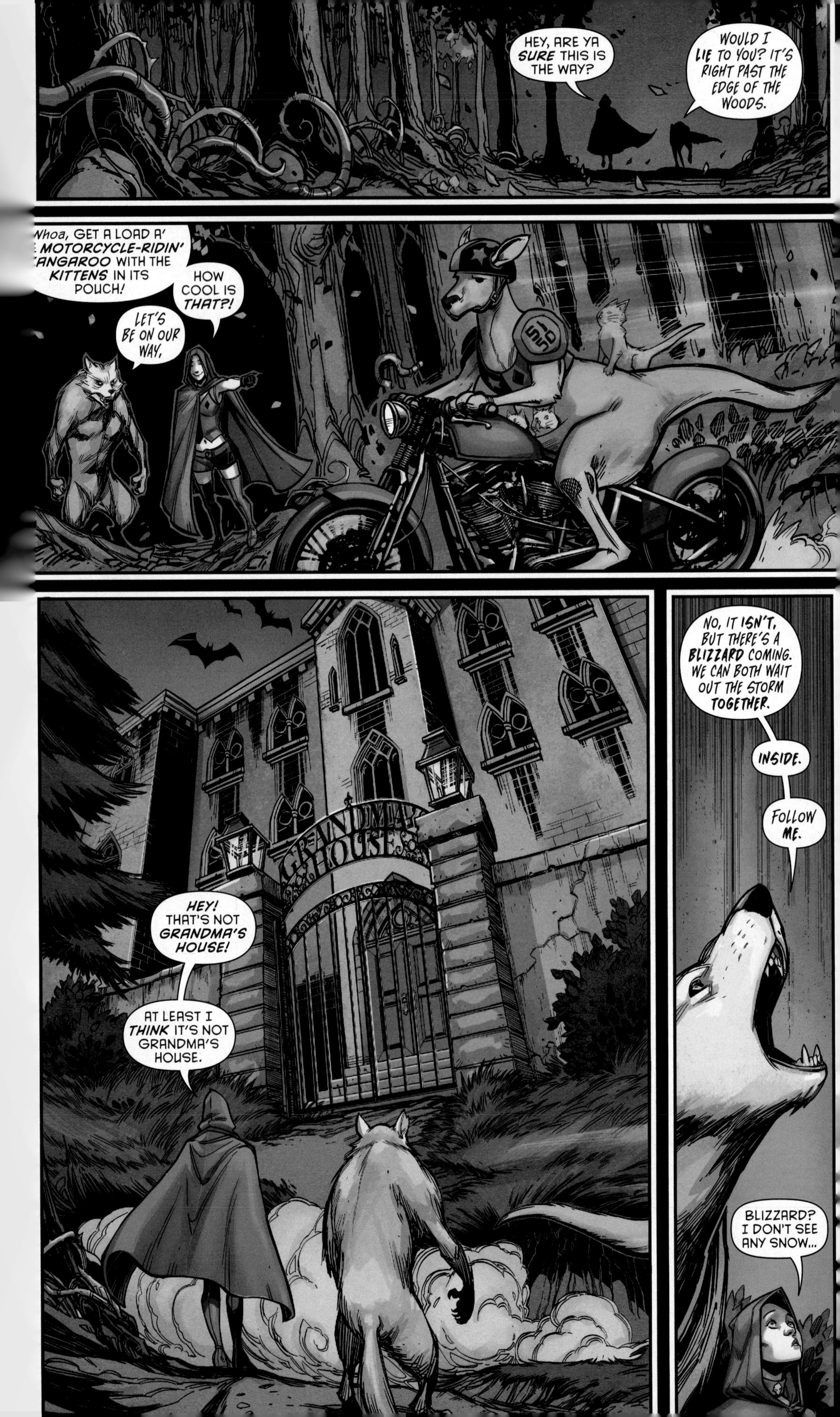
HEY, ARE YA SURE THIS IS THE WAY?
WOULD I LIE TO YOU? IT'S RIGHT PAST THE EDGE OF THE WOODS.
Whoa, GET A LOAD A' E MOTORCYCLE-RIDIN' KANGAROO WITH THE KITTENS IN ITS POUCH!
HOW COOL IS THAT?!
LET'S BE ON OUR WAY.
GRANDMA'S HOUSE
HEY! THAT'S NOT GRANDMA'S HOUSE!
AT LEAST I THINK IT'S NOT GRANDMA'S HOUSE.
NO, IT ISN'T. BUT THERE'S A BLIZZARD COMING. WE CAN BOTH WAIT OUT THE STORM TOGETHER.
INSIDE.
FOLLOW ME.
BLIZZARD? I DON'T SEE ANY SNOW...

GEE, I DUNNO... I FEEL SAFER OUTSIDE.

NONSENSE.

SEE? I LOCKED THE DOOR.

NOW NOTHING CAN HARM YOU.

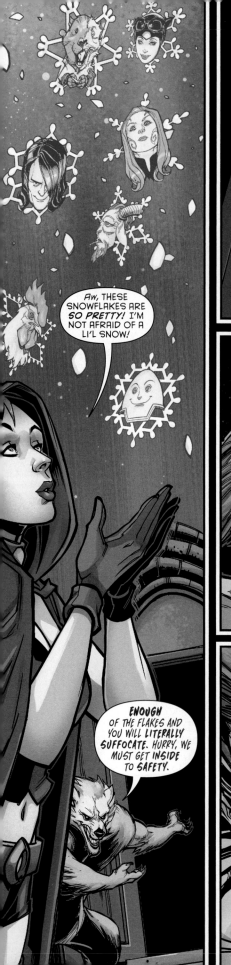

AW, THESE SNOWFLAKES ARE *SO PRETTY!* I'M NOT AFRAID OF A LI'L SNOW!

ENOUGH OF THE FLAKES AND YOU WILL *LITERALLY SUFFOCATE.* HURRY, WE MUST GET *INSIDE* TO *SAFETY.*

~ulp~

UMM...Y-YOU WOULDN'T HURT ME, WOULDJA?

WELL, THAT DEPENDS ON *YOU.*

HARLEY, ARE YOU GOING TO BE A *GOOD GIRL?*

I *AM* A GOOD GIRL. JUST ASK *ANYBODY*...

...WELL, *ALMOST* ANYBODY.

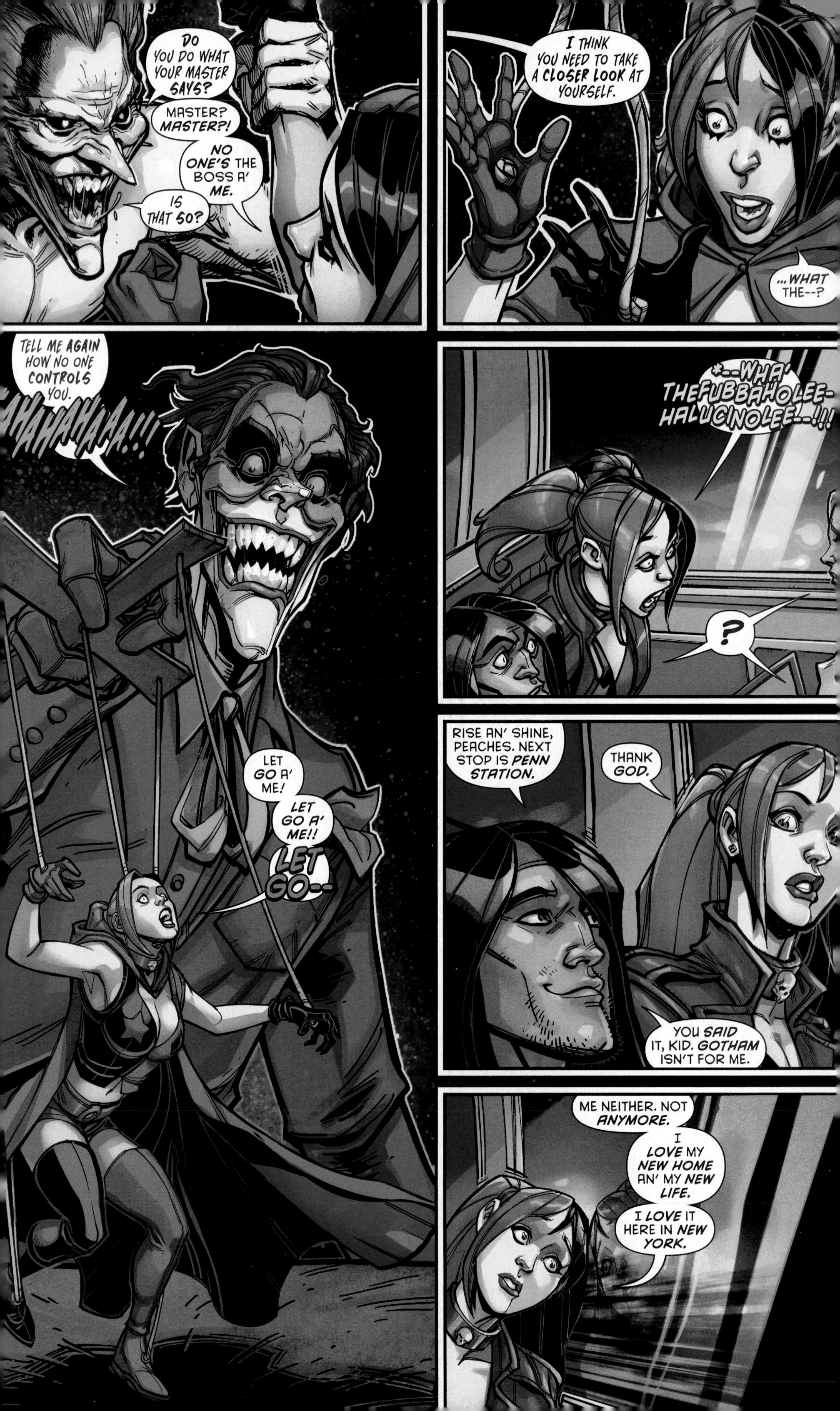
DO YOU DO WHAT YOUR MASTER SAYS?
MASTER? MASTER?!
NO ONE'S THE BOSS A' ME.
IS THAT SO?
I THINK YOU NEED TO TAKE A CLOSER LOOK AT YOURSELF.
...WHAT THE--?
TELL ME AGAIN HOW NO ONE CONTROLS YOU.
AHAHAHAHAA!!!
LET GO A' ME!
LET GO A' ME!!
LET GO--
*--WHA' THEFUBBAHOLEE-HALUCINOLEE--!!!
?
RISE AN' SHINE, PEACHES. NEXT STOP IS PENN STATION.
THANK GOD.
YOU SAID IT, KID. GOTHAM ISN'T FOR ME.
ME NEITHER. NOT ANYMORE.
I LOVE MY NEW HOME AN' MY NEW LIFE.
I LOVE IT HERE IN NEW YORK.

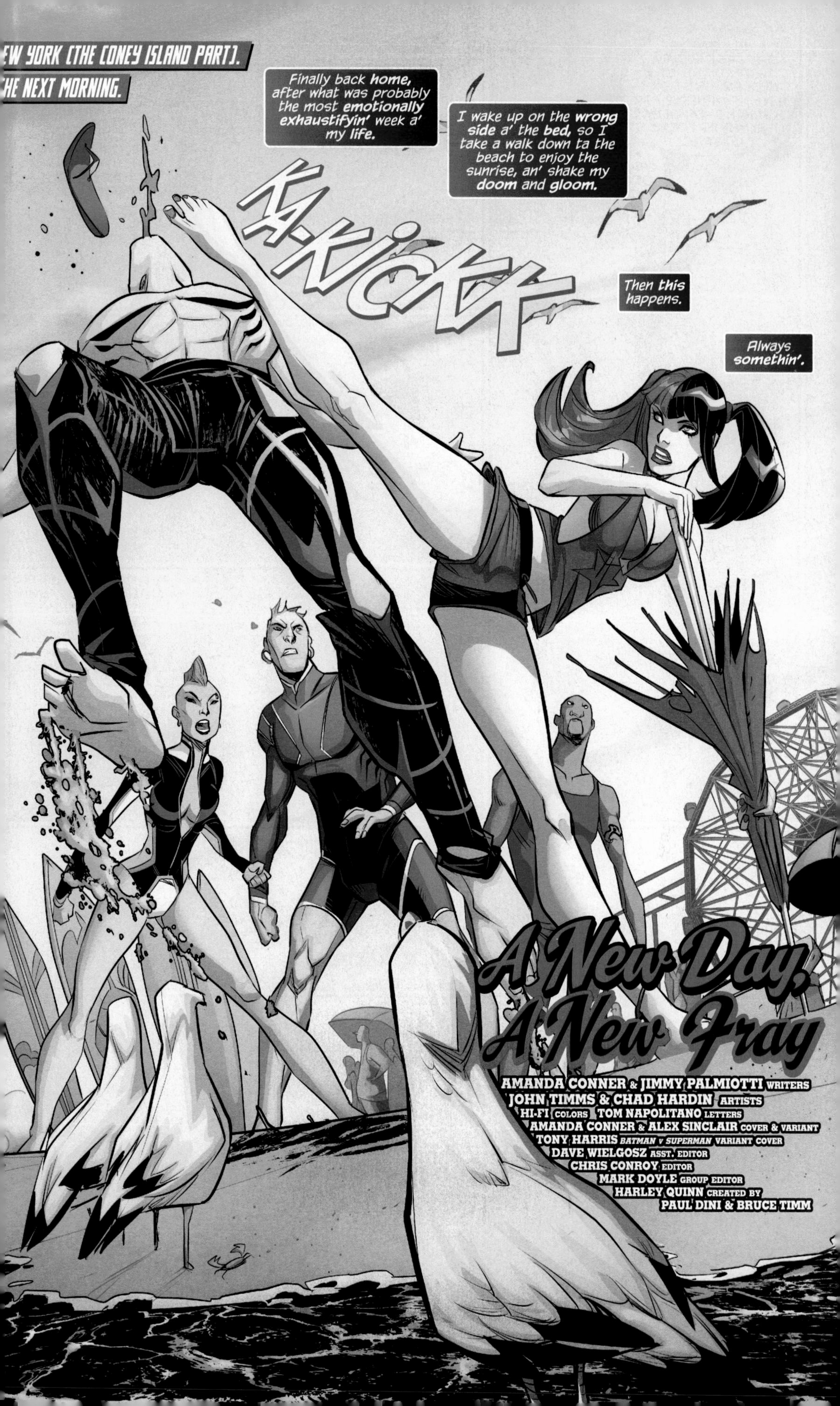

EW YORK (THE CONEY ISLAND PART).
HE NEXT MORNING.
Finally back home, after what was probably the most emotionally exhaustifyin' week a' my life.
I wake up on the wrong side a' the bed, so I take a walk down ta the beach to enjoy the sunrise, an' shake my doom and gloom.
KA-KICKK
Then this happens.
Always somethin'.
A New Day, A New Fray
AMANDA CONNER & JIMMY PALMIOTTI WRITERS
JOHN TIMMS & CHAD HARDIN ARTISTS
HI-FI COLORS TOM NAPOLITANO LETTERS
AMANDA CONNER & ALEX SINCLAIR COVER & VARIANT
TONY HARRIS BATMAN v SUPERMAN VARIANT COVER
DAVE WIELGOSZ ASST. EDITOR
CHRIS CONROY EDITOR
MARK DOYLE GROUP EDITOR
HARLEY QUINN CREATED BY
PAUL DINI & BRUCE TIMM

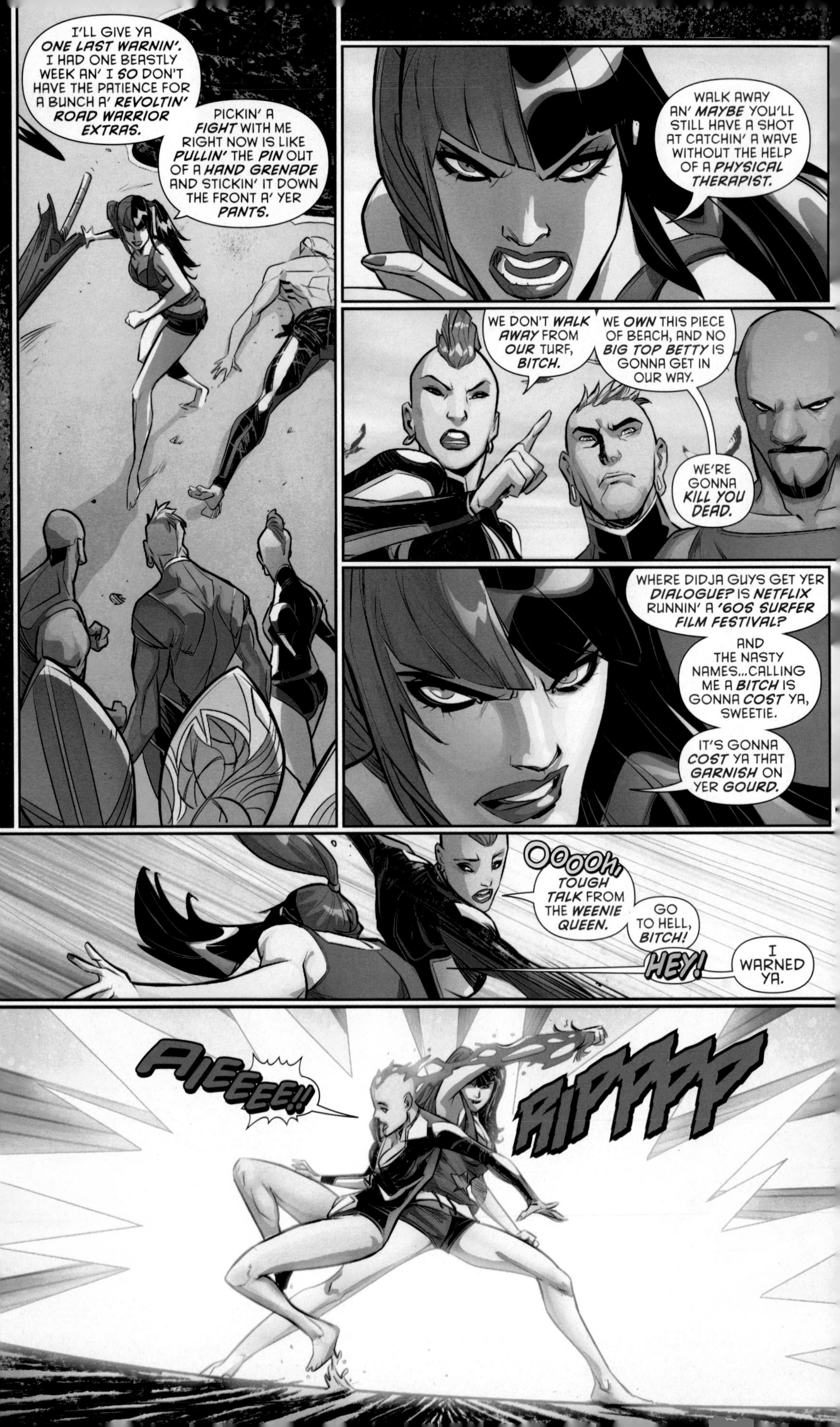

I'LL GIVE YA ONE LAST WARNIN'. I HAD ONE BEASTLY WEEK AN' I SO DON'T HAVE THE PATIENCE FOR A BUNCH A' REVOLTIN' ROAD WARRIOR EXTRAS.
PICKIN' A FIGHT WITH ME RIGHT NOW IS LIKE PULLIN' THE PIN OUT OF A HAND GRENADE AND STICKIN' IT DOWN THE FRONT A' YER PANTS.
WALK AWAY AN' MAYBE YOU'LL STILL HAVE A SHOT AT CATCHIN' A WAVE WITHOUT THE HELP OF A PHYSICAL THERAPIST.
WE DON'T WALK AWAY FROM OUR TURF, BITCH.
WE OWN THIS PIECE OF BEACH, AND NO BIG TOP BETTY IS GONNA GET IN OUR WAY.
WE'RE GONNA KILL YOU DEAD.
WHERE DIDJA GUYS GET YER DIALOGUE? IS NETFLIX RUNNIN' A '60S SURFER FILM FESTIVAL?
AND THE NASTY NAMES...CALLING ME A BITCH IS GONNA COST YA, SWEETIE.
IT'S GONNA COST YA THAT GARNISH ON YER GOURD.
OOOOH, TOUGH TALK FROM THE WEENIE QUEEN.
GO TO HELL, BITCH!
HEY!
I WARNED YA.
AIEEEEE!!
RIPPPP

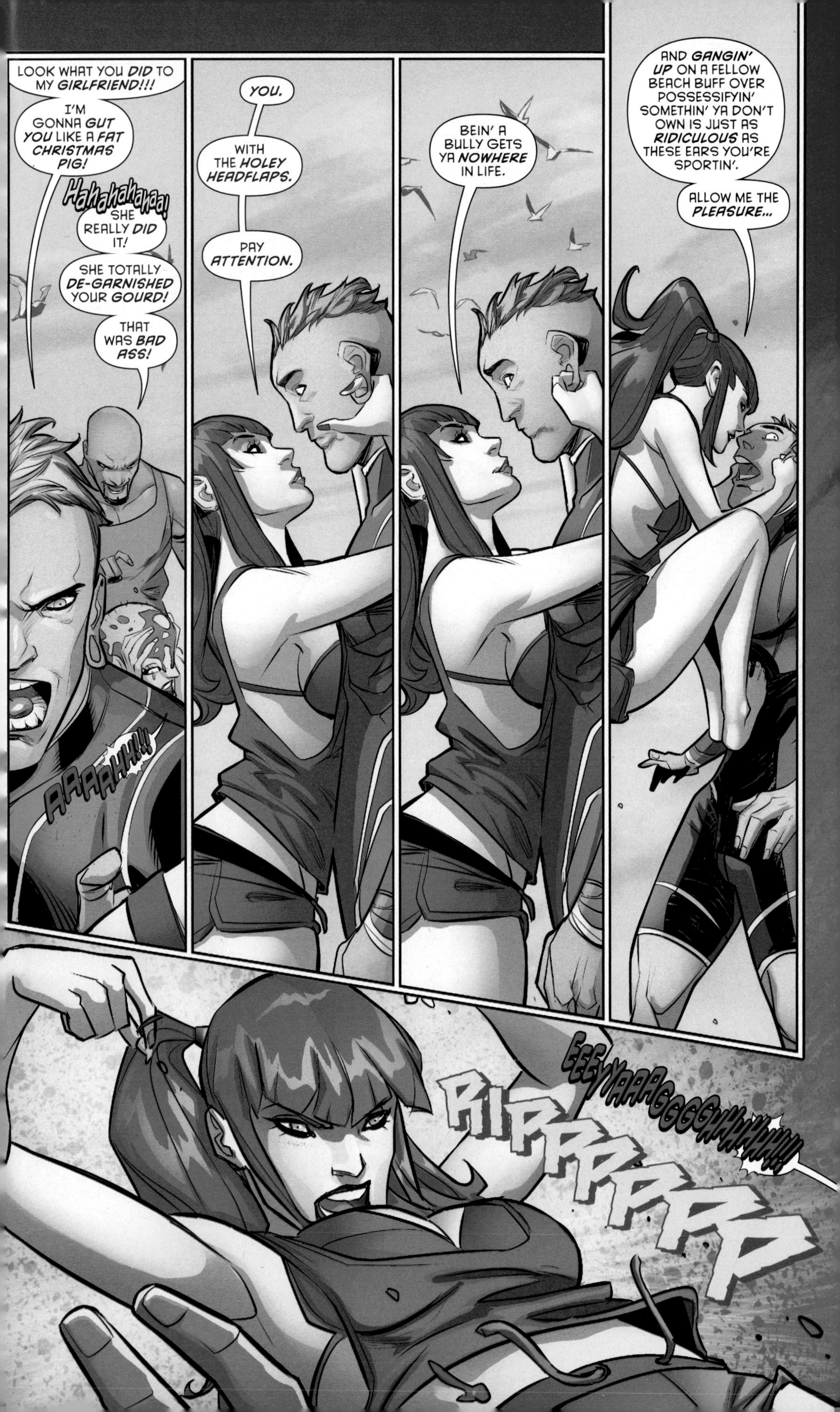

LOOK WHAT YOU DID TO MY GIRLFRIEND!!!
I'M GONNA GUT YOU LIKE A FAT CHRISTMAS PIG!
Hahahahahaa!
SHE REALLY DID IT!
SHE TOTALLY DE-GARNISHED YOUR GOURD!
THAT WAS BAD ASS!
AAAAAHH!!!
YOU.
WITH THE HOLEY HEADFLAPS.
PAY ATTENTION.
BEIN' A BULLY GETS YA NOWHERE IN LIFE.
AND GANGIN' UP ON A FELLOW BEACH BUFF OVER POSSESSIFYIN' SOMETHIN' YA DON'T OWN IS JUST AS RIDICULOUS AS THESE EARS YOU'RE SPORTIN'.
ALLOW ME THE PLEASURE...
EEEYAAAGGGGHHHHH!!!
RIPPPPP

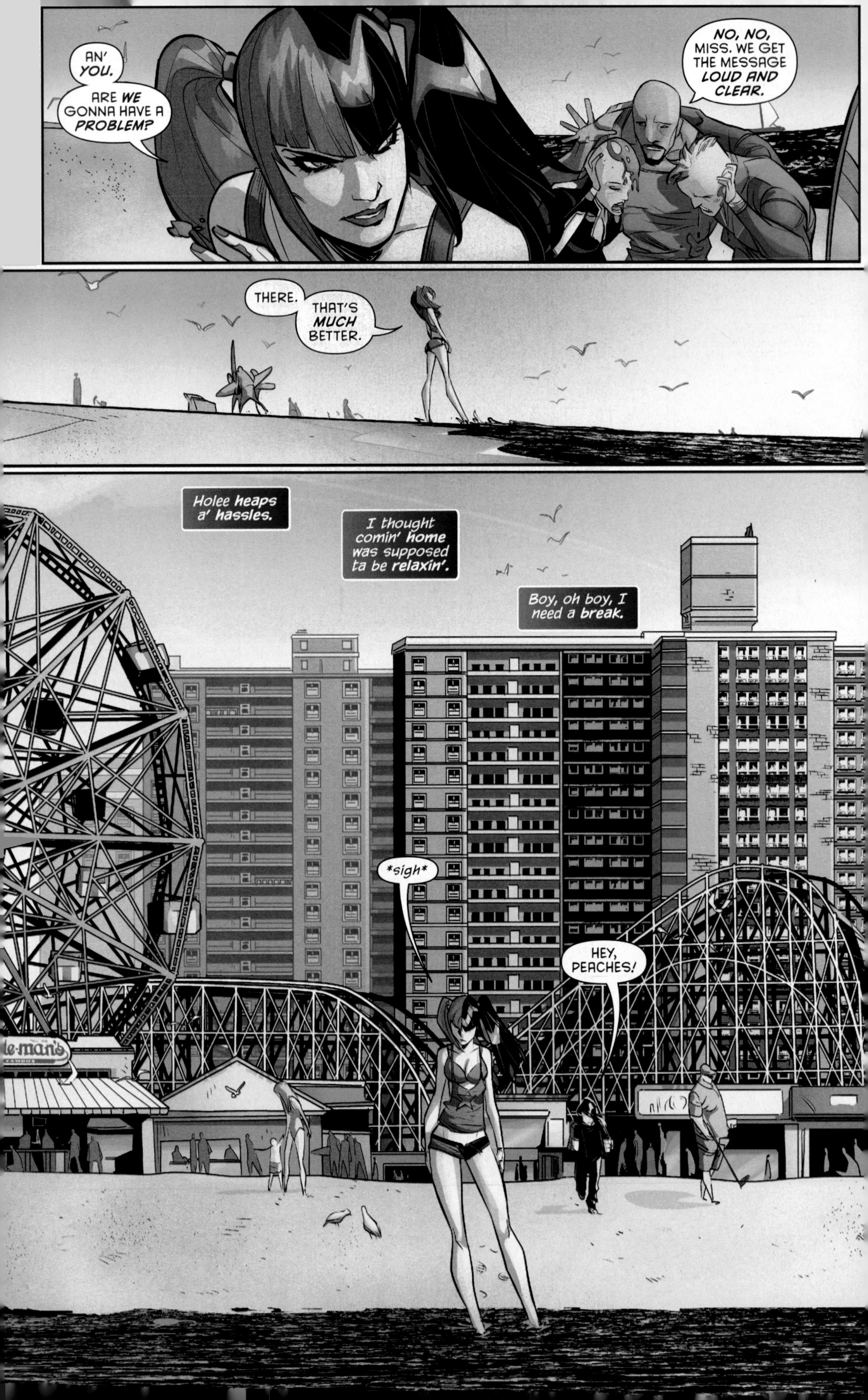
AN' YOU.
ARE WE GONNA HAVE A PROBLEM?
NO, NO, MISS. WE GET THE MESSAGE LOUD AND CLEAR.
THERE.
THAT'S MUCH BETTER.
Holee heaps a' hassles.
I thought comin' home was supposed ta be relaxin'.
Boy, oh boy, I need a break.
sigh
HEY, PEACHES!

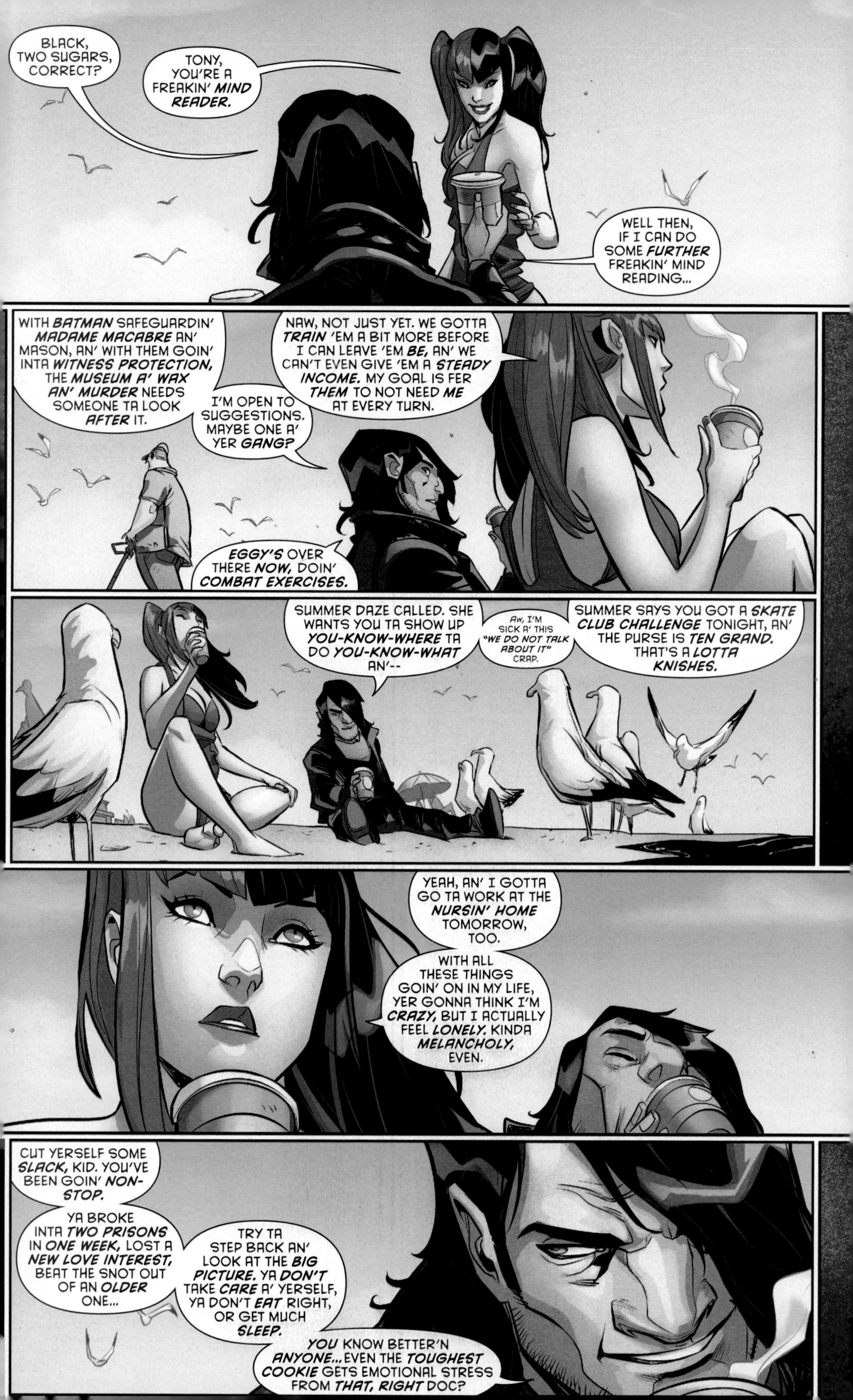
BLACK, TWO SUGARS, CORRECT?
TONY, YOU'RE A FREAKIN' MIND READER.
WELL THEN, IF I CAN DO SOME FURTHER FREAKIN' MIND READING...
WITH BATMAN SAFEGUARDIN' MADAME MACABRE AN' MASON, AN' WITH THEM GOIN' INTA WITNESS PROTECTION, THE MUSEUM A' WAX AN' MURDER NEEDS SOMEONE TA LOOK AFTER IT.
I'M OPEN TO SUGGESTIONS. MAYBE ONE A' YER GANG?
NAW, NOT JUST YET. WE GOTTA TRAIN 'EM A BIT MORE BEFORE I CAN LEAVE 'EM BE, AN' WE CAN'T EVEN GIVE 'EM A STEADY INCOME. MY GOAL IS FER THEM TO NOT NEED ME AT EVERY TURN.
EGGY'S OVER THERE NOW, DOIN' COMBAT EXERCISES.
SUMMER DAZE CALLED. SHE WANTS YOU TA SHOW UP YOU-KNOW-WHERE TA DO YOU-KNOW-WHAT AN'--
AW, I'M SICK A' THIS "WE DO NOT TALK ABOUT IT" CRAP.
SUMMER SAYS YOU GOT A SKATE CLUB CHALLENGE TONIGHT, AN' THE PURSE IS TEN GRAND. THAT'S A LOTTA KNISHES.
YEAH, AN' I GOTTA GO TA WORK AT THE NURSIN' HOME TOMORROW, TOO.
WITH ALL THESE THINGS GOIN' ON IN MY LIFE, YER GONNA THINK I'M CRAZY, BUT I ACTUALLY FEEL LONELY. KINDA MELANCHOLY, EVEN.
CUT YERSELF SOME SLACK, KID. YOU'VE BEEN GOIN' NON-STOP.
YA BROKE INTA TWO PRISONS IN ONE WEEK, LOST A NEW LOVE INTEREST, BEAT THE SNOT OUT OF AN OLDER ONE...
TRY TA STEP BACK AN' LOOK AT THE BIG PICTURE. YA DON'T TAKE CARE A' YERSELF, YA DON'T EAT RIGHT, OR GET MUCH SLEEP.
YOU KNOW BETTER'N ANYONE...EVEN THE TOUGHEST COOKIE GETS EMOTIONAL STRESS FROM THAT, RIGHT DOC?

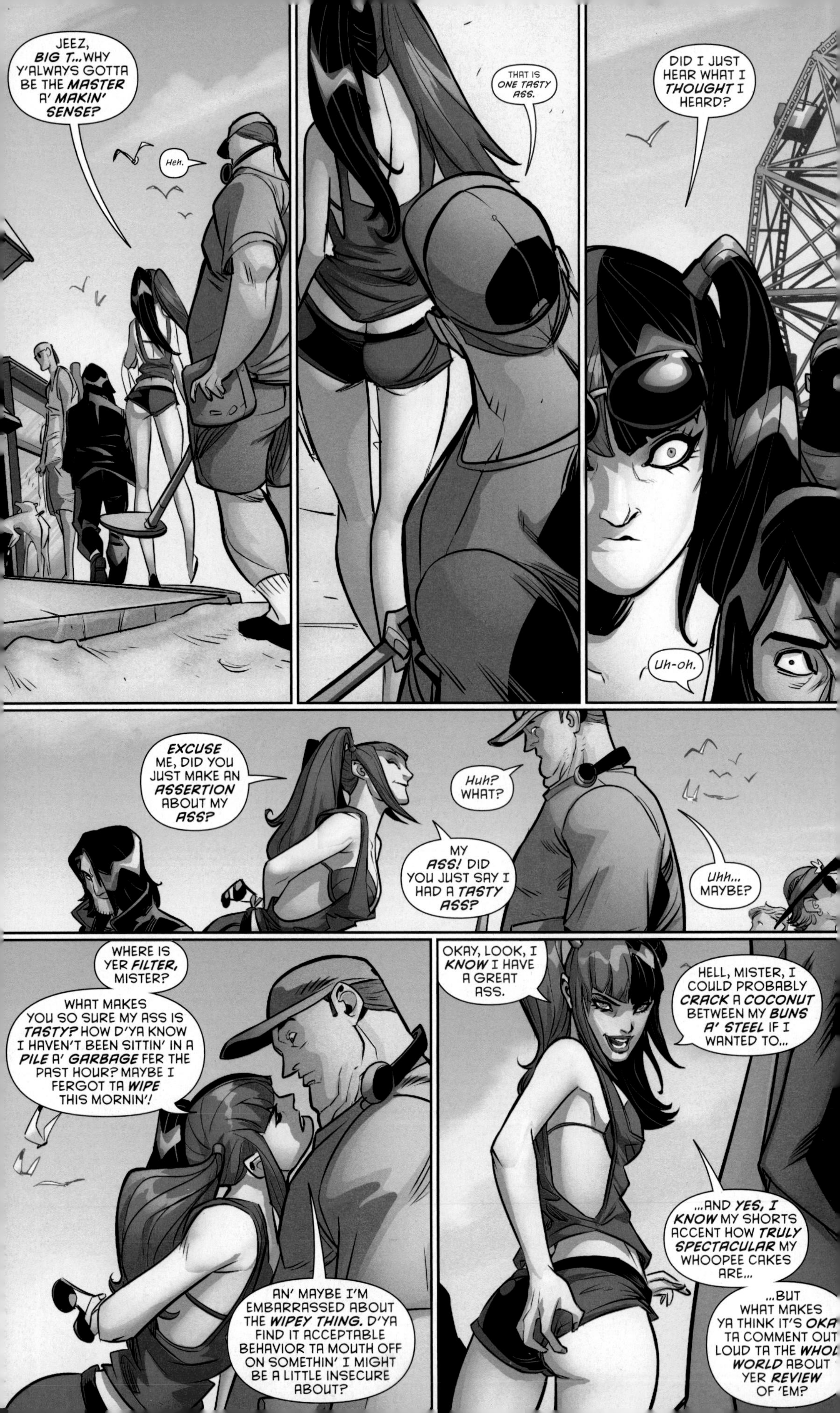
JEEZ, BIG T...WHY Y'ALWAYS GOTTA BE THE MASTER A' MAKIN' SENSE?
Heh.
THAT IS ONE TASTY ASS.
DID I JUST HEAR WHAT I THOUGHT I HEARD?
Uh-oh.
EXCUSE ME, DID YOU JUST MAKE AN ASSERTION ABOUT MY ASS?
Huh? WHAT?
MY ASS! DID YOU JUST SAY I HAD A TASTY ASS?
Uhh... MAYBE?
WHERE IS YER FILTER, MISTER?
WHAT MAKES YOU SO SURE MY ASS IS TASTY? HOW D'YA KNOW I HAVEN'T BEEN SITTIN' IN A PILE A' GARBAGE FER THE PAST HOUR? MAYBE I FERGOT TA WIPE THIS MORNIN'!
AN' MAYBE I'M EMBARRASSED ABOUT THE WIPEY THING. D'YA FIND IT ACCEPTABLE BEHAVIOR TA MOUTH OFF ON SOMETHIN' I MIGHT BE A LITTLE INSECURE ABOUT?
OKAY, LOOK, I KNOW I HAVE A GREAT ASS.
HELL, MISTER, I COULD PROBABLY CRACK A COCONUT BETWEEN MY BUNS A' STEEL IF I WANTED TO...
...AND YES, I KNOW MY SHORTS ACCENT HOW TRULY SPECTACULAR MY WHOOPEE CAKES ARE...
...BUT WHAT MAKES YA THINK IT'S OKA TA COMMENT OUT LOUD TA THE WHOL WORLD ABOUT YER REVIEW OF 'EM?

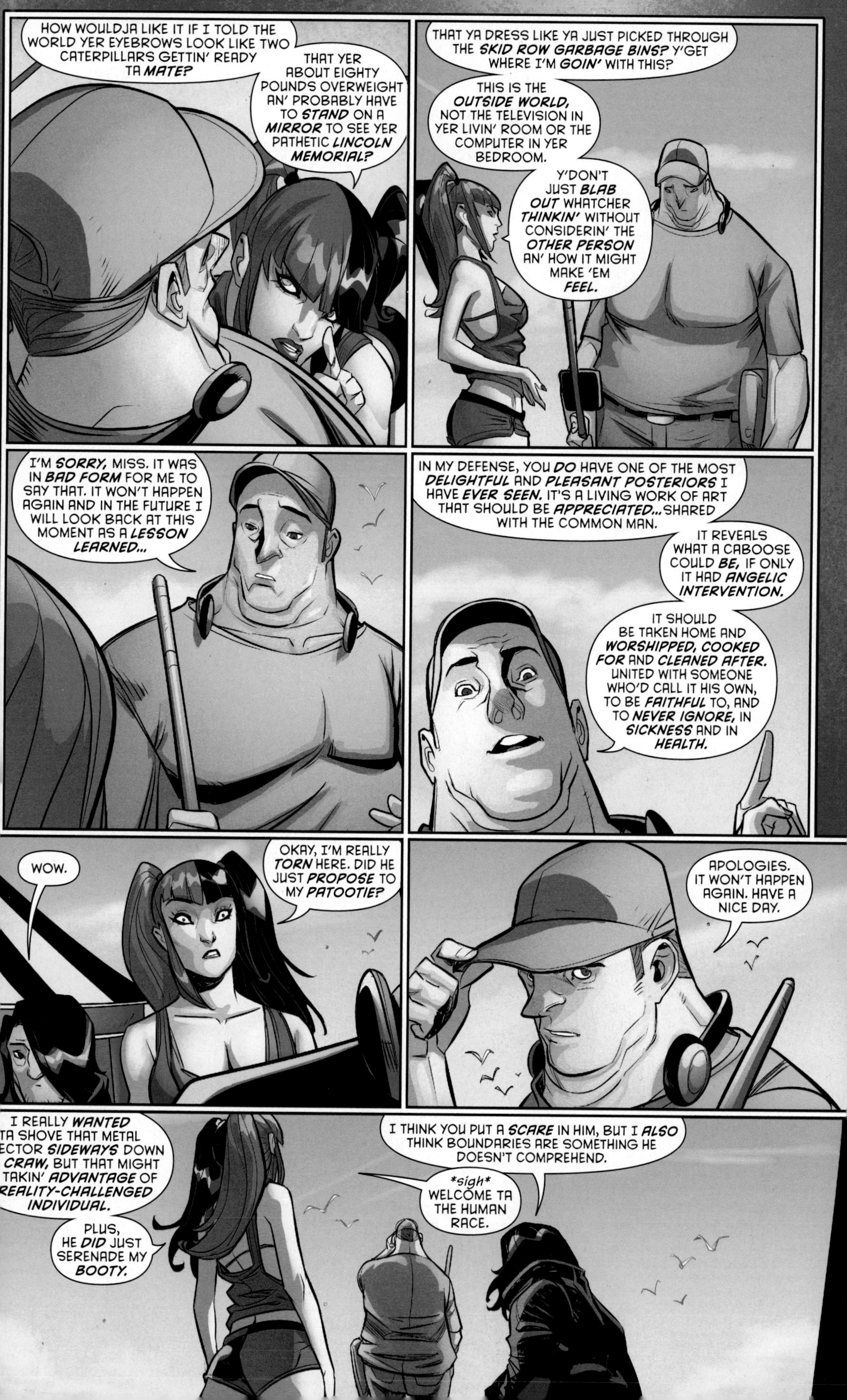
HOW WOULDJA LIKE IT IF I TOLD THE WORLD YER EYEBROWS LOOK LIKE TWO CATERPILLARS GETTIN' READY TA MATE?
THAT YER ABOUT EIGHTY POUNDS OVERWEIGHT AN' PROBABLY HAVE TO STAND ON A MIRROR TO SEE YER PATHETIC LINCOLN MEMORIAL?
THAT YA DRESS LIKE YA JUST PICKED THROUGH THE SKID ROW GARBAGE BINS? Y'GET WHERE I'M GOIN' WITH THIS?
THIS IS THE OUTSIDE WORLD, NOT THE TELEVISION IN YER LIVIN' ROOM OR THE COMPUTER IN YER BEDROOM.
Y'DON'T JUST BLAB OUT WHATCHER THINKIN' WITHOUT CONSIDERIN' THE OTHER PERSON AN' HOW IT MIGHT MAKE 'EM FEEL.
I'M SORRY, MISS. IT WAS IN BAD FORM FOR ME TO SAY THAT. IT WON'T HAPPEN AGAIN AND IN THE FUTURE I WILL LOOK BACK AT THIS MOMENT AS A LESSON LEARNED...
IN MY DEFENSE, YOU DO HAVE ONE OF THE MOST DELIGHTFUL AND PLEASANT POSTERIORS I HAVE EVER SEEN. IT'S A LIVING WORK OF ART THAT SHOULD BE APPRECIATED...SHARED WITH THE COMMON MAN.
IT REVEALS WHAT A CABOOSE COULD BE, IF ONLY IT HAD ANGELIC INTERVENTION.
IT SHOULD BE TAKEN HOME AND WORSHIPPED, COOKED FOR AND CLEANED AFTER. UNITED WITH SOMEONE WHO'D CALL IT HIS OWN, TO BE FAITHFUL TO, AND TO NEVER IGNORE, IN SICKNESS AND IN HEALTH.
WOW.
OKAY, I'M REALLY TORN HERE. DID HE JUST PROPOSE TO MY PATOOTIE?
APOLOGIES. IT WON'T HAPPEN AGAIN. HAVE A NICE DAY.
I REALLY WANTED TA SHOVE THAT METAL ECTOR SIDEWAYS DOWN CRAW, BUT THAT MIGHT TAKIN' ADVANTAGE OF REALITY-CHALLENGED INDIVIDUAL.
PLUS, HE DID JUST SERENADE MY BOOTY.
I THINK YOU PUT A SCARE IN HIM, BUT I ALSO THINK BOUNDARIES ARE SOMETHING HE DOESN'T COMPREHEND.
sigh WELCOME TA THE HUMAN RACE.

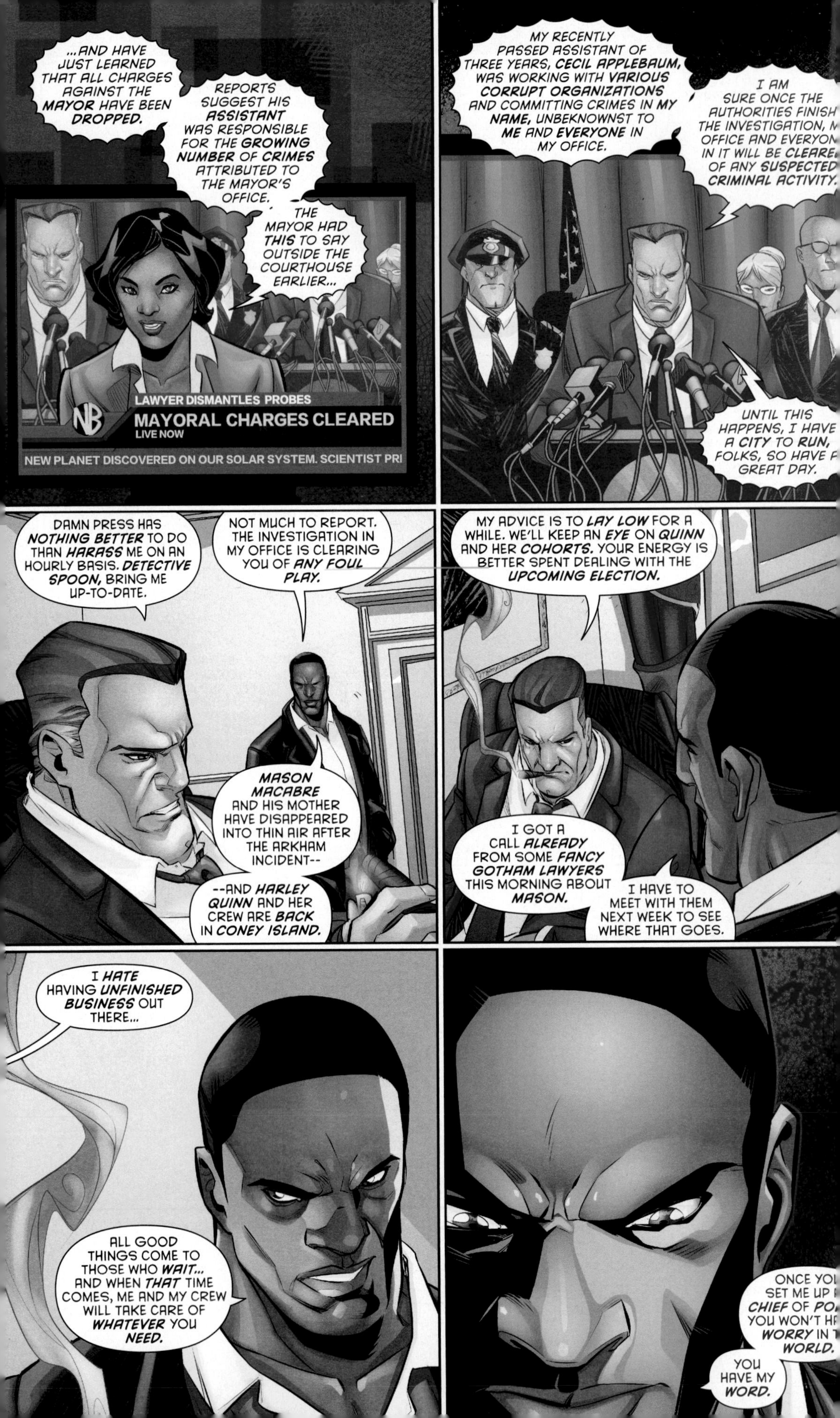
...AND HAVE JUST LEARNED THAT ALL CHARGES AGAINST THE MAYOR HAVE BEEN DROPPED.
REPORTS SUGGEST HIS ASSISTANT WAS RESPONSIBLE FOR THE GROWING NUMBER OF CRIMES ATTRIBUTED TO THE MAYOR'S OFFICE.
THE MAYOR HAD THIS TO SAY OUTSIDE THE COURTHOUSE EARLIER...
LAWYER DISMANTLES PROBES
MAYORAL CHARGES CLEARED
LIVE NOW
NEW PLANET DISCOVERED ON OUR SOLAR SYSTEM. SCIENTIST PRI
MY RECENTLY PASSED ASSISTANT OF THREE YEARS, CECIL APPLEBAUM, WAS WORKING WITH VARIOUS CORRUPT ORGANIZATIONS AND COMMITTING CRIMES IN MY NAME, UNBEKNOWNST TO ME AND EVERYONE IN MY OFFICE.
I AM SURE ONCE THE AUTHORITIES FINISH THE INVESTIGATION, M OFFICE AND EVERYON IN IT WILL BE CLEARE OF ANY SUSPECTED CRIMINAL ACTIVITY.
UNTIL THIS HAPPENS, I HAVE A CITY TO RUN, FOLKS, SO HAVE A GREAT DAY.
DAMN PRESS HAS NOTHING BETTER TO DO THAN HARASS ME ON AN HOURLY BASIS. DETECTIVE SPOON, BRING ME UP-TO-DATE.
NOT MUCH TO REPORT. THE INVESTIGATION IN MY OFFICE IS CLEARING YOU OF ANY FOUL PLAY.
MASON MACABRE AND HIS MOTHER HAVE DISAPPEARED INTO THIN AIR AFTER THE ARKHAM INCIDENT--
--AND HARLEY QUINN AND HER CREW ARE BACK IN CONEY ISLAND.
MY ADVICE IS TO LAY LOW FOR A WHILE. WE'LL KEEP AN EYE ON QUINN AND HER COHORTS. YOUR ENERGY IS BETTER SPENT DEALING WITH THE UPCOMING ELECTION.
I GOT A CALL ALREADY FROM SOME FANCY GOTHAM LAWYERS THIS MORNING ABOUT MASON.
I HAVE TO MEET WITH THEM NEXT WEEK TO SEE WHERE THAT GOES.
I HATE HAVING UNFINISHED BUSINESS OUT THERE...
ALL GOOD THINGS COME TO THOSE WHO WAIT... AND WHEN THAT TIME COMES, ME AND MY CREW WILL TAKE CARE OF WHATEVER YOU NEED.
ONCE YO SET ME UP CHIEF OF PO YOU WON'T HA WORRY IN T WORLD.
YOU HAVE MY WORD.

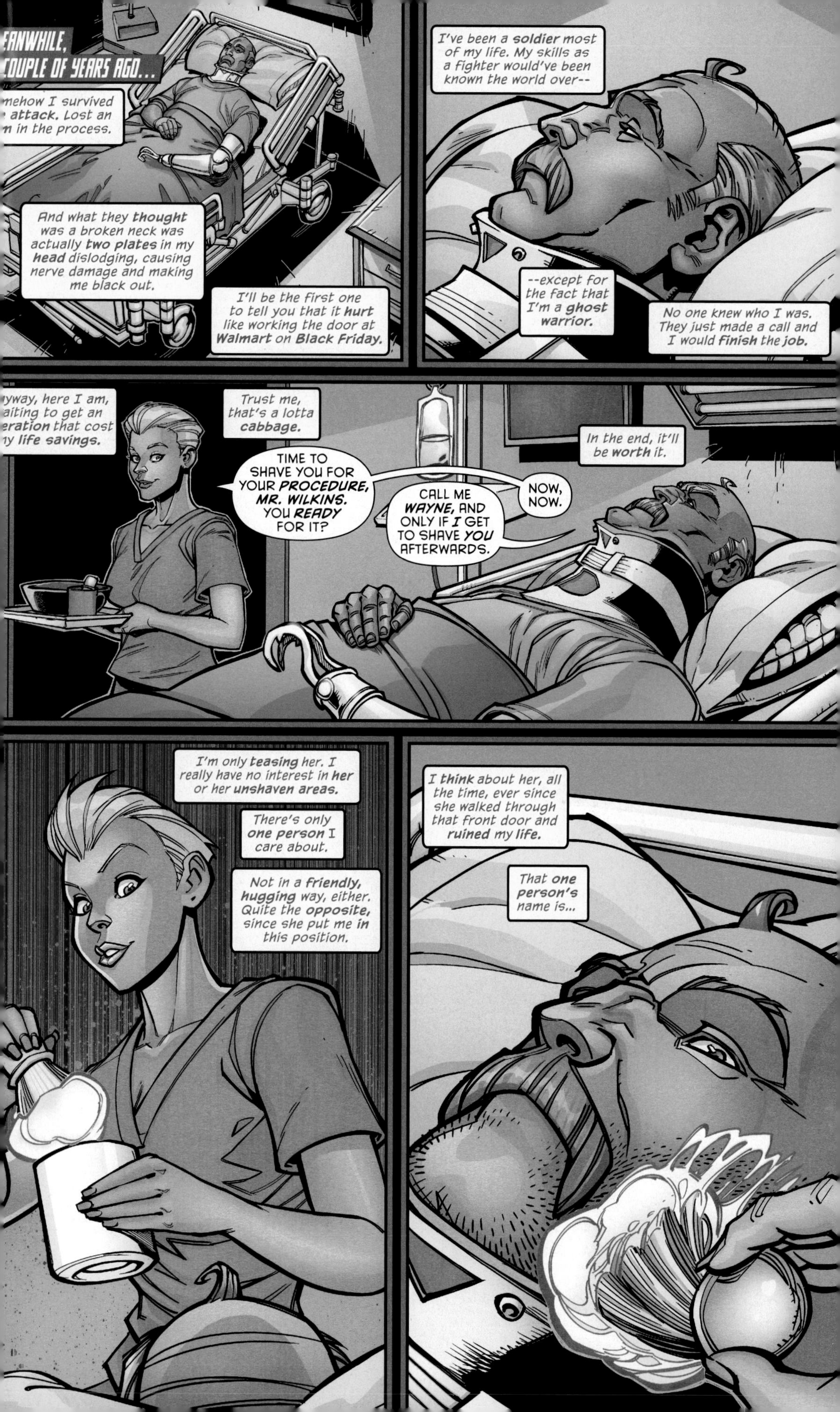
EANWHILE, COUPLE OF YEARS AGO...
mehow I survived attack. Lost an n in the process.
And what they thought was a broken neck was actually two plates in my head dislodging, causing nerve damage and making me black out.
I'll be the first one to tell you that it hurt like working the door at Walmart on Black Friday.
I've been a soldier most of my life. My skills as a fighter would've been known the world over--
--except for the fact that I'm a ghost warrior.
No one knew who I was. They just made a call and I would finish the job.
yway, here I am, aiting to get an eration that cost y life savings.
Trust me, that's a lotta cabbage.
In the end, it'll be worth it.
TIME TO SHAVE YOU FOR YOUR PROCEDURE, MR. WILKINS. YOU READY FOR IT?
NOW, NOW.
CALL ME WAYNE, AND ONLY IF I GET TO SHAVE YOU AFTERWARDS.
I'm only teasing her. I really have no interest in her or her unshaven areas.
There's only one person I care about.
Not in a friendly, hugging way, either. Quite the opposite, since she put me in this position.
I think about her, all the time, ever since she walked through that front door and ruined my life.
That one person's name is...

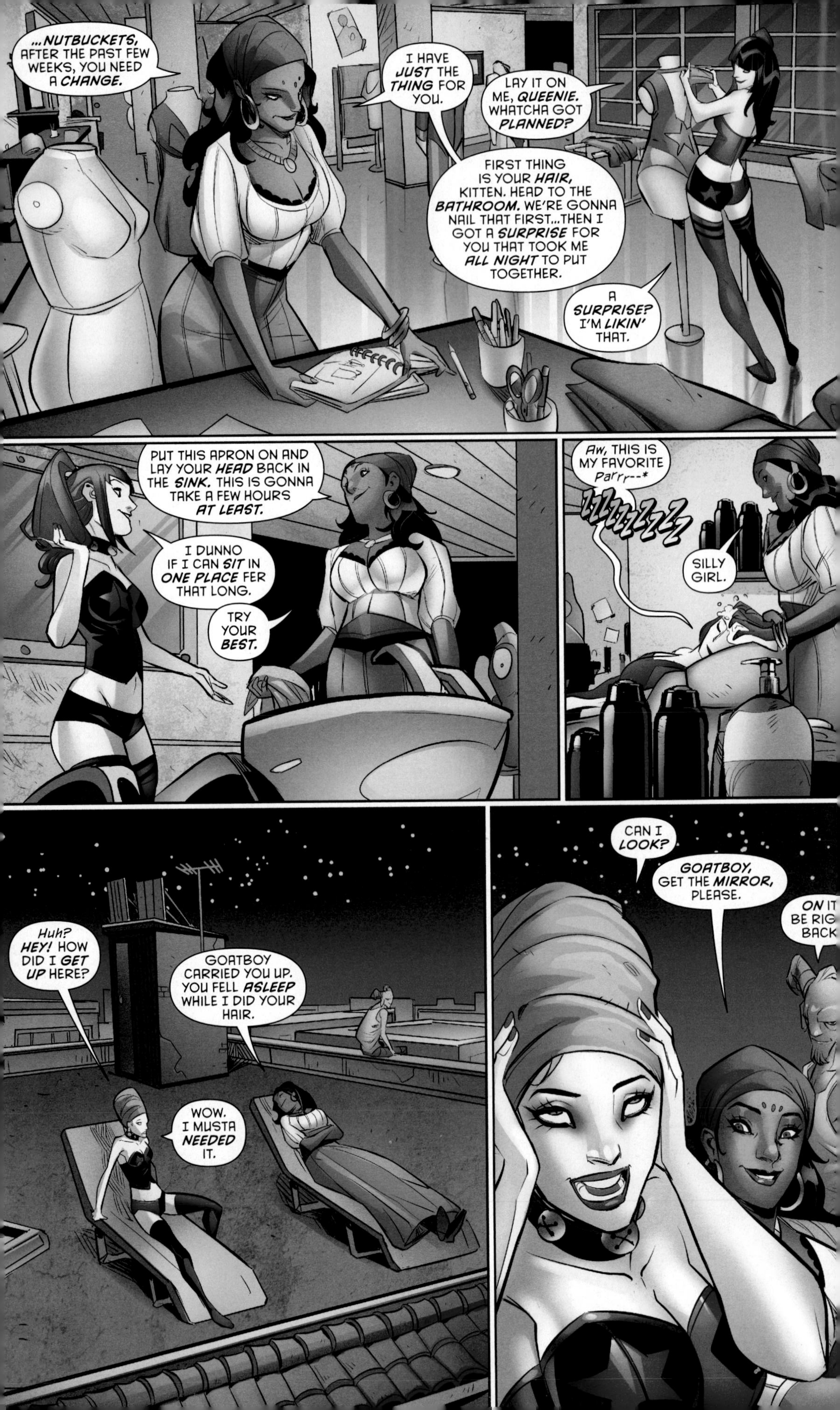

...NUTBUCKETS, AFTER THE PAST FEW WEEKS, YOU NEED A CHANGE.
I HAVE JUST THE THING FOR YOU.
LAY IT ON ME, QUEENIE. WHATCHA GOT PLANNED?
FIRST THING IS YOUR HAIR, KITTEN. HEAD TO THE BATHROOM. WE'RE GONNA NAIL THAT FIRST...THEN I GOT A SURPRISE FOR YOU THAT TOOK ME ALL NIGHT TO PUT TOGETHER.
A SURPRISE? I'M LIKIN' THAT.
PUT THIS APRON ON AND LAY YOUR HEAD BACK IN THE SINK. THIS IS GONNA TAKE A FEW HOURS AT LEAST.
I DUNNO IF I CAN SIT IN ONE PLACE FER THAT LONG.
TRY YOUR BEST.
Aw, THIS IS MY FAVORITE Parrr--*
ZZZZZZZZZ
SILLY GIRL.
Huh? HEY! HOW DID I GET UP HERE?
GOATBOY CARRIED YOU UP. YOU FELL ASLEEP WHILE I DID YOUR HAIR.
WOW. I MUSTA NEEDED IT.
CAN I LOOK?
GOATBOY, GET THE MIRROR, PLEASE.
ON IT BE RIG BACK

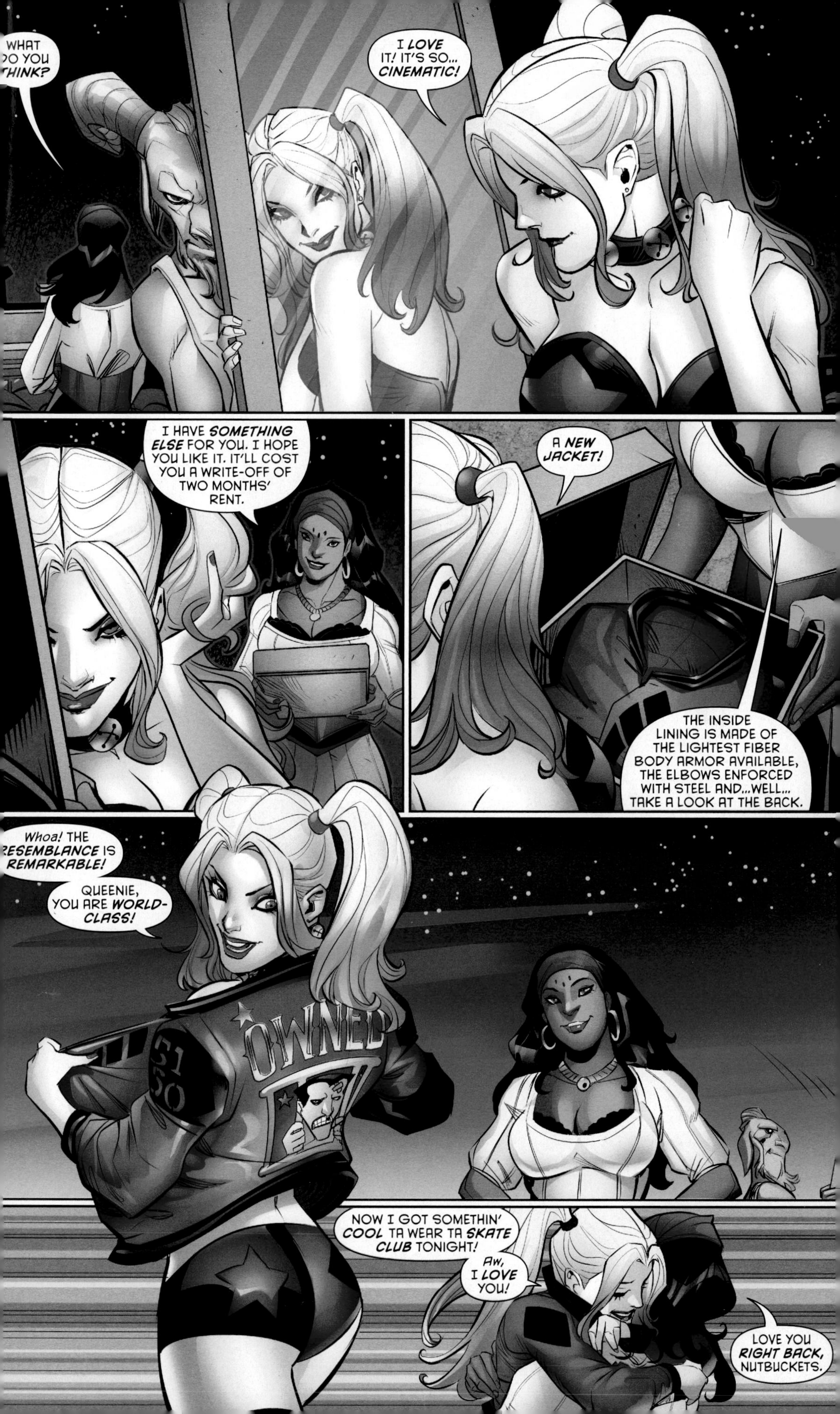

WHAT DO YOU THINK?
I LOVE IT! IT'S SO... CINEMATIC!
I HAVE SOMETHING ELSE FOR YOU. I HOPE YOU LIKE IT. IT'LL COST YOU A WRITE-OFF OF TWO MONTHS' RENT.
A NEW JACKET!
THE INSIDE LINING IS MADE OF THE LIGHTEST FIBER BODY ARMOR AVAILABLE, THE ELBOWS ENFORCED WITH STEEL AND...WELL... TAKE A LOOK AT THE BACK.
Whoa! THE RESEMBLANCE IS REMARKABLE!
QUEENIE, YOU ARE WORLD-CLASS!
OWNED
5150
NOW I GOT SOMETHIN' COOL TA WEAR TA SKATE CLUB TONIGHT!
Aw, I LOVE YOU!
LOVE YOU RIGHT BACK, NUTBUCKETS.

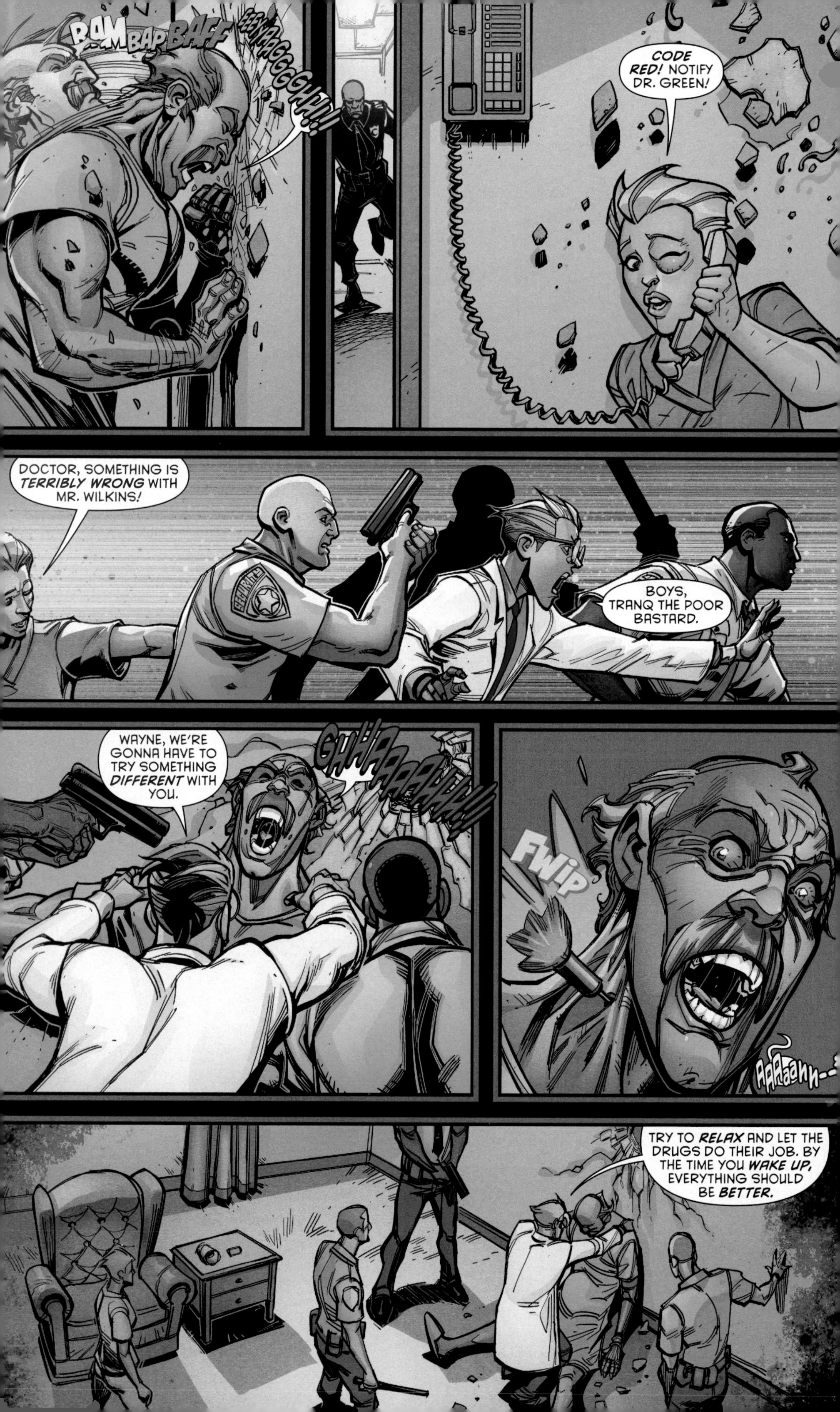
BAM BAP BAFF
EEEYAAGGGHH!!!
CODE RED! NOTIFY DR. GREEN!
DOCTOR, SOMETHING IS TERRIBLY WRONG WITH MR. WILKINS!
BOYS, TRANQ THE POOR BASTARD.
WAYNE, WE'RE GONNA HAVE TO TRY SOMETHING DIFFERENT WITH YOU.
GHHAAAAAHH!!!
FWIP
AAAaann--
TRY TO RELAX AND LET THE DRUGS DO THEIR JOB. BY THE TIME YOU WAKE UP, EVERYTHING SHOULD BE BETTER.

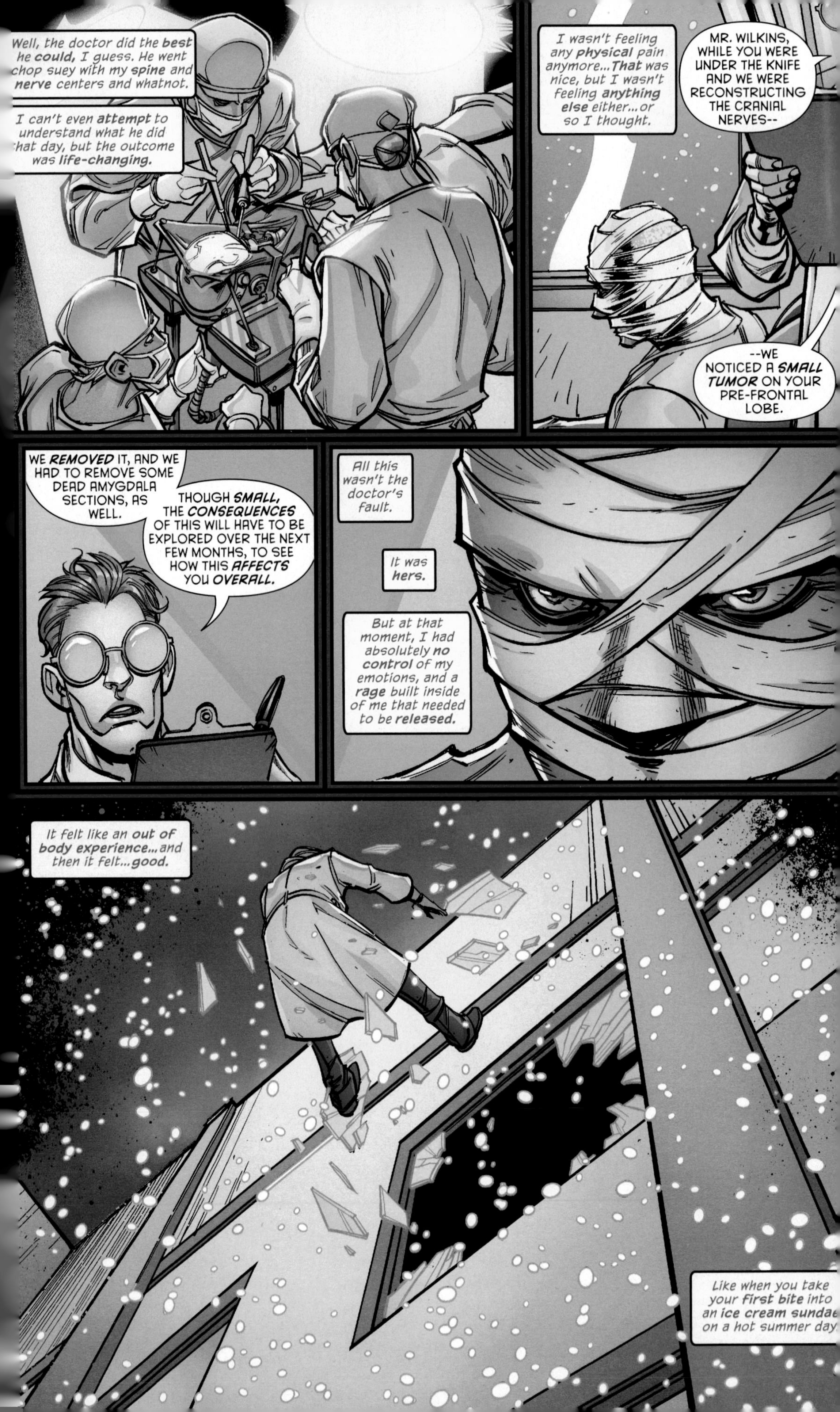

Well, the doctor did the best he could, I guess. He went chop suey with my spine and nerve centers and whatnot.
I can't even attempt to understand what he did that day, but the outcome was life-changing.
I wasn't feeling any physical pain anymore...That was nice, but I wasn't feeling anything else either...or so I thought.
MR. WILKINS, WHILE YOU WERE UNDER THE KNIFE AND WE WERE RECONSTRUCTING THE CRANIAL NERVES--
--WE NOTICED A SMALL TUMOR ON YOUR PRE-FRONTAL LOBE.
WE REMOVED IT, AND WE HAD TO REMOVE SOME DEAD AMYGDALA SECTIONS, AS WELL.
THOUGH SMALL, THE CONSEQUENCES OF THIS WILL HAVE TO BE EXPLORED OVER THE NEXT FEW MONTHS, TO SEE HOW THIS AFFECTS YOU OVERALL.
All this wasn't the doctor's fault.
It was hers.
But at that moment, I had absolutely no control of my emotions, and a rage built inside of me that needed to be released.
It felt like an out of body experience...and then it felt...good.
Like when you take your first bite into an ice cream sundae on a hot summer day

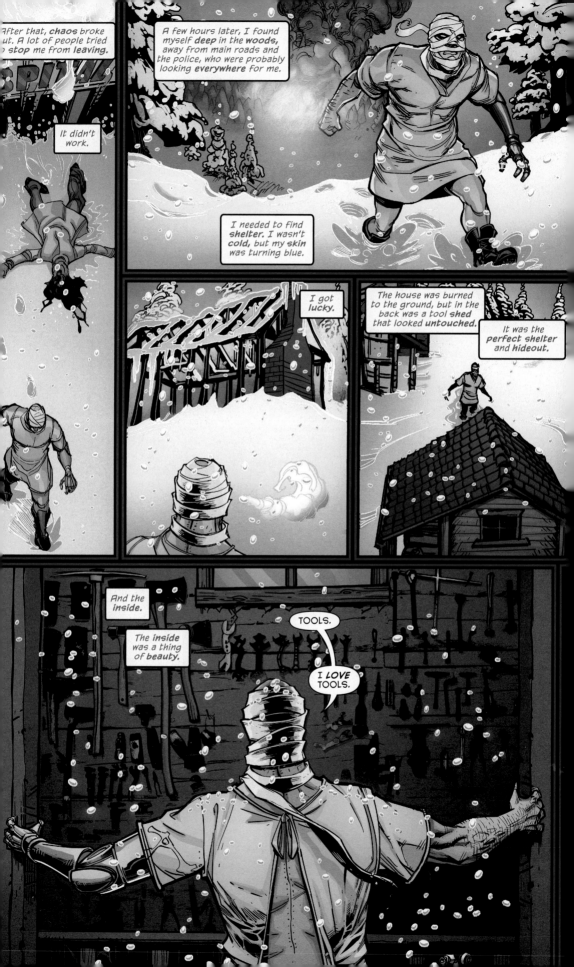

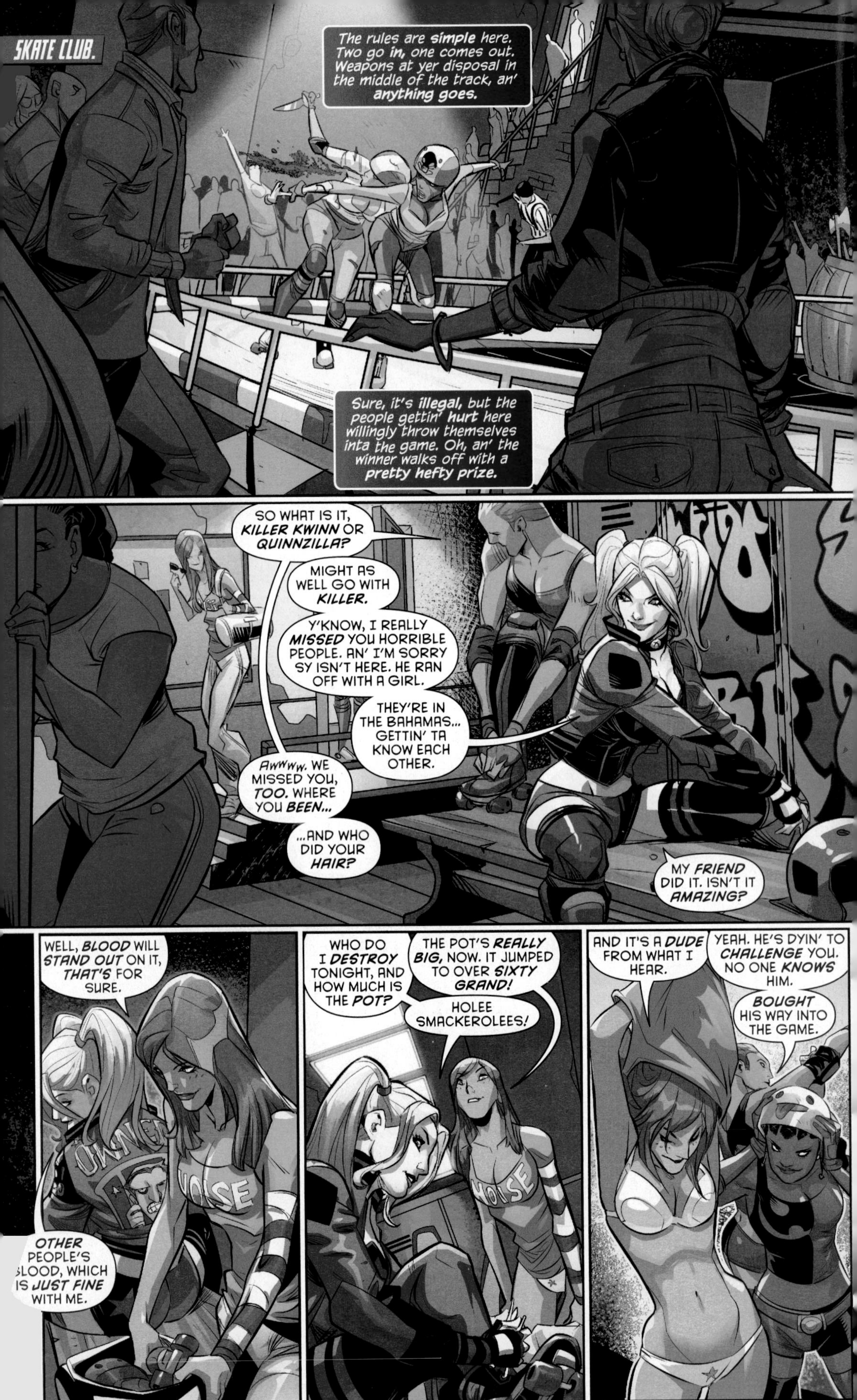
SKATE CLUB.
The rules are simple here. Two go in, one comes out. Weapons at yer disposal in the middle of the track, an' anything goes.
Sure, it's illegal, but the people gettin' hurt here willingly throw themselves inta the game. Oh, an' the winner walks off with a pretty hefty prize.
SO WHAT IS IT, KILLER KWINN OR QUINNZILLA?
MIGHT AS WELL GO WITH KILLER.
Y'KNOW, I REALLY MISSED YOU HORRIBLE PEOPLE. AN' I'M SORRY SY ISN'T HERE. HE RAN OFF WITH A GIRL.
THEY'RE IN THE BAHAMAS... GETTIN' TA KNOW EACH OTHER.
AWWWW. WE MISSED YOU, TOO. WHERE YOU BEEN...
...AND WHO DID YOUR HAIR?
MY FRIEND DID IT. ISN'T IT AMAZING?
WELL, BLOOD WILL STAND OUT ON IT, THAT'S FOR SURE.
OTHER PEOPLE'S BLOOD, WHICH IS JUST FINE WITH ME.
WHO DO I DESTROY TONIGHT, AND HOW MUCH IS THE POT?
THE POT'S REALLY BIG, NOW. IT JUMPED TO OVER SIXTY GRAND!
HOLEE SMACKEROLEES!
AND IT'S A DUDE FROM WHAT I HEAR.
YEAH. HE'S DYIN' TO CHALLENGE YOU. NO ONE KNOWS HIM.
BOUGHT HIS WAY INTO THE GAME.

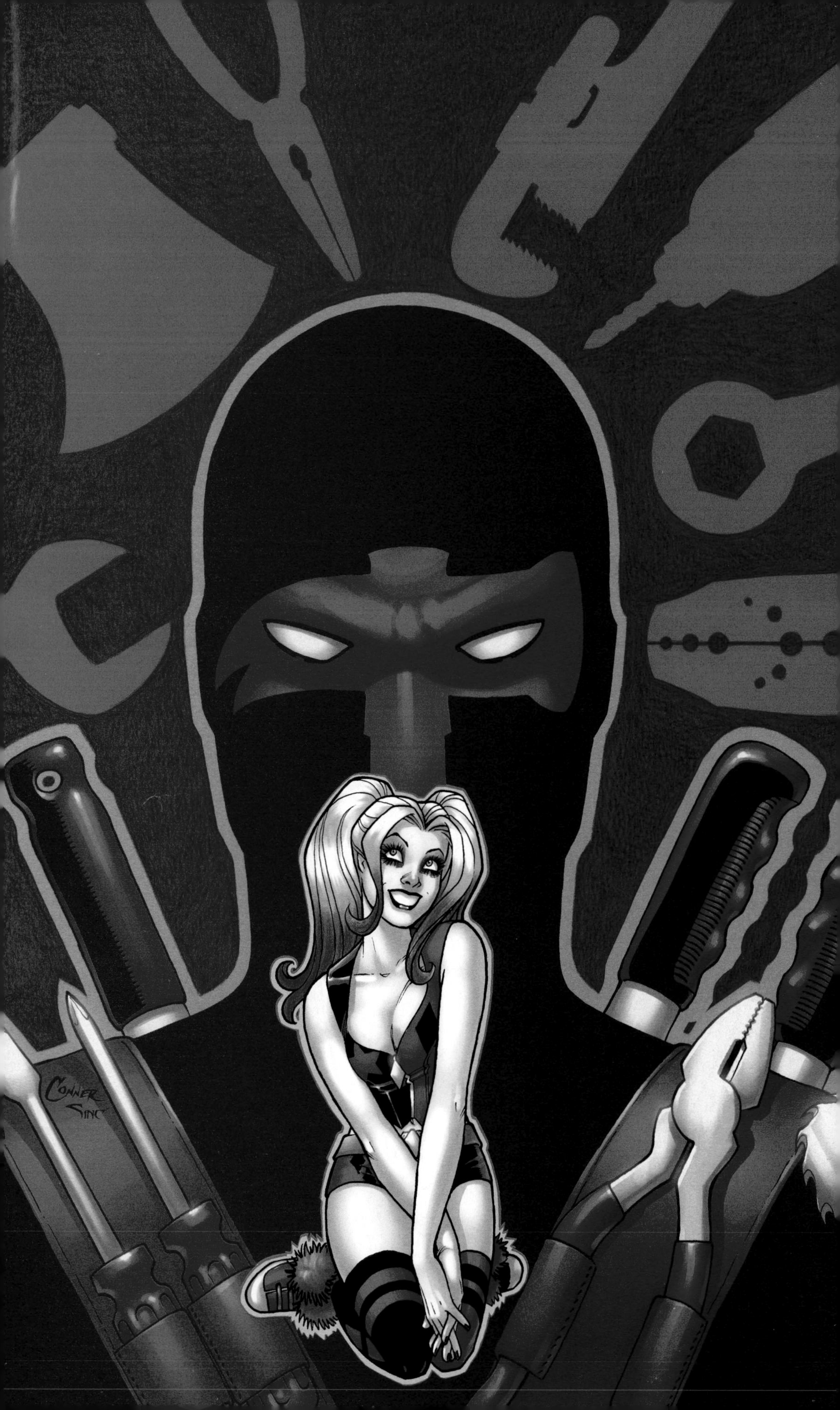

CONNER
SINC

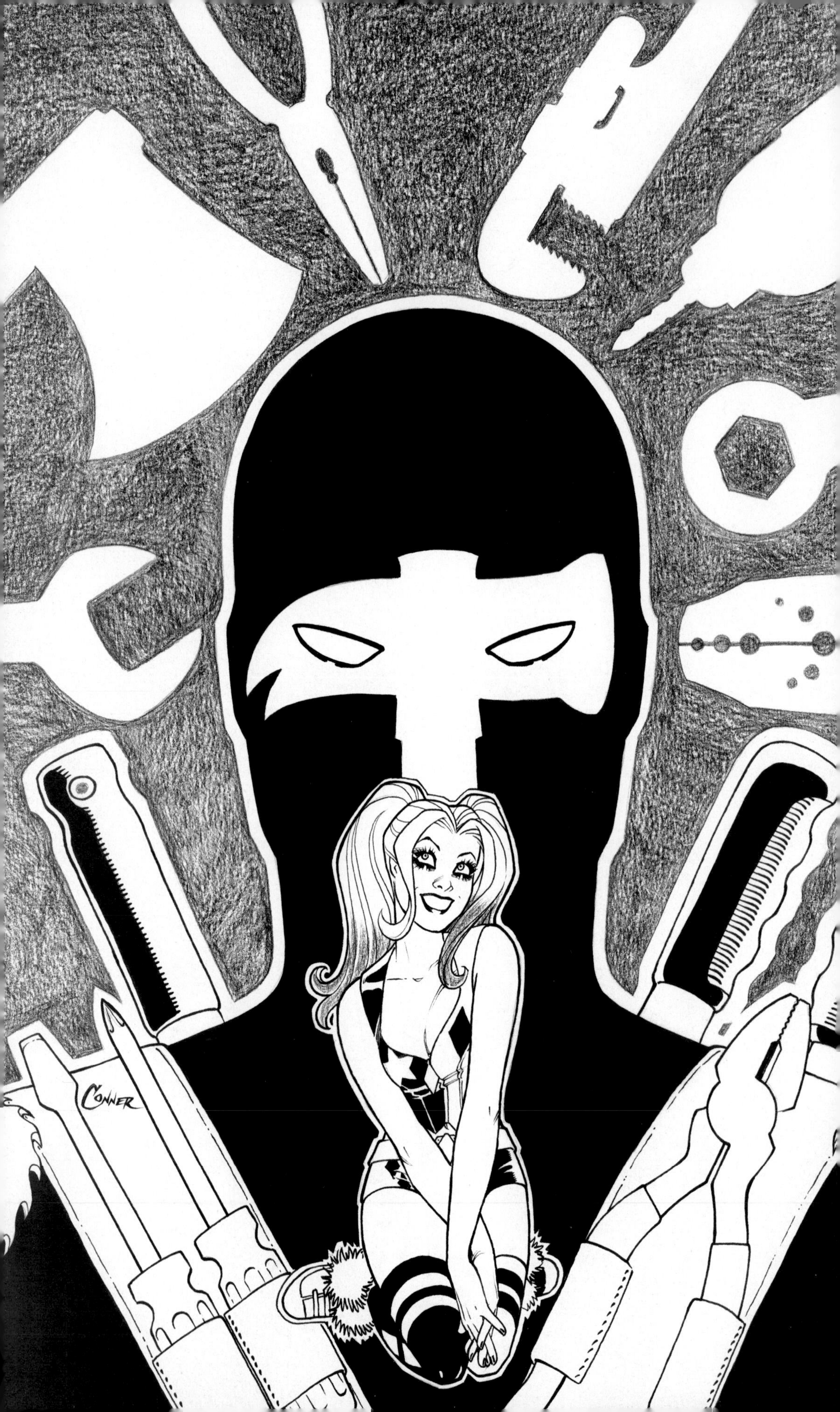
CONNER

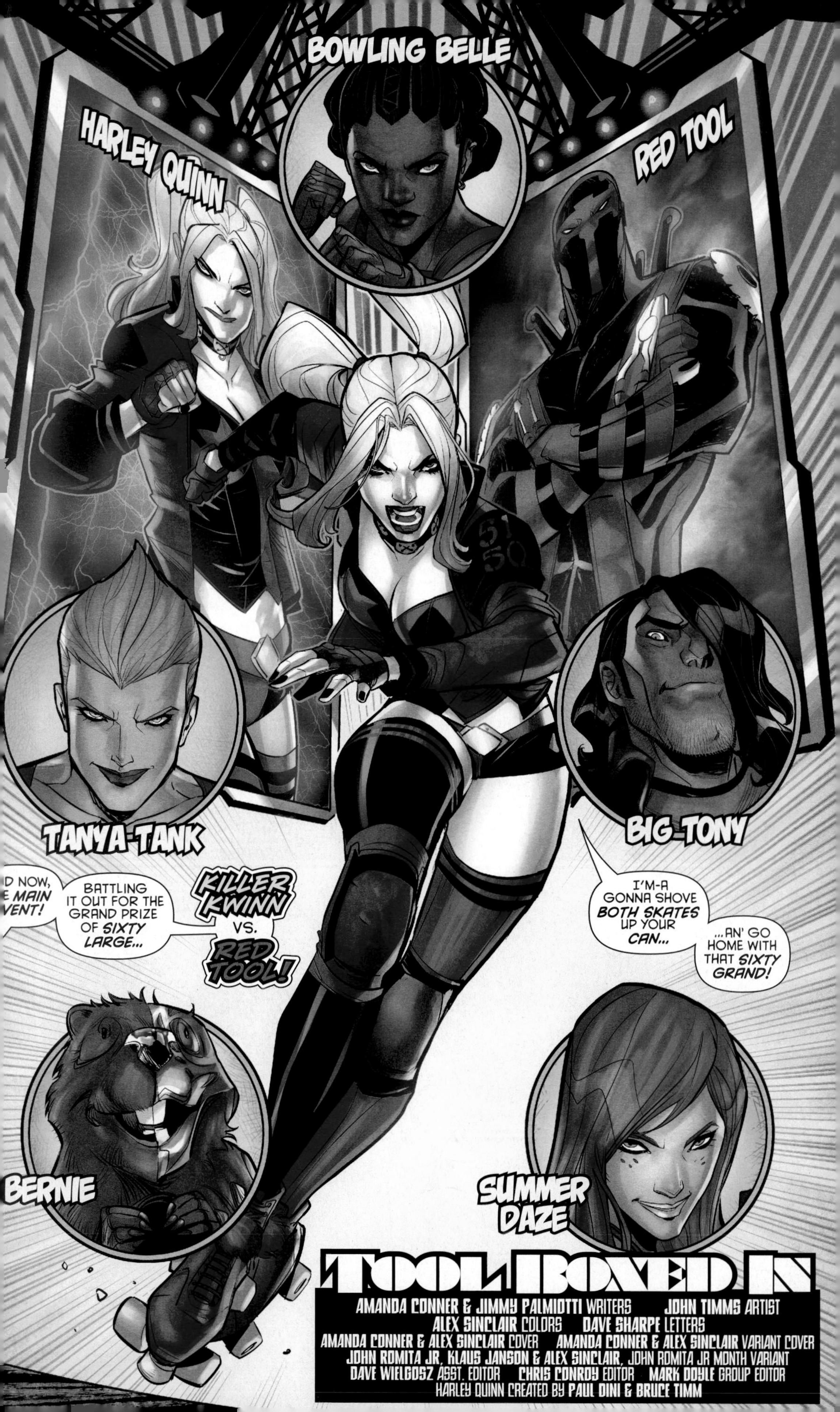
BOWLING BELLE
HARLEY QUINN
RED TOOL
TANYA TANK
BIG TONY
D NOW, E MAIN VENT!
BATTLING IT OUT FOR THE GRAND PRIZE OF SIXTY LARGE...
KILLER KWINN VS. RED TOOL!
I'M-A GONNA SHOVE BOTH SKATES UP YOUR CAN...
...AN' GO HOME WITH THAT SIXTY GRAND!
BERNIE
SUMMER DAZE
TOOL BOXED IN
AMANDA CONNER & JIMMY PALMIOTTI WRITERS JOHN TIMMS ARTIST
ALEX SINCLAIR COLORS DAVE SHARPE LETTERS
AMANDA CONNER & ALEX SINCLAIR COVER AMANDA CONNER & ALEX SINCLAIR VARIANT COVER
JOHN ROMITA JR, KLAUS JANSON & ALEX SINCLAIR, JOHN ROMITA JR MONTH VARIANT
DAVE WIELGOSZ ASST. EDITOR CHRIS CONROY EDITOR MARK DOYLE GROUP EDITOR
HARLEY QUINN CREATED BY PAUL DINI & BRUCE TIMM

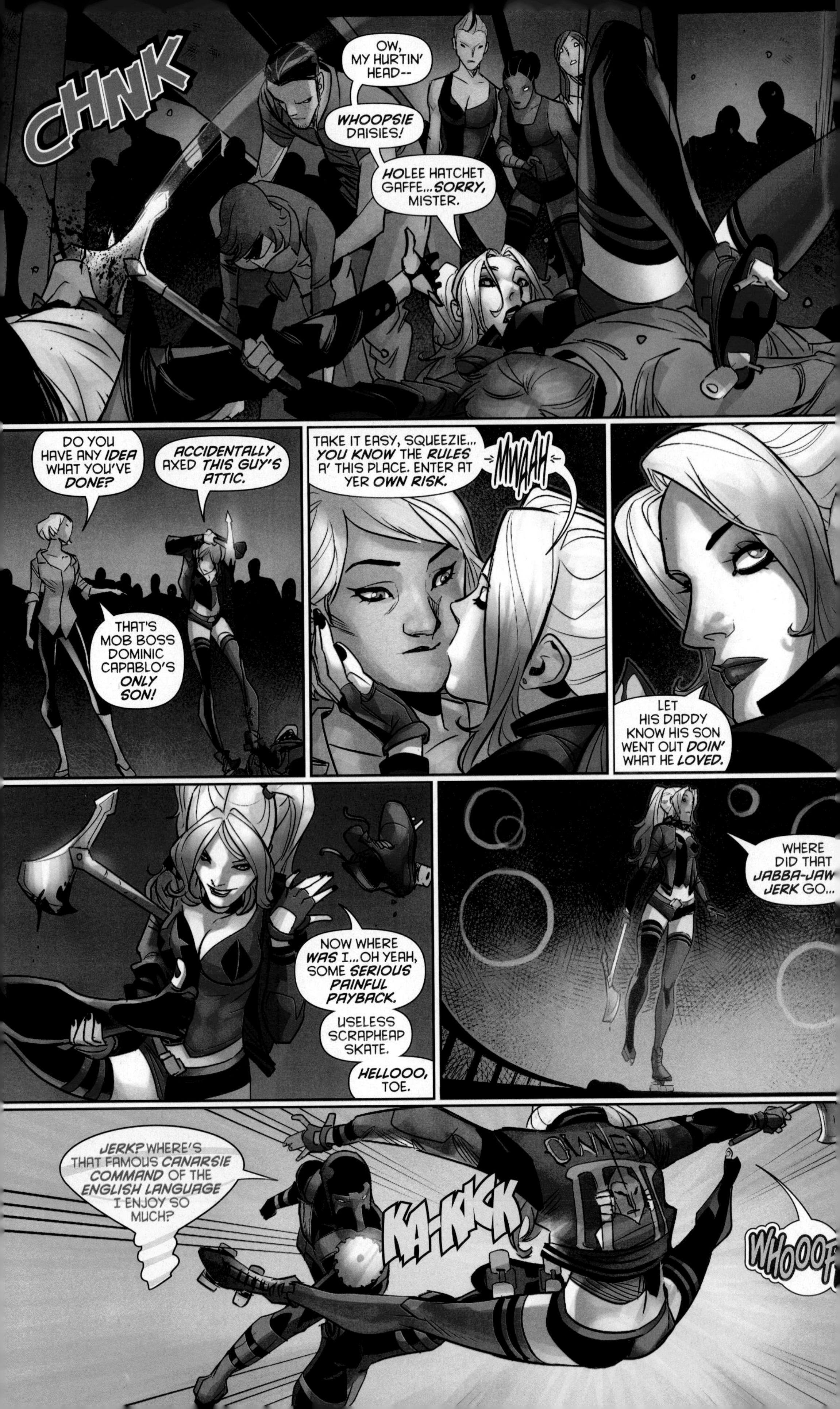

CHNK
OW, MY HURTIN' HEAD--
WHOOPSIE DAISIES!
HOLEE HATCHET GAFFE...SORRY, MISTER.
DO YOU HAVE ANY IDEA WHAT YOU'VE DONE?
ACCIDENTALLY AXED THIS GUY'S ATTIC.
THAT'S MOB BOSS DOMINIC CAPABLO'S ONLY SON!
TAKE IT EASY, SQUEEZIE... YOU KNOW THE RULES A' THIS PLACE. ENTER AT YER OWN RISK.
MWAAH
LET HIS DADDY KNOW HIS SON WENT OUT DOIN' WHAT HE LOVED.
NOW WHERE WAS I...OH YEAH, SOME SERIOUS PAINFUL PAYBACK.
USELESS SCRAPHEAP SKATE.
HELLOOO, TOE.
WHERE DID THAT JABBA-JAW JERK GO...
JERK? WHERE'S THAT FAMOUS CANARSIE COMMAND OF THE ENGLISH LANGUAGE I ENJOY SO MUCH?
KA-KICK
WHOOOF

SKA-BOOF

NOT YET, ANYWAY.

SHHKK D-CAPP THUNKK

SKEWER

STABB

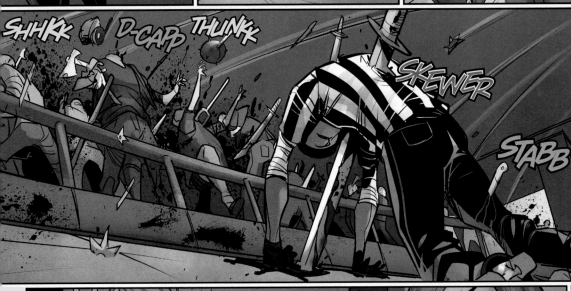

OH MY... EEEEWWW!

OH, I PITY THE CLEANING CREW TONIGHT.

WELL AIN'T THIS *IRONICAL!* I'M GONNA BEAT YOU *UP, DOWN, SIDEWAYS,* AN' *DIAGONALLY* WITH ONE A' YER *VERY OWN* CUSTOM RED *HAMMERS!*

TIME TO *FINISH* THIS ROMP AND GET TO THE *NEXT* ONE.

THIS WAS *FUN.*

WE *GOTTA* DO IT AGAIN.

BWEEEEP

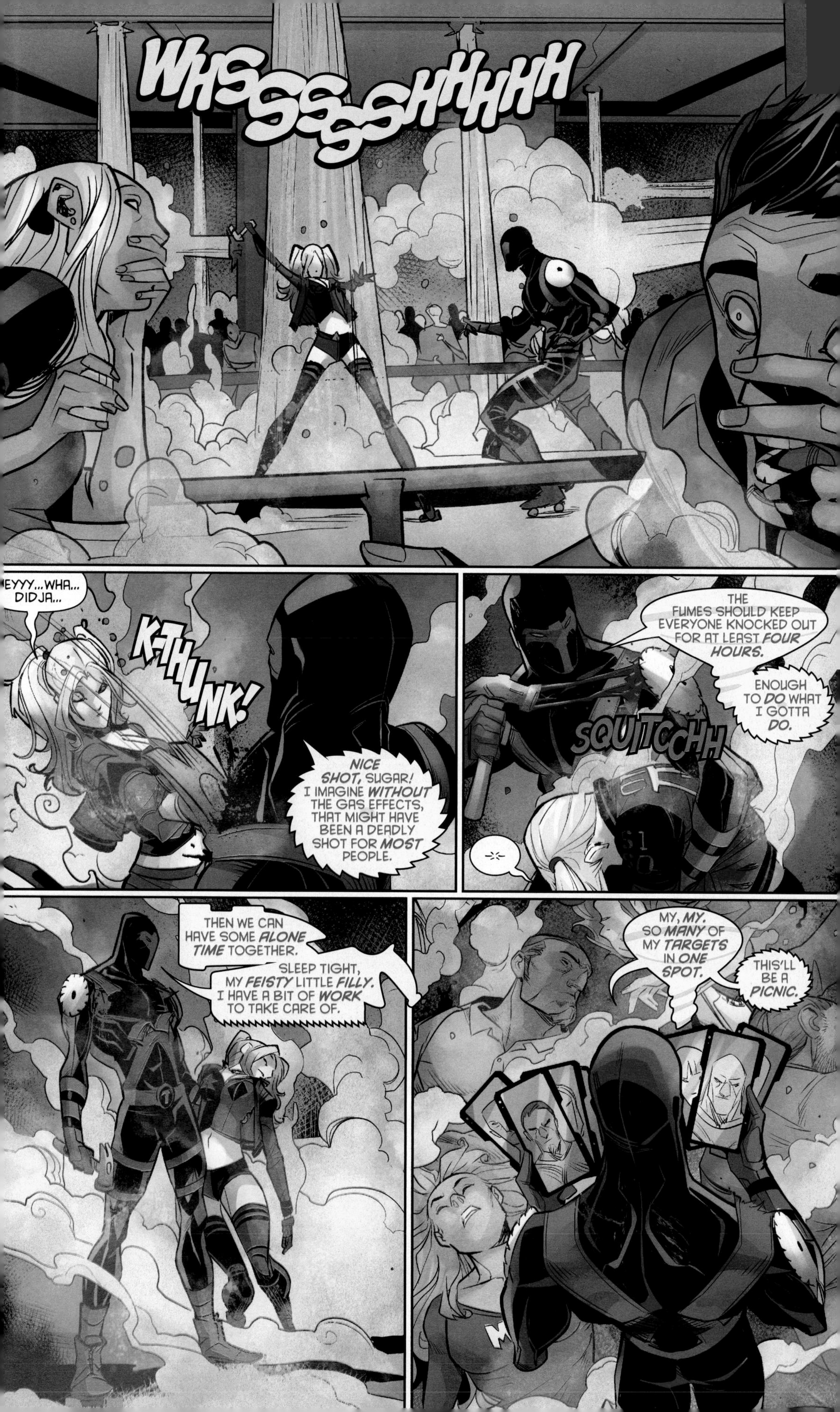
WHSSSSSHHHHHH
EYYY...WHA... DIDJA...
K-THUNK!
NICE SHOT, SUGAR! I IMAGINE WITHOUT THE GAS EFFECTS, THAT MIGHT HAVE BEEN A DEADLY SHOT FOR MOST PEOPLE.
THE FUMES SHOULD KEEP EVERYONE KNOCKED OUT FOR AT LEAST FOUR HOURS.
ENOUGH TO DO WHAT I GOTTA DO.
SQUITCCHH
THEN WE CAN HAVE SOME ALONE TIME TOGETHER.
SLEEP TIGHT, MY FEISTY LITTLE FILLY. I HAVE A BIT OF WORK TO TAKE CARE OF.
MY, MY. SO MANY OF MY TARGETS IN ONE SPOT.
THIS'LL BE A PICNIC.

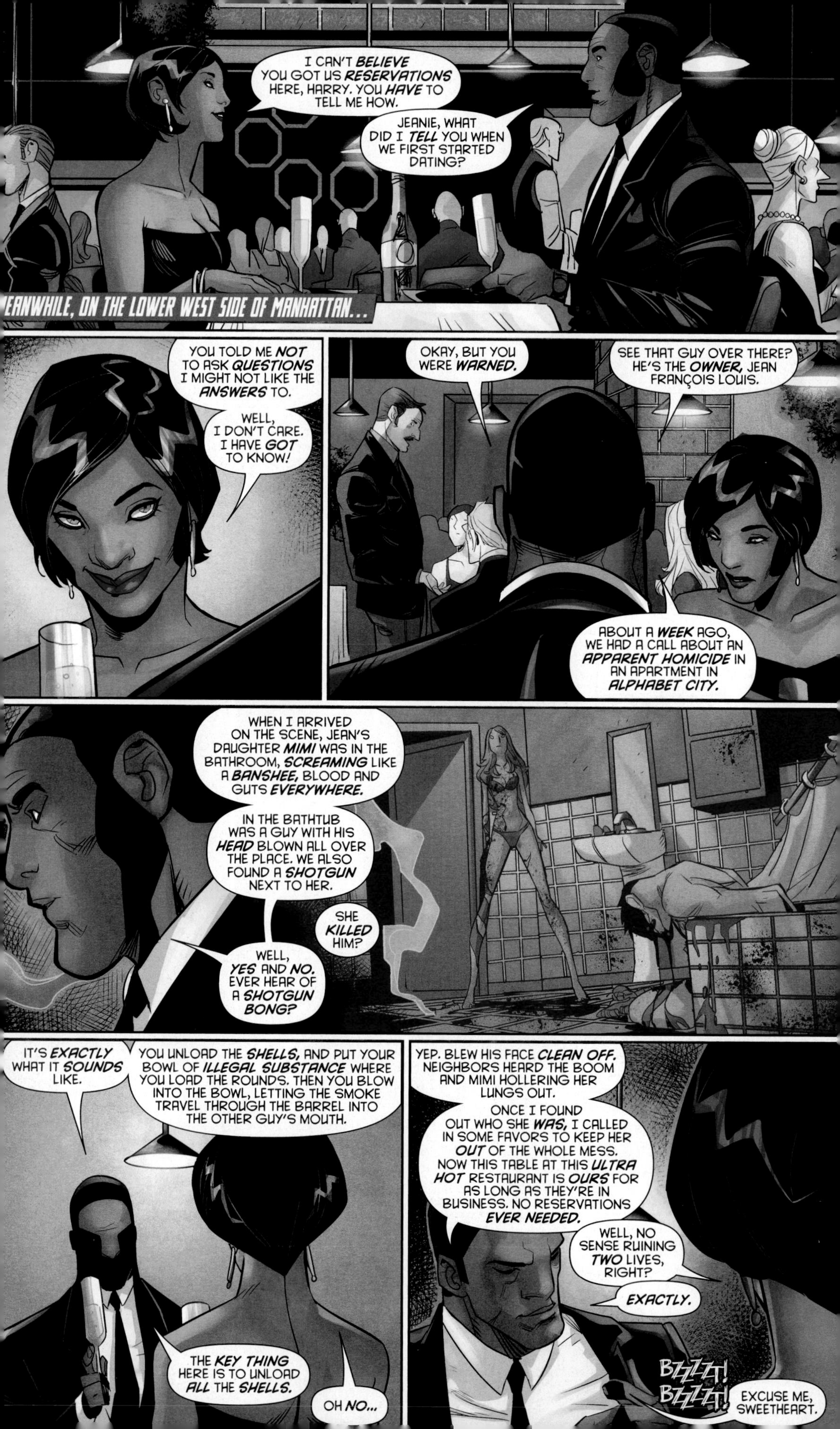
I CAN'T BELIEVE YOU GOT US RESERVATIONS HERE, HARRY. YOU HAVE TO TELL ME HOW.
JEANIE, WHAT DID I TELL YOU WHEN WE FIRST STARTED DATING?
EANWHILE, ON THE LOWER WEST SIDE OF MANHATTAN...
YOU TOLD ME NOT TO ASK QUESTIONS I MIGHT NOT LIKE THE ANSWERS TO.
WELL, I DON'T CARE. I HAVE GOT TO KNOW!
OKAY, BUT YOU WERE WARNED.
SEE THAT GUY OVER THERE? HE'S THE OWNER, JEAN FRANÇOIS LOUIS.
ABOUT A WEEK AGO, WE HAD A CALL ABOUT AN APPARENT HOMICIDE IN AN APARTMENT IN ALPHABET CITY.
WHEN I ARRIVED ON THE SCENE, JEAN'S DAUGHTER MIMI WAS IN THE BATHROOM, SCREAMING LIKE A BANSHEE, BLOOD AND GUTS EVERYWHERE.
IN THE BATHTUB WAS A GUY WITH HIS HEAD BLOWN ALL OVER THE PLACE. WE ALSO FOUND A SHOTGUN NEXT TO HER.
SHE KILLED HIM?
WELL, YES AND NO. EVER HEAR OF A SHOTGUN BONG?
IT'S EXACTLY WHAT IT SOUNDS LIKE.
YOU UNLOAD THE SHELLS, AND PUT YOUR BOWL OF ILLEGAL SUBSTANCE WHERE YOU LOAD THE ROUNDS. THEN YOU BLOW INTO THE BOWL, LETTING THE SMOKE TRAVEL THROUGH THE BARREL INTO THE OTHER GUY'S MOUTH.
THE KEY THING HERE IS TO UNLOAD ALL THE SHELLS.
OH NO...
YEP. BLEW HIS FACE CLEAN OFF. NEIGHBORS HEARD THE BOOM AND MIMI HOLLERING HER LUNGS OUT.
ONCE I FOUND OUT WHO SHE WAS, I CALLED IN SOME FAVORS TO KEEP HER OUT OF THE WHOLE MESS. NOW THIS TABLE AT THIS ULTRA HOT RESTAURANT IS OURS FOR AS LONG AS THEY'RE IN BUSINESS. NO RESERVATIONS EVER NEEDED.
WELL, NO SENSE RUINING TWO LIVES, RIGHT?
EXACTLY.
BZZZZT! BZZZZT!
EXCUSE ME, SWEETHEART.

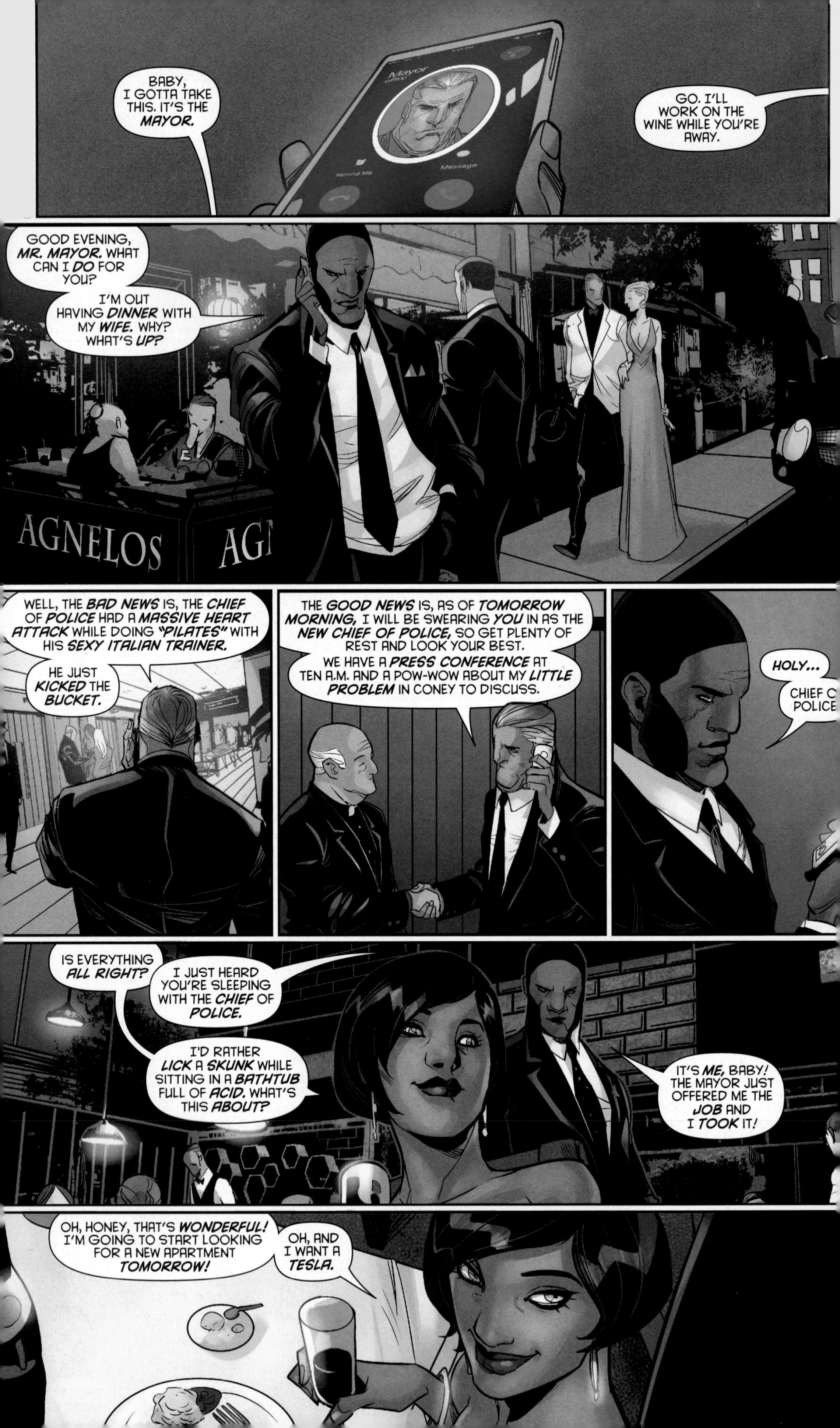

BABY, I GOTTA TAKE THIS. IT'S THE MAYOR.
GO. I'LL WORK ON THE WINE WHILE YOU'RE AWAY.
GOOD EVENING, MR. MAYOR. WHAT CAN I DO FOR YOU?
I'M OUT HAVING DINNER WITH MY WIFE. WHY? WHAT'S UP?
AGNELOS
AGN
WELL, THE BAD NEWS IS, THE CHIEF OF POLICE HAD A MASSIVE HEART ATTACK WHILE DOING "PILATES" WITH HIS SEXY ITALIAN TRAINER.
HE JUST KICKED THE BUCKET.
THE GOOD NEWS IS, AS OF TOMORROW MORNING, I WILL BE SWEARING YOU IN AS THE NEW CHIEF OF POLICE, SO GET PLENTY OF REST AND LOOK YOUR BEST.
WE HAVE A PRESS CONFERENCE AT TEN A.M. AND A POW-WOW ABOUT MY LITTLE PROBLEM IN CONEY TO DISCUSS.
HOLY...
CHIEF O POLICE
IS EVERYTHING ALL RIGHT?
I JUST HEARD YOU'RE SLEEPING WITH THE CHIEF OF POLICE.
I'D RATHER LICK A SKUNK WHILE SITTING IN A BATHTUB FULL OF ACID. WHAT'S THIS ABOUT?
IT'S ME, BABY! THE MAYOR JUST OFFERED ME THE JOB AND I TOOK IT!
OH, HONEY, THAT'S WONDERFUL! I'M GOING TO START LOOKING FOR A NEW APARTMENT TOMORROW!
OH, AND I WANT A TESLA.

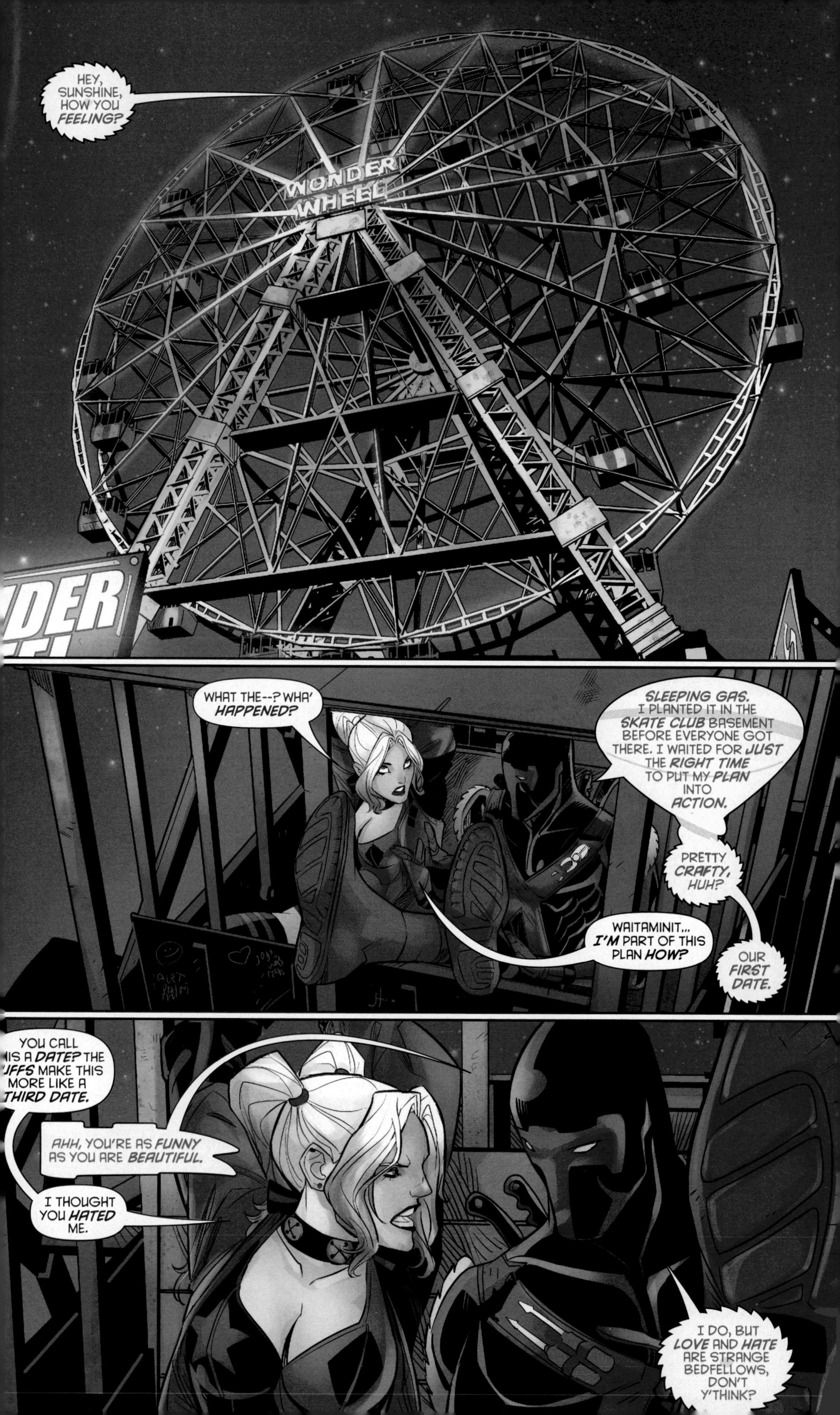
HEY, SUNSHINE, HOW YOU FEELING?
WONDER WHEEL
DER
WHAT THE--? WHA' HAPPENED?
SLEEPING GAS. I PLANTED IT IN THE SKATE CLUB BASEMENT BEFORE EVERYONE GOT THERE. I WAITED FOR JUST THE RIGHT TIME TO PUT MY PLAN INTO ACTION.
PRETTY CRAFTY, HUH?
WAITAMINIT... I'M PART OF THIS PLAN HOW?
OUR FIRST DATE.
YOU CALL IS A DATE? THE UFFS MAKE THIS MORE LIKE A THIRD DATE.
AHH, YOU'RE AS FUNNY AS YOU ARE BEAUTIFUL.
I THOUGHT YOU HATED ME.
I DO, BUT LOVE AND HATE ARE STRANGE BEDFELLOWS, DON'T Y'THINK?

WH... WHA' *HIT* ME?

Ow.

WHAT HIT *EVERYBODY*, YOU MEAN. SMELLED LIKE *KNOCKOUT* GAS, AND THE *HEADACHE* I HAVE *CONFIRMS* IT.

HARLEY AND *RED TOOL* ARE GONE...AN'...

...*OH*... OH *MY*.

ARE THOSE... *TATTOOS?*

OH, *OW*... WHAT HAPPENED?

OUCH, WHAT THE *HELL?*

MIGOD, IS THERE *ANYTHING*...

NO, NO, YOU'RE *FINE*. NO TATTOOS...

WHAT ABOUT *MY* HEAD?

YOU'RE GOOD. IS MINE OKAY?

NO TATTOO ON YOU. WHAT THE HELL'S GOING *ON?*

TRY HARLEY'S CELL...

GOOD IDEA!

IT'S RINGING.

HELLO, *HARLEY?*

I'M SORRY; HARLEY IS *TIED UP* AT THE MOMENT. MAY I TAKE A *MESSAGE?*

WHO *IS* THIS?

HER *ASSISTANT*. IF YOU'D *LIKE* TO LEAVE A *MESSAGE*, I'LL MAKE SURE SHE *GETS* IT.

RELAX, BELLE. YOUR GIRL IS *FINE*. SHE HAS HER *MOUTH FULL* AT THE MOMENT.

ISN'T THAT *RIGHT*, HARLEY?

YOU'RE *OKAY*, RIGHT?

NEFFR BMM BEFFR!

YURRPPP!

I'LL HAVE HER CALL YOU *BACK* AS SOON AS SHE CAN. BUH-BYE.

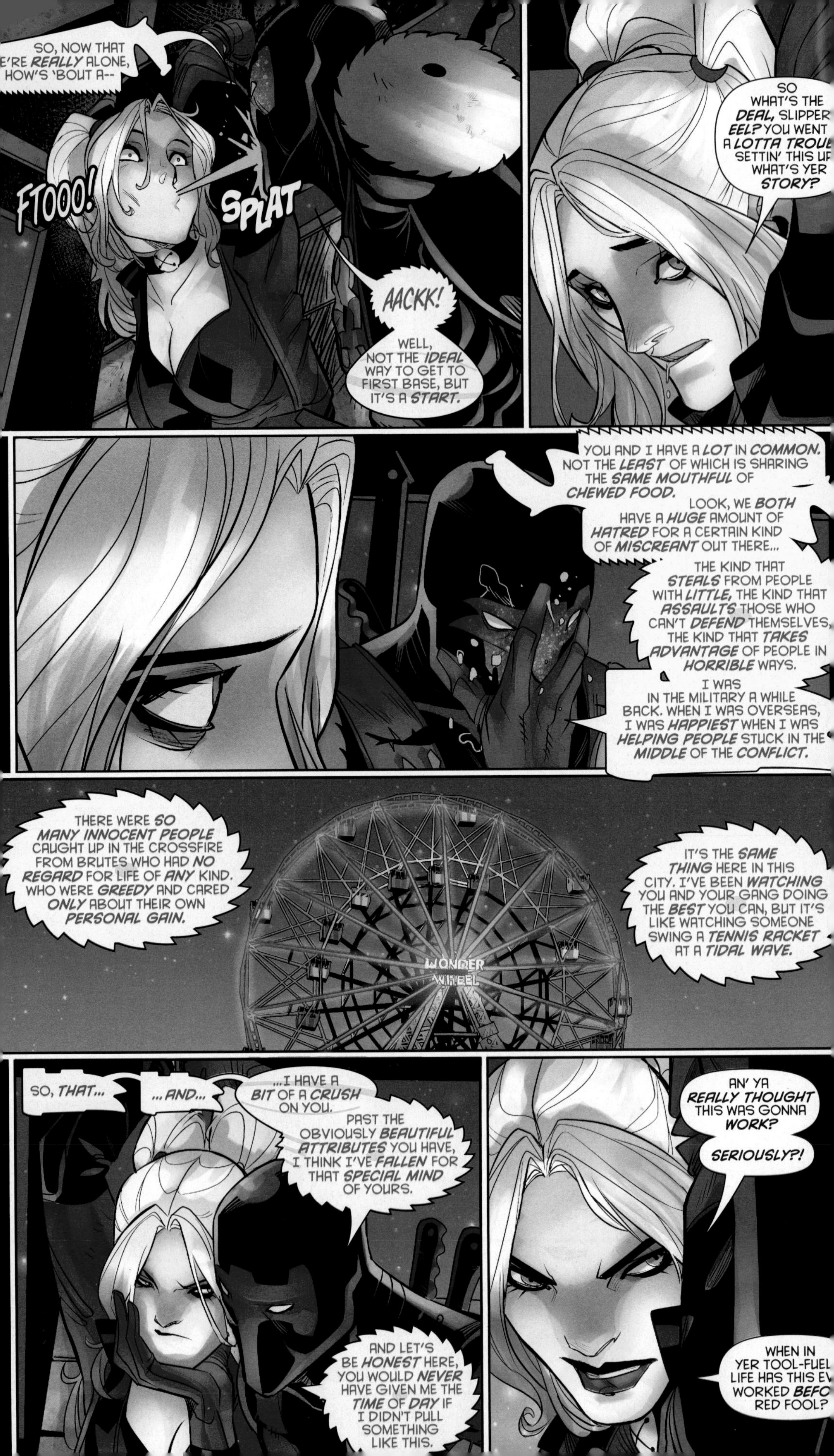
SO, NOW THAT 'E'RE REALLY ALONE, HOW'S 'BOUT A--
FTOOO!
SPLAT
AACKK!
WELL, NOT THE IDEAL WAY TO GET TO FIRST BASE, BUT IT'S A START.
SO WHAT'S THE DEAL, SLIPPER EEL? YOU WENT A LOTTA TROUI SETTIN' THIS UP WHAT'S YER STORY?
YOU AND I HAVE A LOT IN COMMON. NOT THE LEAST OF WHICH IS SHARING THE SAME MOUTHFUL OF CHEWED FOOD.
LOOK, WE BOTH HAVE A HUGE AMOUNT OF HATRED FOR A CERTAIN KIND OF MISCREANT OUT THERE...
THE KIND THAT STEALS FROM PEOPLE WITH LITTLE, THE KIND THAT ASSAULTS THOSE WHO CAN'T DEFEND THEMSELVES, THE KIND THAT TAKES ADVANTAGE OF PEOPLE IN HORRIBLE WAYS.
I WAS IN THE MILITARY A WHILE BACK. WHEN I WAS OVERSEAS, I WAS HAPPIEST WHEN I WAS HELPING PEOPLE STUCK IN THE MIDDLE OF THE CONFLICT.
THERE WERE SO MANY INNOCENT PEOPLE CAUGHT UP IN THE CROSSFIRE FROM BRUTES WHO HAD NO REGARD FOR LIFE OF ANY KIND. WHO WERE GREEDY AND CARED ONLY ABOUT THEIR OWN PERSONAL GAIN.
WONDER WHEEL
IT'S THE SAME THING HERE IN THIS CITY. I'VE BEEN WATCHING YOU AND YOUR GANG DOING THE BEST YOU CAN, BUT IT'S LIKE WATCHING SOMEONE SWING A TENNIS RACKET AT A TIDAL WAVE.
SO, THAT...
...AND...
...I HAVE A BIT OF A CRUSH ON YOU.
PAST THE OBVIOUSLY BEAUTIFUL ATTRIBUTES YOU HAVE, I THINK I'VE FALLEN FOR THAT SPECIAL MIND OF YOURS.
AND LET'S BE HONEST HERE, YOU WOULD NEVER HAVE GIVEN ME THE TIME OF DAY IF I DIDN'T PULL SOMETHING LIKE THIS.
AN' YA REALLY THOUGHT THIS WAS GONNA WORK?
SERIOUSLY?!
WHEN IN YER TOOL-FUEL LIFE HAS THIS EV WORKED BEFC RED FOOL?

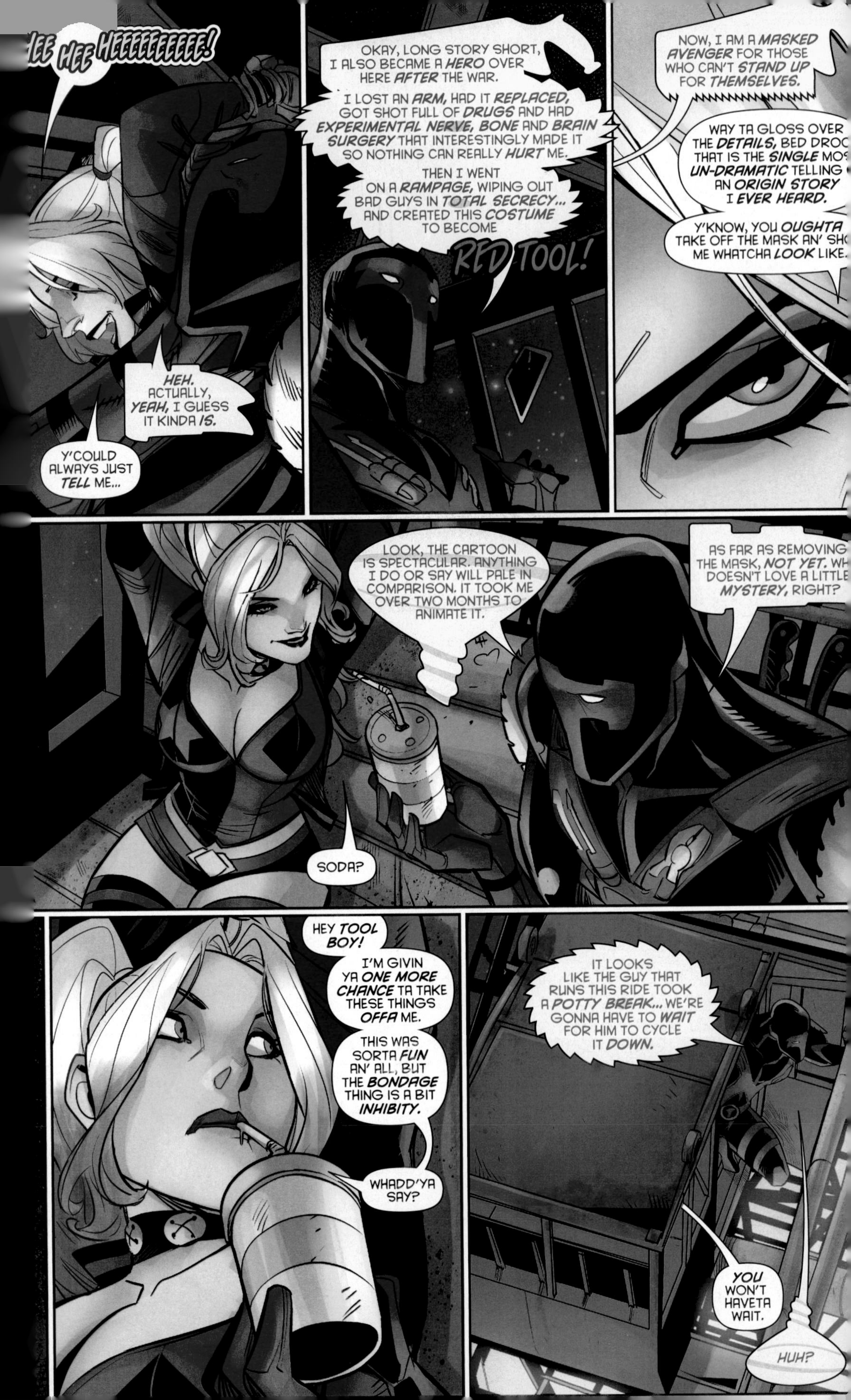

HEE HEE HEEEEEEEEEEE!
OKAY, LONG STORY SHORT, I ALSO BECAME A HERO OVER HERE AFTER THE WAR.
I LOST AN ARM, HAD IT REPLACED, GOT SHOT FULL OF DRUGS AND HAD EXPERIMENTAL NERVE, BONE AND BRAIN SURGERY THAT INTERESTINGLY MADE IT SO NOTHING CAN REALLY HURT ME.
THEN I WENT ON A RAMPAGE, WIPING OUT BAD GUYS IN TOTAL SECRECY... AND CREATED THIS COSTUME TO BECOME
RED TOOL!
NOW, I AM A MASKED AVENGER FOR THOSE WHO CAN'T STAND UP FOR THEMSELVES.
WAY TA GLOSS OVER THE DETAILS, BED DRO THAT IS THE SINGLE MO UN-DRAMATIC TELLING AN ORIGIN STORY I EVER HEARD.
Y'KNOW, YOU OUGHTA TAKE OFF THE MASK AN' SH ME WHATCHA LOOK LIKE.
HEH. ACTUALLY, YEAH, I GUESS IT KINDA IS.
Y'COULD ALWAYS JUST TELL ME...
LOOK, THE CARTOON IS SPECTACULAR. ANYTHING I DO OR SAY WILL PALE IN COMPARISON. IT TOOK ME OVER TWO MONTHS TO ANIMATE IT.
AS FAR AS REMOVING THE MASK, NOT YET. WH DOESN'T LOVE A LITTLE MYSTERY, RIGHT?
SODA?
HEY TOOL BOY!
I'M GIVIN YA ONE MORE CHANCE TA TAKE THESE THINGS OFFA ME.
THIS WAS SORTA FUN AN' ALL, BUT THE BONDAGE THING IS A BIT INHIBITY.
WHADD'YA SAY?
IT LOOKS LIKE THE GUY THAT RUNS THIS RIDE TOOK A POTTY BREAK... WE'RE GONNA HAVE TO WAIT FOR HIM TO CYCLE IT DOWN.
YOU WON'T HAVETA WAIT.
HUH?

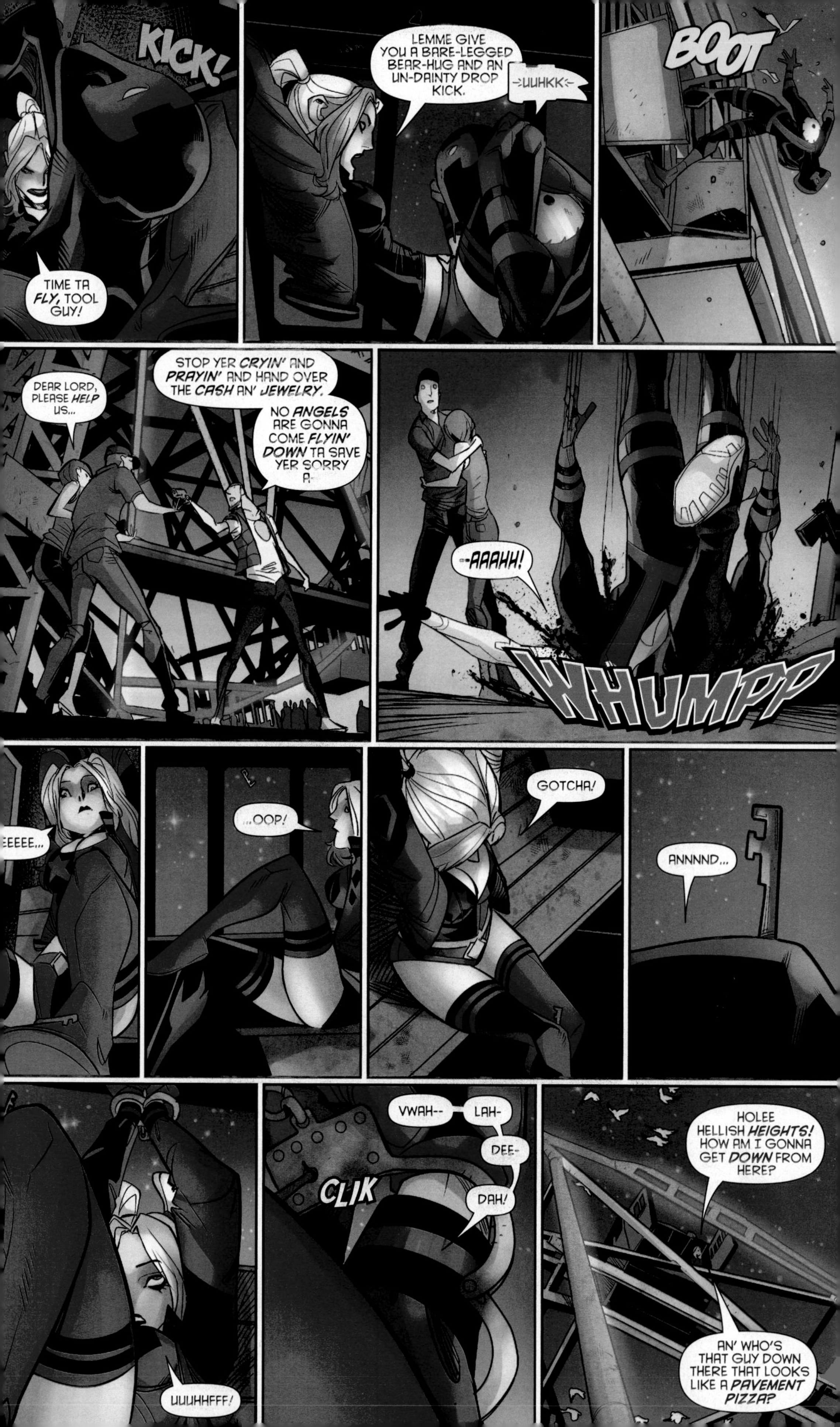
KICK!
TIME TA FLY, TOOL GUY!
LEMME GIVE YOU A BARE-LEGGED BEAR-HUG AND AN UN-DAINTY DROP KICK.
UUHKK
BOOT
DEAR LORD, PLEASE HELP US...
STOP YER CRYIN' AND PRAYIN' AND HAND OVER THE CASH AN' JEWELRY.
NO ANGELS ARE GONNA COME FLYIN' DOWN TA SAVE YER SORRY A-
--AAAHH!
WHUMPP
EEEEE...
...OOP!
GOTCHA!
ANNNND...
UUUHHFFF!
VWAH--
LAH-
DEE-
DAH!
CLIK
HOLEE HELLISH HEIGHTS! HOW AM I GONNA GET DOWN FROM HERE?
AN' WHO'S THAT GUY DOWN THERE THAT LOOKS LIKE A PAVEMENT PIZZA?

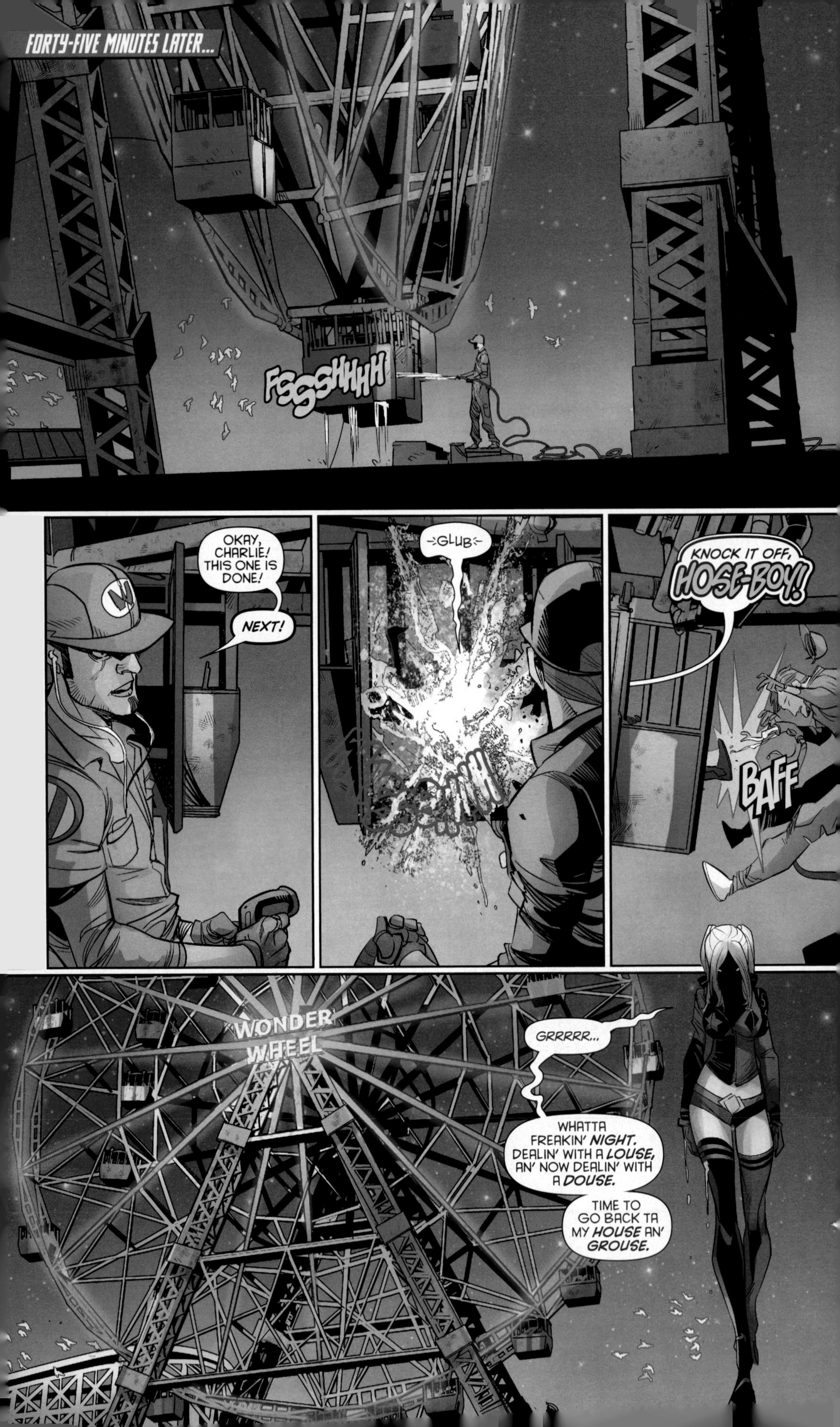
FORTY-FIVE MINUTES LATER...
FSSSHHHH
OKAY, CHARLIE! THIS ONE IS DONE!
NEXT!
GLUB
KNOCK IT OFF, HOSE-BOY!
BAFF
WONDER WHEEL
GRRRRR...
WHATTA FREAKIN' NIGHT. DEALIN' WITH A LOUSE, AN' NOW DEALIN' WITH A DOUSE.
TIME TO GO BACK TA MY HOUSE AN' GROUSE.

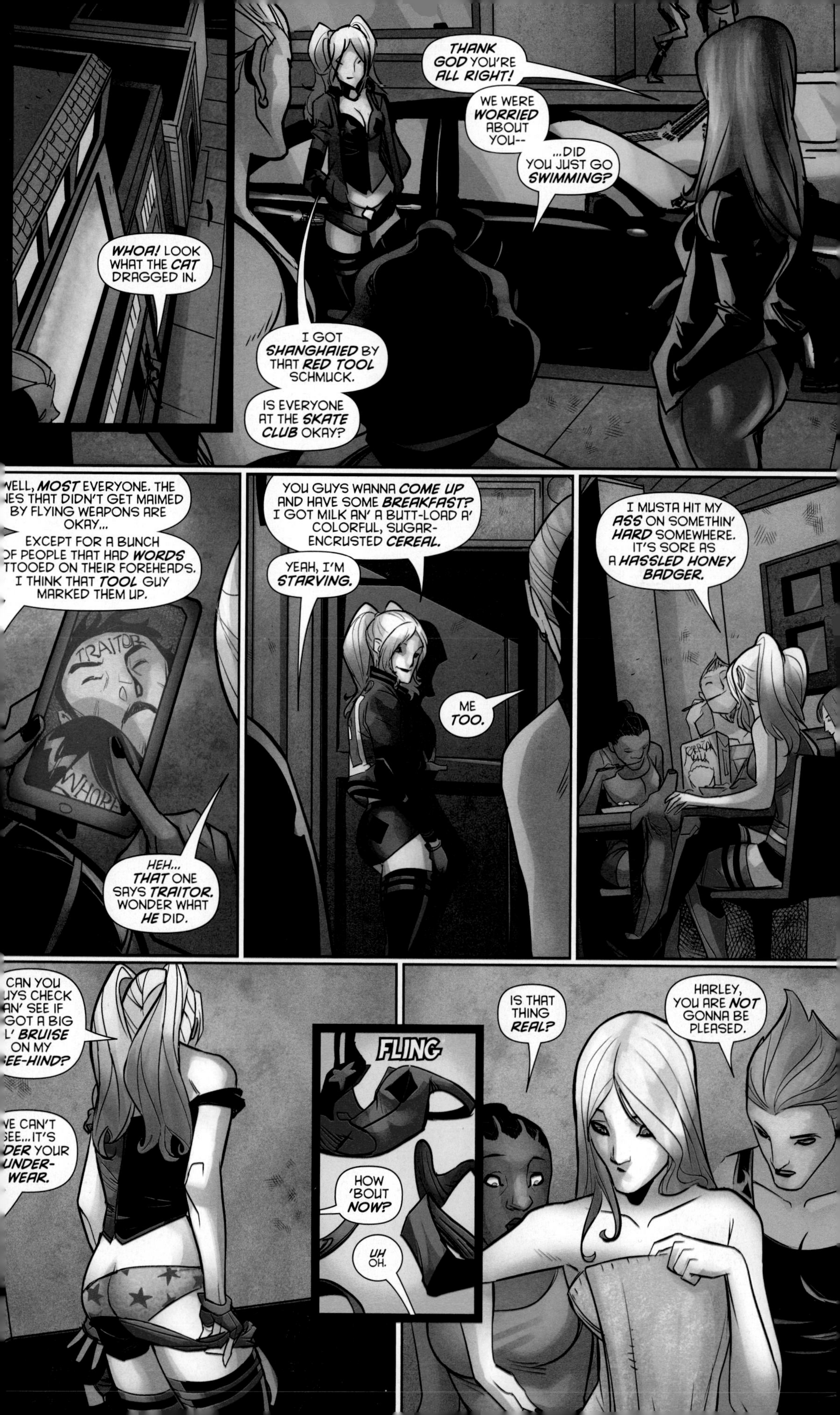
THANK GOD YOU'RE ALL RIGHT!
WE WERE WORRIED ABOUT YOU--
...DID YOU JUST GO SWIMMING?
WHOA! LOOK WHAT THE CAT DRAGGED IN.
I GOT SHANGHAIED BY THAT RED TOOL SCHMUCK.
IS EVERYONE AT THE SKATE CLUB OKAY?
WELL, MOST EVERYONE. THE NES THAT DIDN'T GET MAIMED BY FLYING WEAPONS ARE OKAY...
EXCEPT FOR A BUNCH OF PEOPLE THAT HAD WORDS TTOOED ON THEIR FOREHEADS. I THINK THAT TOOL GUY MARKED THEM UP.
TRAITOR
WHORE
HEH... THAT ONE SAYS TRAITOR. WONDER WHAT HE DID.
YOU GUYS WANNA COME UP AND HAVE SOME BREAKFAST? I GOT MILK AN' A BUTT-LOAD A' COLORFUL, SUGAR-ENCRUSTED CEREAL.
YEAH, I'M STARVING.
ME TOO.
I MUSTA HIT MY ASS ON SOMETHIN' HARD SOMEWHERE. IT'S SORE AS A HASSLED HONEY BADGER.
CAN YOU UYS CHECK AN' SEE IF GOT A BIG L' BRUISE ON MY EE-HIND?
WE CAN'T EE...IT'S DER YOUR UNDER-WEAR.
FLING
HOW 'BOUT NOW?
UH OH.
IS THAT THING REAL?
HARLEY, YOU ARE NOT GONNA BE PLEASED.

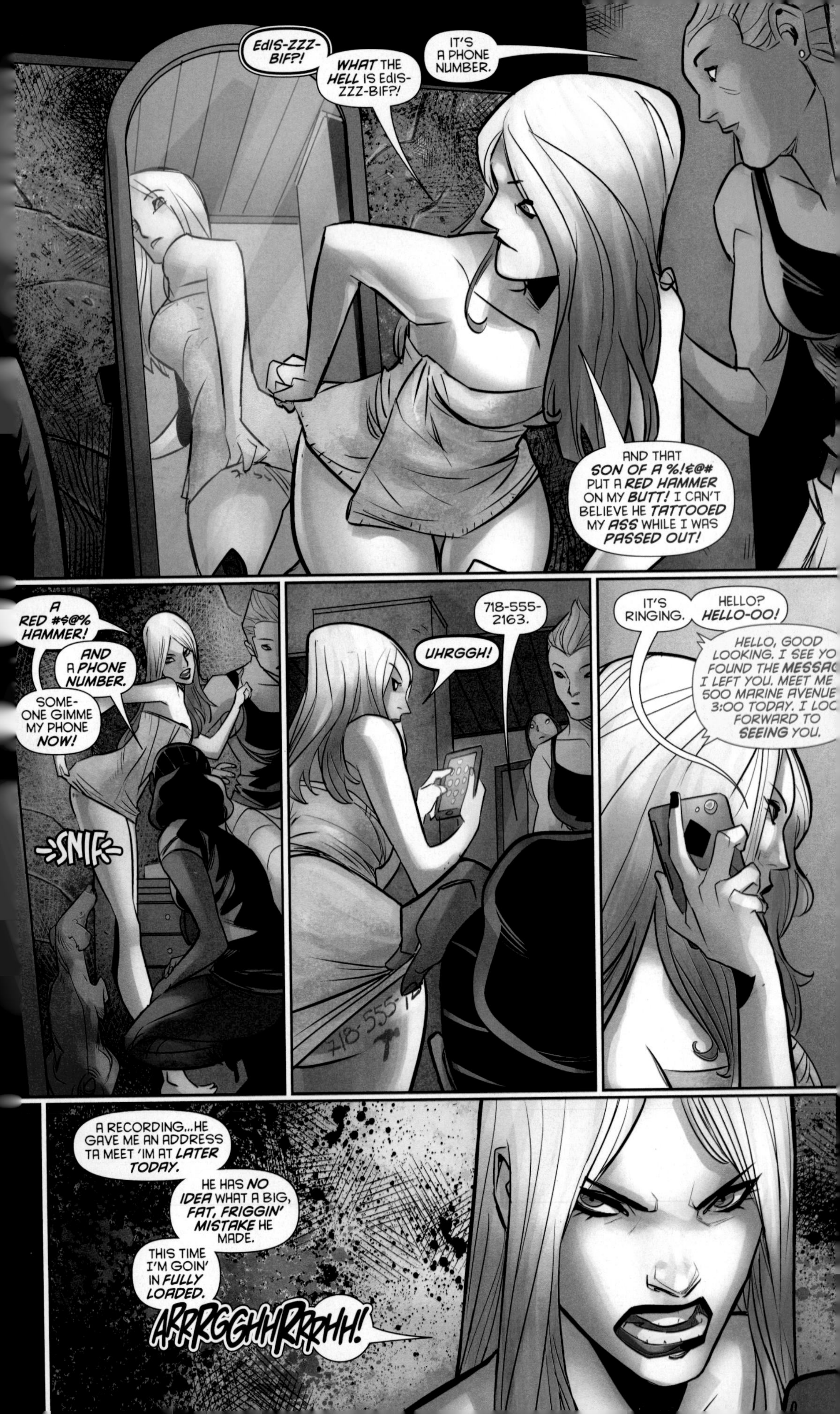
EdIS-ZZZ-BIF?!
WHAT THE HELL IS EdIS-ZZZ-BIF?!
IT'S A PHONE NUMBER.
AND THAT SON OF A %!¢@# PUT A RED HAMMER ON MY BUTT! I CAN'T BELIEVE HE TATTOOED MY ASS WHILE I WAS PASSED OUT!
A RED #$@% HAMMER!
AND A PHONE NUMBER.
SOME-ONE GIMME MY PHONE NOW!
SNIF
718-555-2163.
UHRGGH!
718-555-
IT'S RINGING.
HELLO? HELLO-OO!
HELLO, GOOD LOOKING. I SEE YO FOUND THE MESSAG I LEFT YOU. MEET ME 500 MARINE AVENUE 3:00 TODAY. I LOO FORWARD TO SEEING YOU.
A RECORDING...HE GAVE ME AN ADDRESS TA MEET 'IM AT LATER TODAY.
HE HAS NO IDEA WHAT A BIG, FAT, FRIGGIN' MISTAKE HE MADE.
THIS TIME I'M GOIN' IN FULLY LOADED.
ARRRGGHHRRRHH!

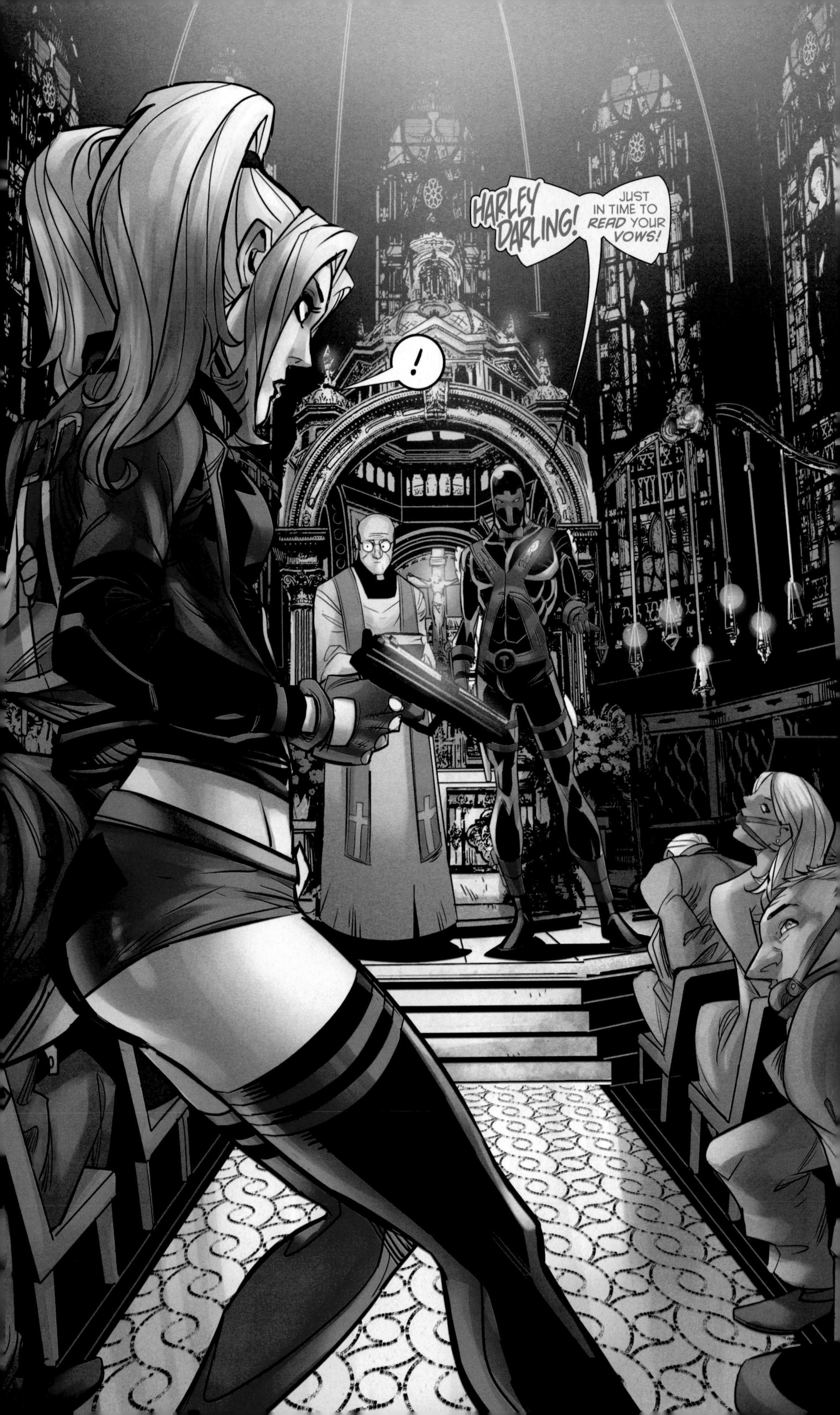
!
HARLEY DARLING! JUST IN TIME TO READ YOUR VOWS!

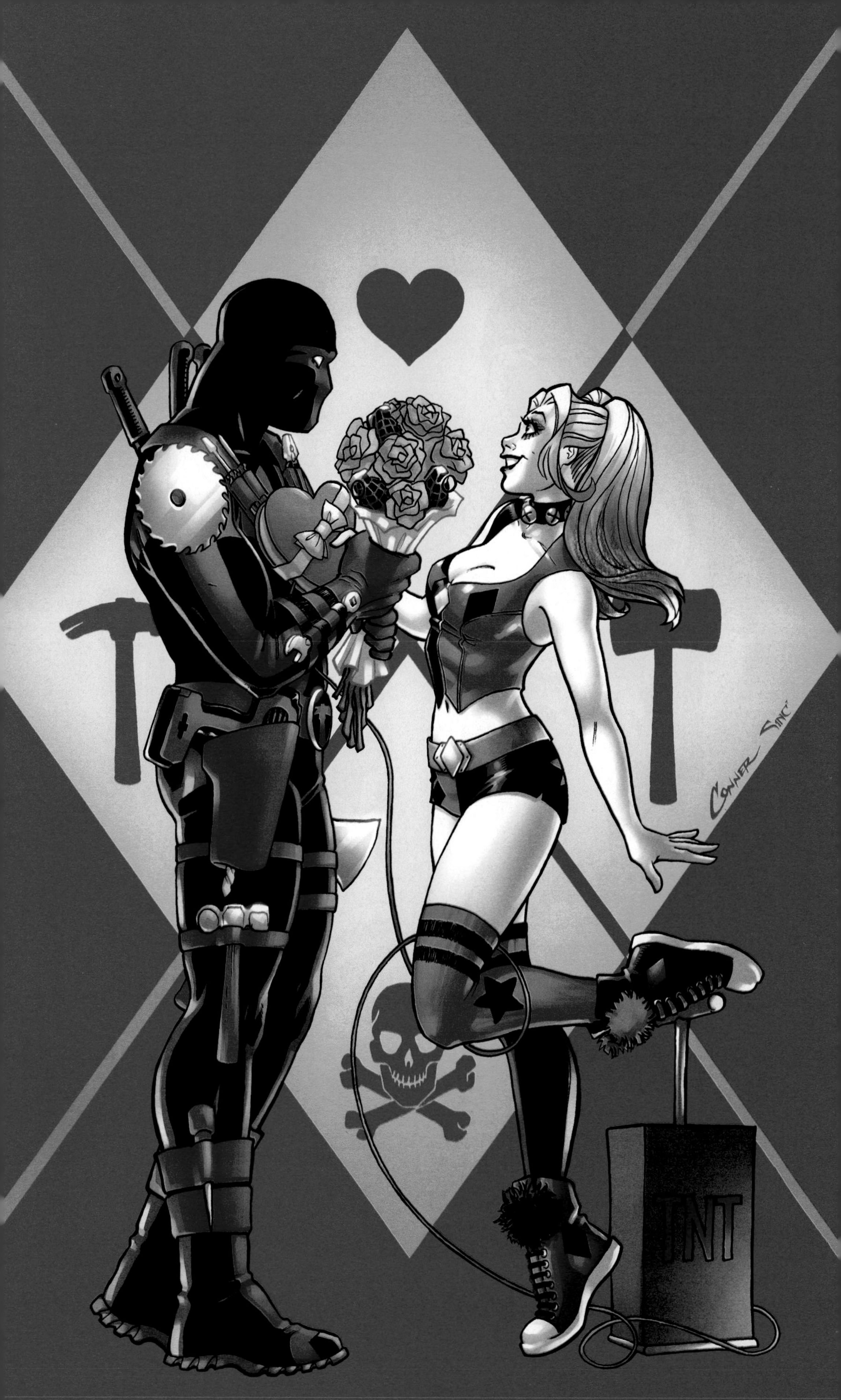
TNT

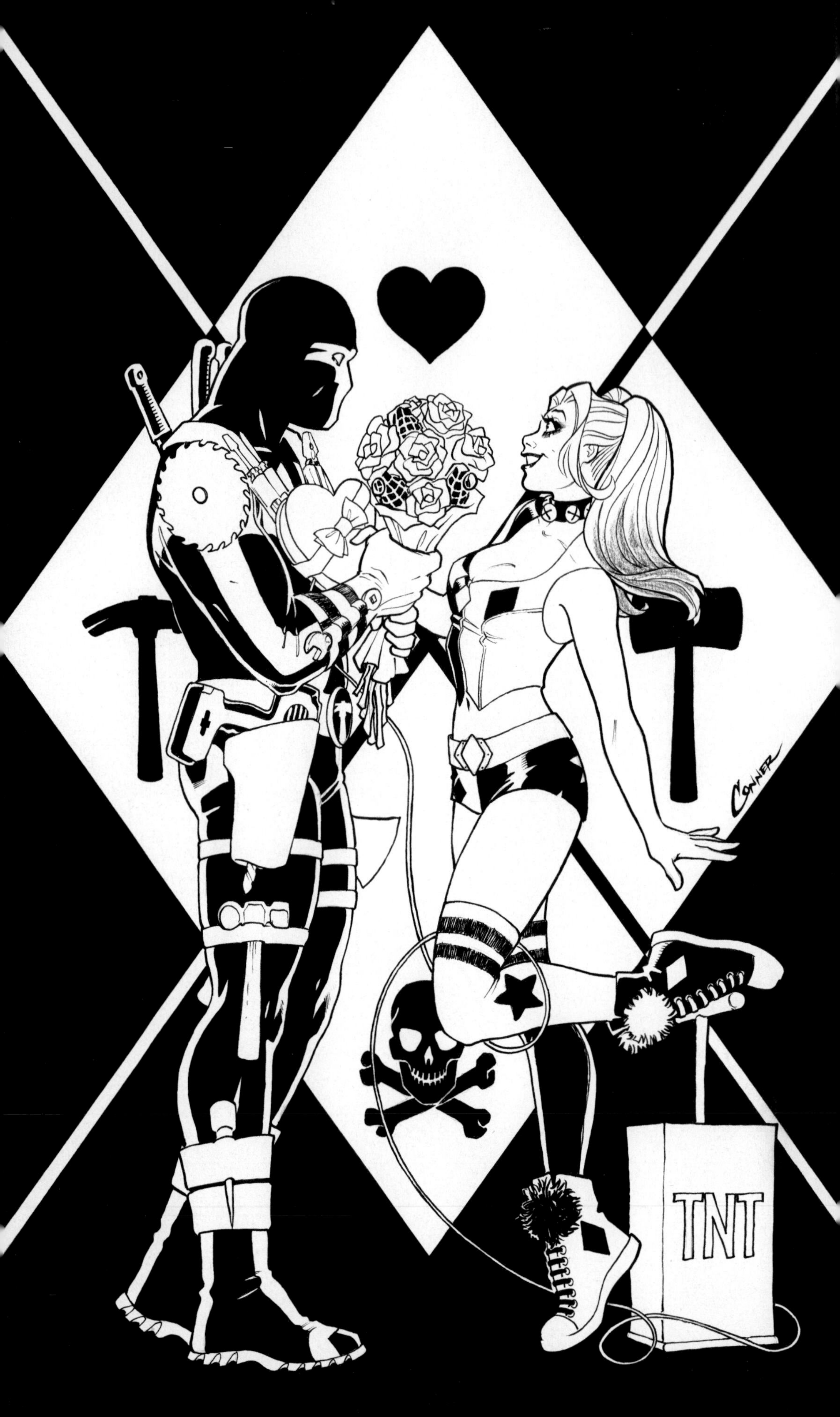
CONNER
TNT

MR. SPOONSDALE, I'M CALLING 'CAUSE I JUST DROPPED OFF THE *PERSON* YOU'RE LOOKING FOR AT A *CHURCH* HERE IN *BROOKLYN*.

YES, IT'S *HER*. DO I GET MY *GRAND*?

GREAT. THE ADDRESS HERE IS...

...AND NOW I WOULD LIKE TO INTRODUCE THE NEW CHIEF OF POLICE... *HARRY SPOONSDALE*!

GOT IT. SORRY. I HAVE TO GO.

IT'S QUINN, WE HAVE A *LOCATION* ON HER. WANT ME TO HANDLE IT *NOW*?

GO *GET* HER. DO WHAT WE *PLANNED*. I'LL *COVER* FOR YOU, SPOON.

CHIEF SPOONSDALE FROM NOW ON, PLEASE.

APOLOGIES, LADIES AND GENTLEMEN. OUR NEW *CHIEF OF POLICE* IS TAKING CARE OF AN *URGENT SITUATION*.

Heh. NOTHING LIKE JUMPING RIGHT INTO THE JOB WITH *BOTH FEET*!

AS YOU CAN SEE, *CHIEF SPOONSDALE* WILL BE DOING HIS *ABSOLUTE BEST* TO KEEP OUR FINE CITY *SAFE* FOR *EVERYONE*.

ROUND UP THE TROOPS...

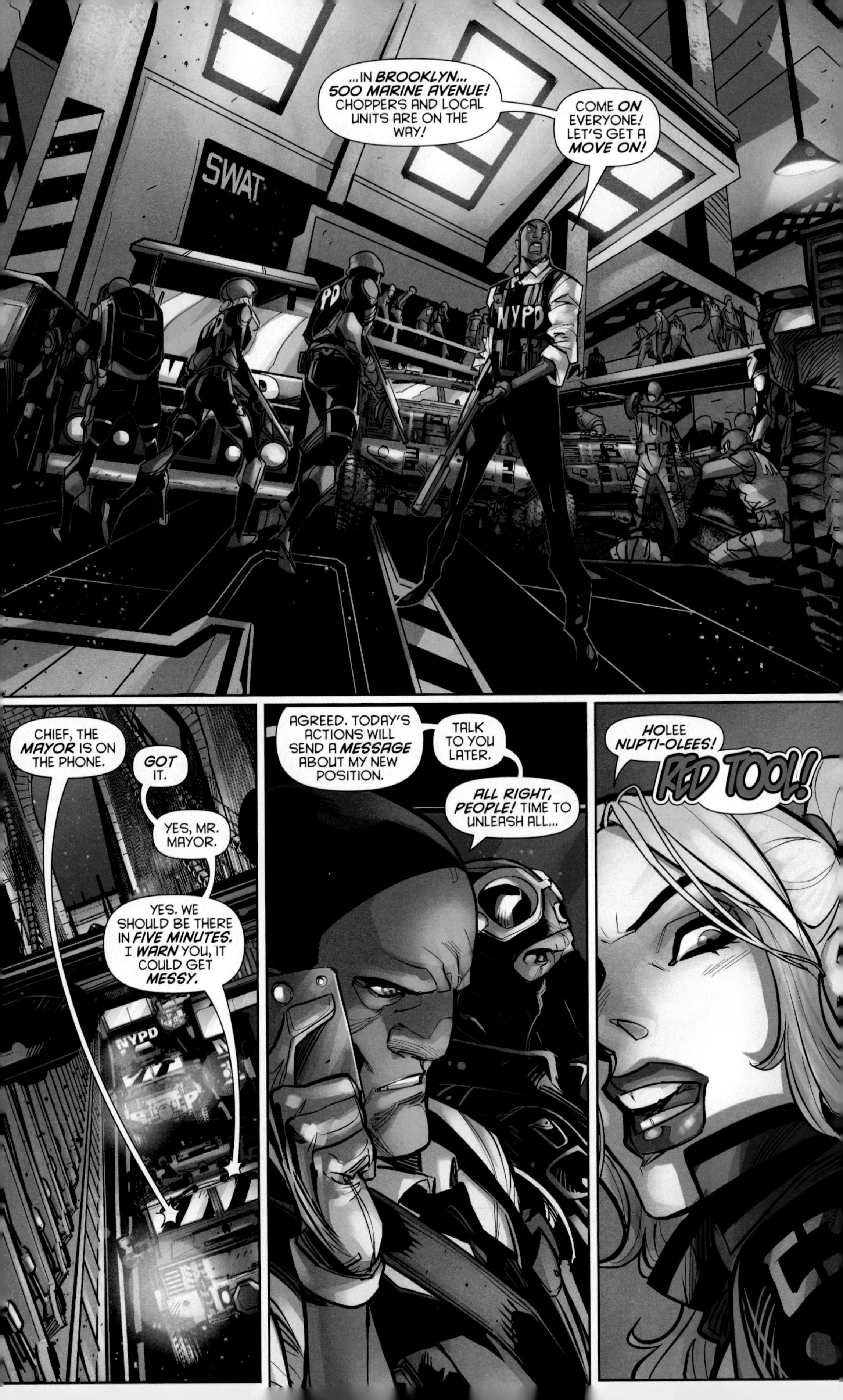

...IN BROOKLYN... 500 MARINE AVENUE! CHOPPERS AND LOCAL UNITS ARE ON THE WAY!
COME ON EVERYONE! LET'S GET A MOVE ON!
SWAT
NYPD
CHIEF, THE MAYOR IS ON THE PHONE.
GOT IT.
YES, MR. MAYOR.
YES. WE SHOULD BE THERE IN FIVE MINUTES. I WARN YOU, IT COULD GET MESSY.
AGREED. TODAY'S ACTIONS WILL SEND A MESSAGE ABOUT MY NEW POSITION.
TALK TO YOU LATER.
ALL RIGHT, PEOPLE! TIME TO UNLEASH ALL...
HOLEE NUPTI-OLEES!
RED TOOL!

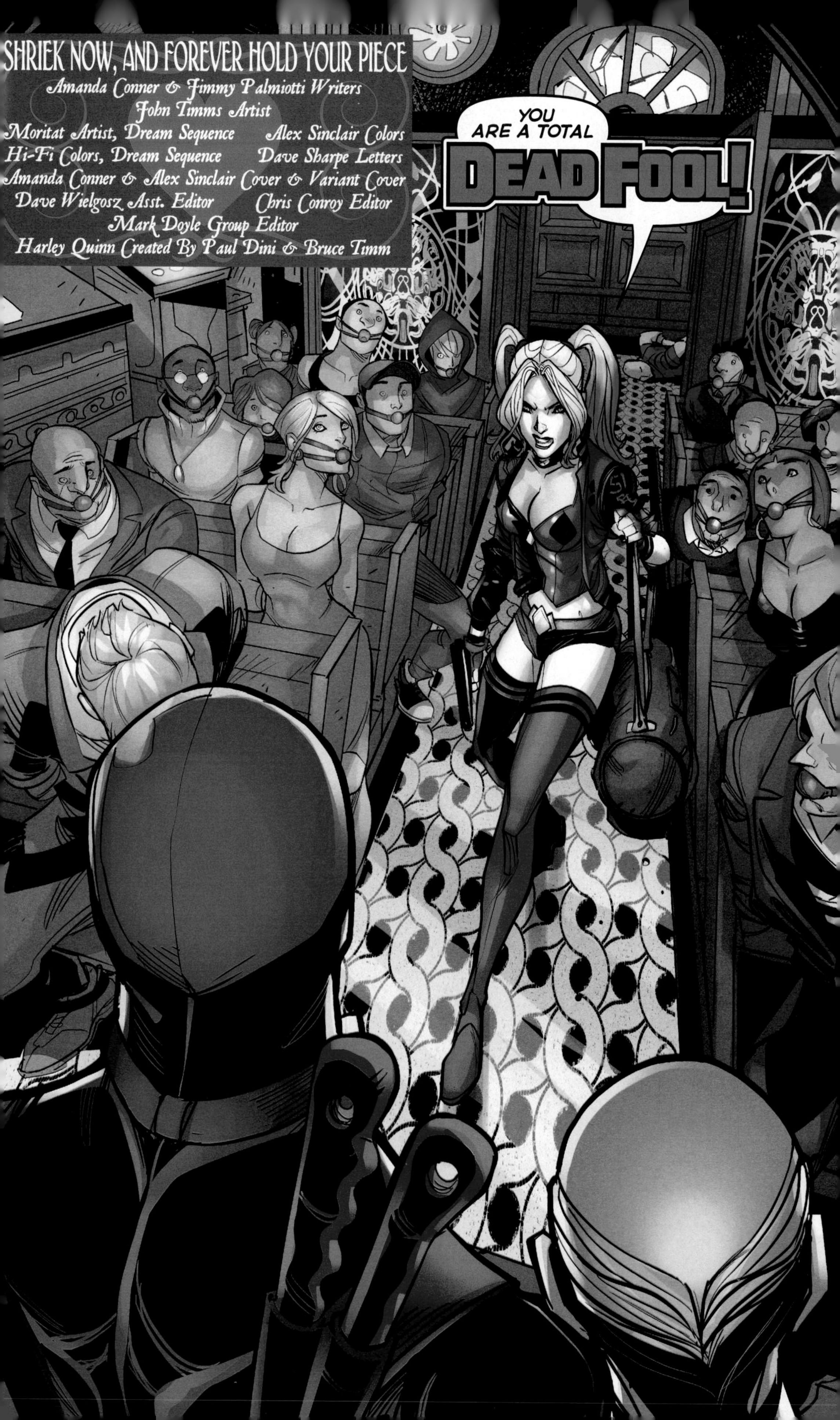
SHRIEK NOW, AND FOREVER HOLD YOUR PIECE
Amanda Conner & Jimmy Palmiotti Writers
John Timms Artist
Moritat Artist, Dream Sequence
Alex Sinclair Colors
Hi-Fi Colors, Dream Sequence
Dave Sharpe Letters
Amanda Conner & Alex Sinclair Cover & Variant Cover
Dave Wielgosz Asst. Editor
Chris Conroy Editor
Mark Doyle Group Editor
Harley Quinn Created By Paul Dini & Bruce Timm
YOU ARE A TOTAL DEAD FOOL!

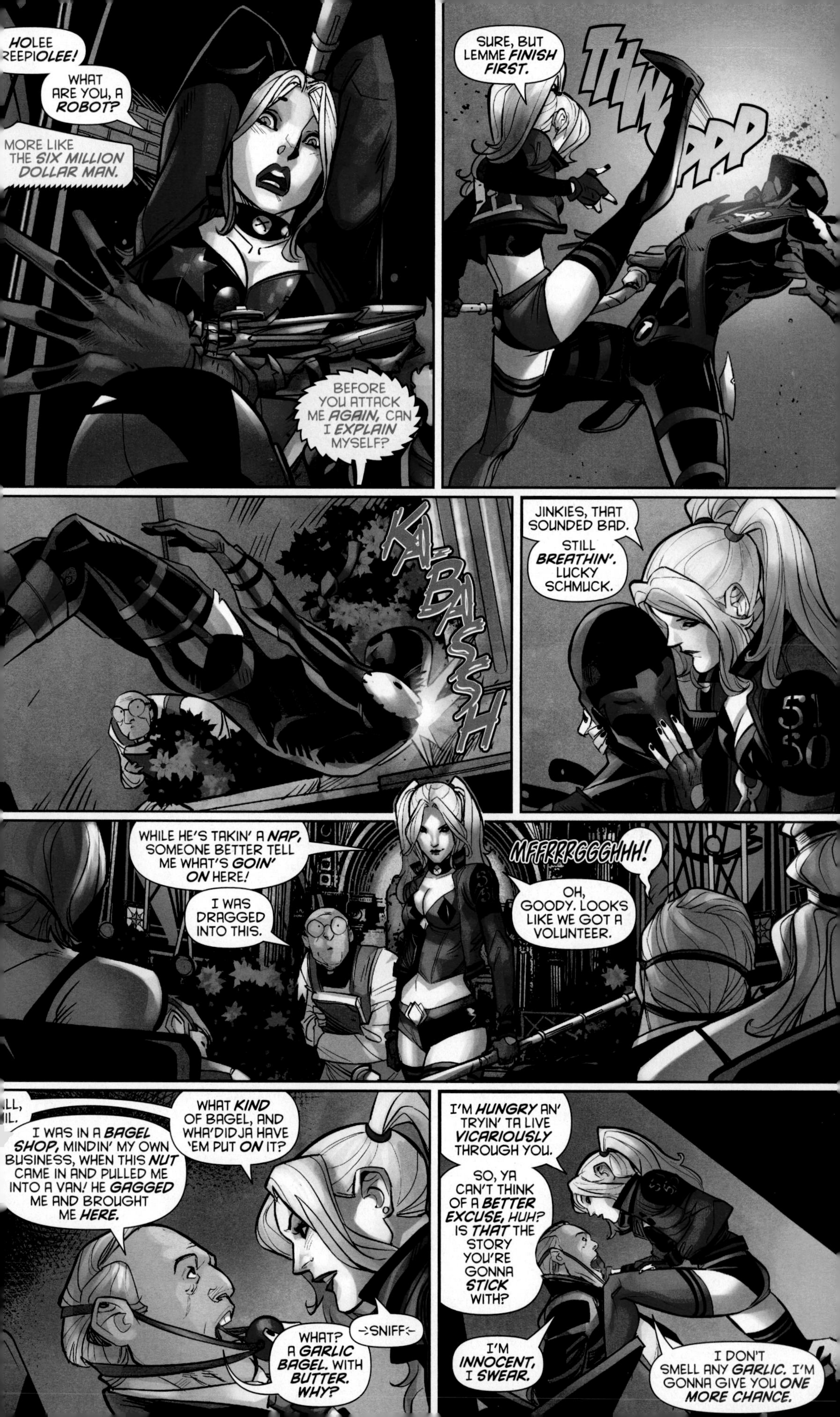
HOLEE
REEPIOLEE!
WHAT ARE YOU, A ROBOT?
MORE LIKE THE SIX MILLION DOLLAR MAN.
BEFORE YOU ATTACK ME AGAIN, CAN I EXPLAIN MYSELF?
SURE, BUT LEMME FINISH FIRST.
KA-BASSSH
JINKIES, THAT SOUNDED BAD.
STILL BREATHIN'. LUCKY SCHMUCK.
WHILE HE'S TAKIN' A NAP, SOMEONE BETTER TELL ME WHAT'S GOIN' ON HERE!
I WAS DRAGGED INTO THIS.
MFFRRRGGGHHH!
OH, GOODY. LOOKS LIKE WE GOT A VOLUNTEER.
I WAS IN A BAGEL SHOP, MINDIN' MY OWN BUSINESS, WHEN THIS NUT CAME IN AND PULLED ME INTO A VAN! HE GAGGED ME AND BROUGHT ME HERE.
WHAT KIND OF BAGEL, AND WHA'DIDJA HAVE 'EM PUT ON IT?
-SNIFF-
WHAT? A GARLIC BAGEL. WITH BUTTER. WHY?
I'M HUNGRY AN' TRYIN' TA LIVE VICARIOUSLY THROUGH YOU.
SO, YA CAN'T THINK OF A BETTER EXCUSE, HUH? IS THAT THE STORY YOU'RE GONNA STICK WITH?
I'M INNOCENT, I SWEAR.
I DON'T SMELL ANY GARLIC. I'M GONNA GIVE YOU ONE MORE CHANCE.

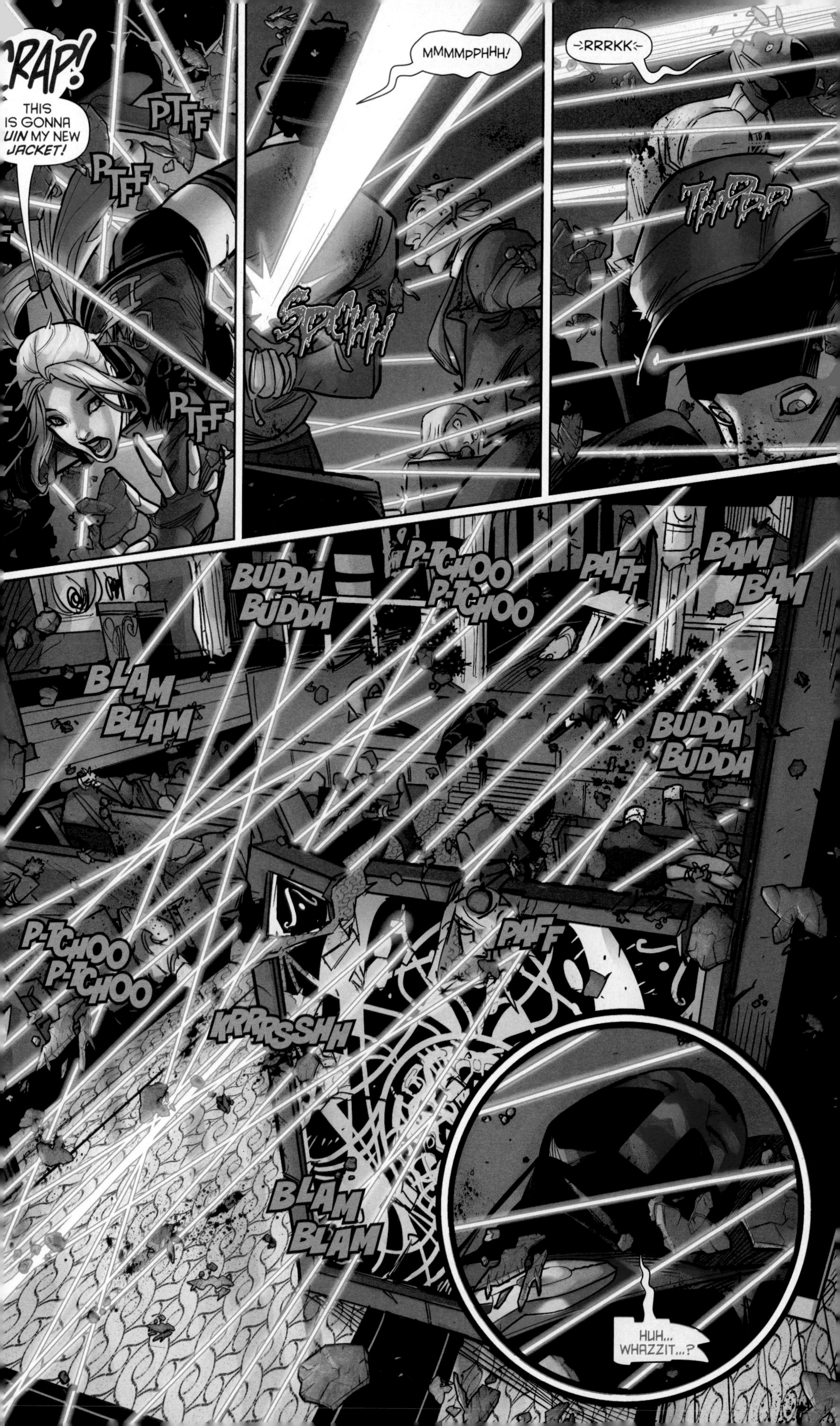
RAP!
THIS IS GONNA UIN MY NEW JACKET!
PTFF
PTFF
PTFF
MMMMPHHH!
SPLUTH
-RRRKK-
THPP
BUDDA BUDDA
P-TCHOO P-TCHOO
PAFF
BAM BAM
BLAM BLAM
BUDDA BUDDA
P-TCHOO P-TCHOO
PAFF
KRRRSSHH
BLAM BLAM
HUH... WHAZZIT...?

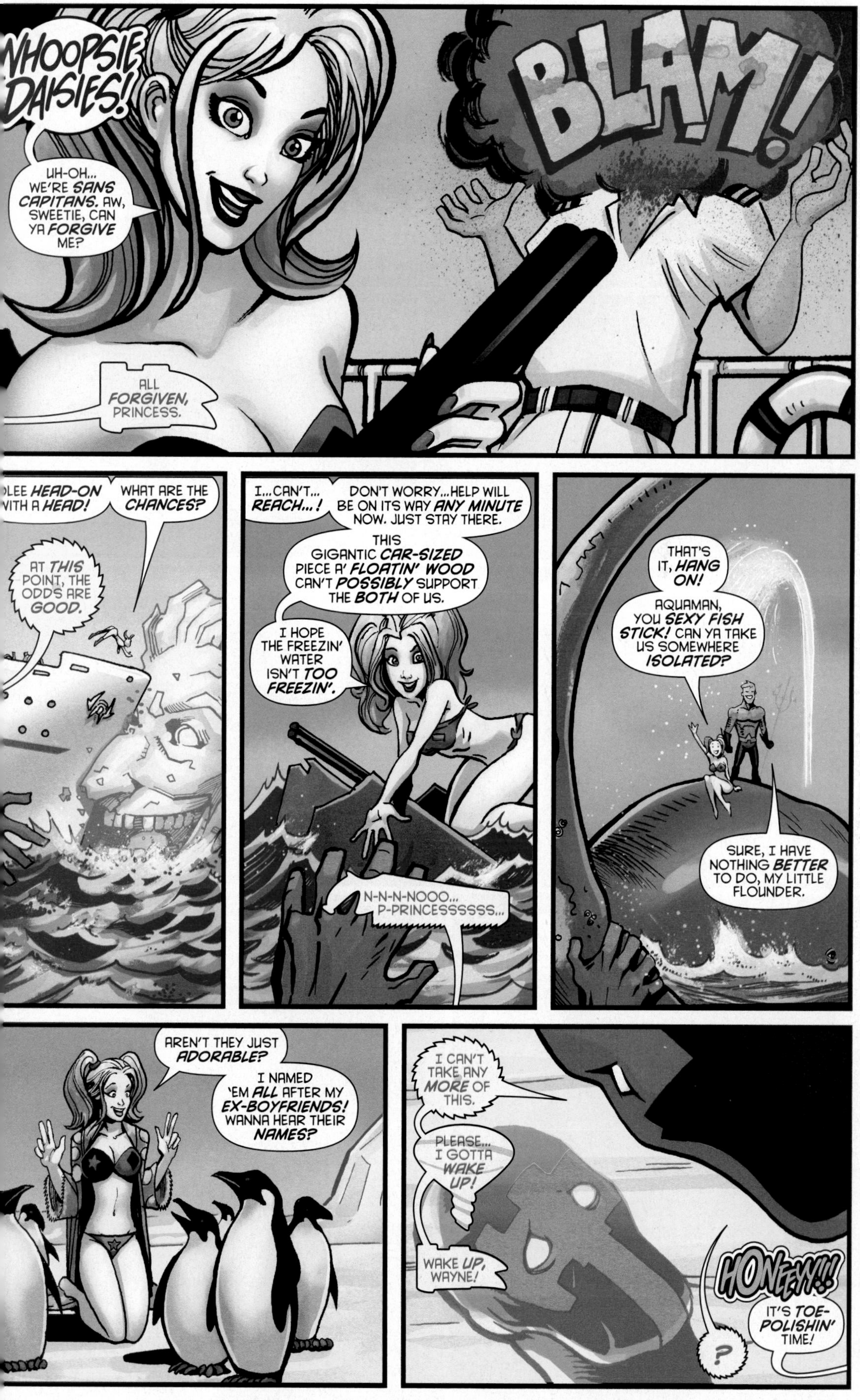
WHOOPSIE DAISIES!
UH-OH... WE'RE SANS CAPITANS. AW, SWEETIE, CAN YA FORGIVE ME?
BLAM!
ALL FORGIVEN, PRINCESS.
OLEE HEAD-ON WITH A HEAD!
WHAT ARE THE CHANCES?
AT THIS POINT, THE ODDS ARE GOOD.
I...CAN'T... REACH...!
DON'T WORRY...HELP WILL BE ON ITS WAY ANY MINUTE NOW. JUST STAY THERE.
THIS GIGANTIC CAR-SIZED PIECE A' FLOATIN' WOOD CAN'T POSSIBLY SUPPORT THE BOTH OF US.
I HOPE THE FREEZIN' WATER ISN'T TOO FREEZIN'.
N-N-N-NOOO... P-PRINCESSSSSS...
THAT'S IT, HANG ON!
AQUAMAN, YOU SEXY FISH STICK! CAN YA TAKE US SOMEWHERE ISOLATED?
SURE, I HAVE NOTHING BETTER TO DO, MY LITTLE FLOUNDER.
AREN'T THEY JUST ADORABLE?
I NAMED 'EM ALL AFTER MY EX-BOYFRIENDS! WANNA HEAR THEIR NAMES?
I CAN'T TAKE ANY MORE OF THIS.
PLEASE... I GOTTA WAKE UP!
WAKE UP, WAYNE!
HONEYY!!!
IT'S TOE-POLISHIN' TIME!
?

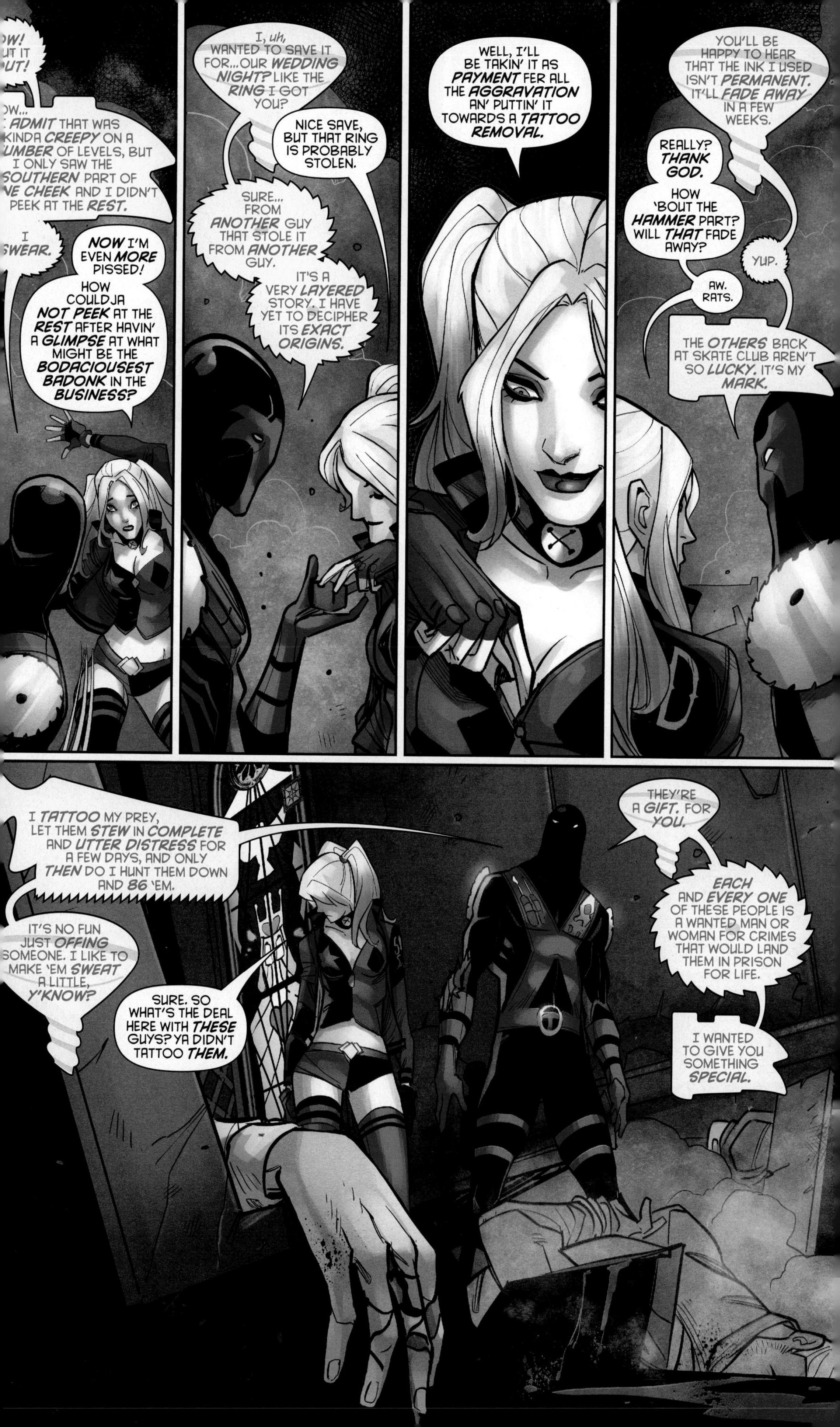
OW! UT IT OUT!
OW... ADMIT THAT WAS KINDA CREEPY ON A UMBER OF LEVELS, BUT I ONLY SAW THE SOUTHERN PART OF NE CHEEK AND I DIDN'T PEEK AT THE REST.
I SWEAR.
NOW I'M EVEN MORE PISSED!
HOW COULDJA NOT PEEK AT THE REST AFTER HAVIN' A GLIMPSE AT WHAT MIGHT BE THE BODACIOUSEST BADONK IN THE BUSINESS?
I, uh, WANTED TO SAVE IT FOR...OUR WEDDING NIGHT? LIKE THE RING I GOT YOU?
NICE SAVE, BUT THAT RING IS PROBABLY STOLEN.
SURE... FROM ANOTHER GUY THAT STOLE IT FROM ANOTHER GUY.
IT'S A VERY LAYERED STORY. I HAVE YET TO DECIPHER ITS EXACT ORIGINS.
WELL, I'LL BE TAKIN' IT AS PAYMENT FER ALL THE AGGRAVATION AN' PUTTIN' IT TOWARDS A TATTOO REMOVAL.
YOU'LL BE HAPPY TO HEAR THAT THE INK I USED ISN'T PERMANENT. IT'LL FADE AWAY IN A FEW WEEKS.
REALLY? THANK GOD.
HOW 'BOUT THE HAMMER PART? WILL THAT FADE AWAY?
YUP.
AW. RATS.
THE OTHERS BACK AT SKATE CLUB AREN'T SO LUCKY. IT'S MY MARK.
I TATTOO MY PREY, LET THEM STEW IN COMPLETE AND UTTER DISTRESS FOR A FEW DAYS, AND ONLY THEN DO I HUNT THEM DOWN AND 86 'EM.
IT'S NO FUN JUST OFFING SOMEONE. I LIKE TO MAKE 'EM SWEAT A LITTLE, Y'KNOW?
SURE. SO WHAT'S THE DEAL HERE WITH THESE GUYS? YA DIDN'T TATTOO THEM.
THEY'RE A GIFT. FOR YOU.
EACH AND EVERY ONE OF THESE PEOPLE IS A WANTED MAN OR WOMAN FOR CRIMES THAT WOULD LAND THEM IN PRISON FOR LIFE.
I WANTED TO GIVE YOU SOMETHING SPECIAL.

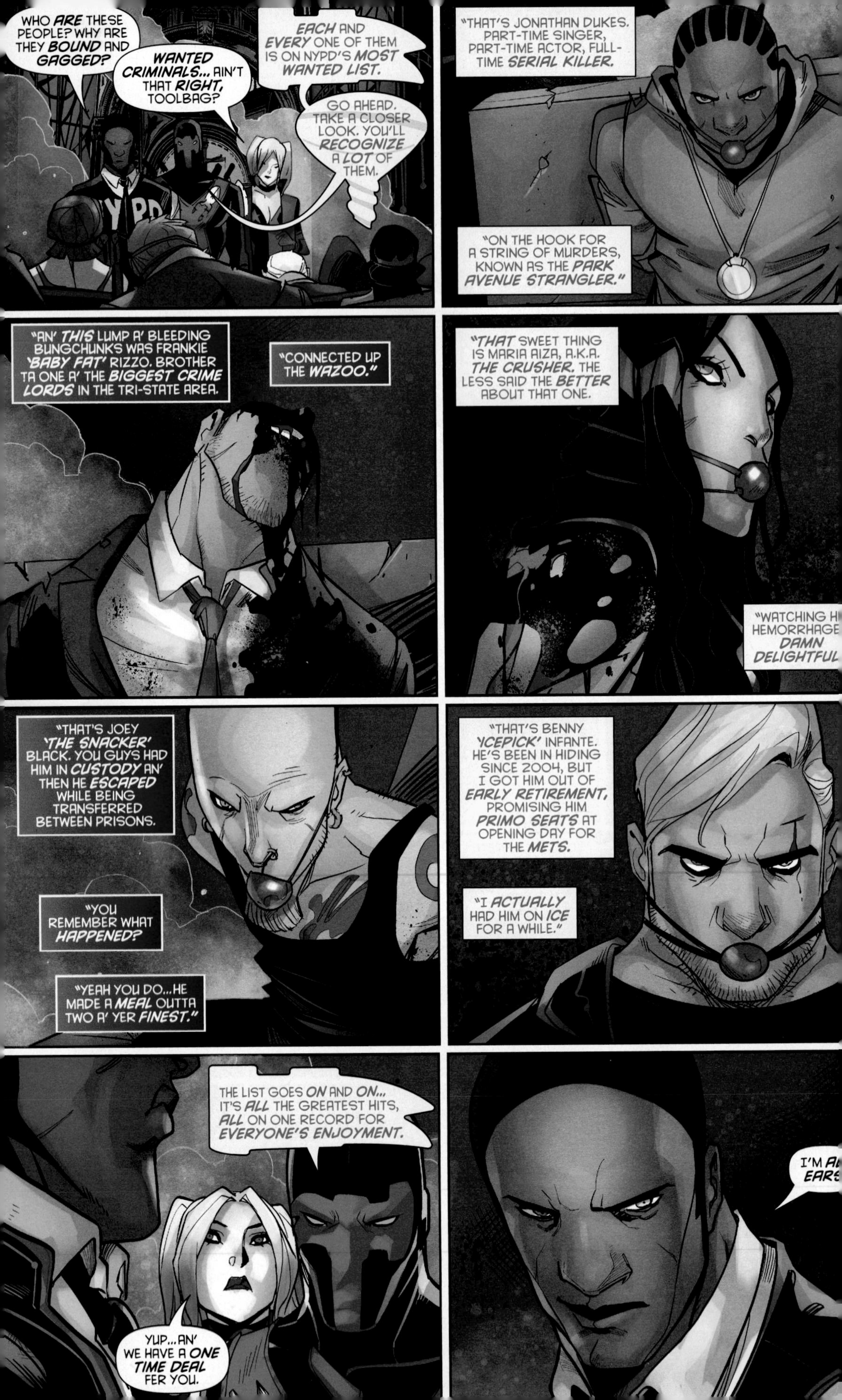
WHO ARE THESE PEOPLE? WHY ARE THEY BOUND AND GAGGED?
WANTED CRIMINALS... AIN'T THAT RIGHT, TOOLBAG?
EACH AND EVERY ONE OF THEM IS ON NYPD'S MOST WANTED LIST.
GO AHEAD. TAKE A CLOSER LOOK. YOU'LL RECOGNIZE A LOT OF THEM.
"THAT'S JONATHAN DUKES. PART-TIME SINGER, PART-TIME ACTOR, FULL-TIME SERIAL KILLER.
"ON THE HOOK FOR A STRING OF MURDERS, KNOWN AS THE PARK AVENUE STRANGLER."
"AN' THIS LUMP A' BLEEDING BUNGCHUNKS WAS FRANKIE 'BABY FAT' RIZZO. BROTHER TA ONE A' THE BIGGEST CRIME LORDS IN THE TRI-STATE AREA.
"CONNECTED UP THE WAZOO."
"THAT SWEET THING IS MARIA AIZA, A.K.A. THE CRUSHER. THE LESS SAID THE BETTER ABOUT THAT ONE.
"WATCHING H HEMORRHAGE DAMN DELIGHTFUL
"THAT'S JOEY 'THE SNACKER' BLACK. YOU GUYS HAD HIM IN CUSTODY AN' THEN HE ESCAPED WHILE BEING TRANSFERRED BETWEEN PRISONS.
"YOU REMEMBER WHAT HAPPENED?
"YEAH YOU DO...HE MADE A MEAL OUTTA TWO A' YER FINEST."
"THAT'S BENNY 'ICEPICK' INFANTE. HE'S BEEN IN HIDING SINCE 2004, BUT I GOT HIM OUT OF EARLY RETIREMENT, PROMISING HIM PRIMO SEATS AT OPENING DAY FOR THE METS.
"I ACTUALLY HAD HIM ON ICE FOR A WHILE."
THE LIST GOES ON AND ON... IT'S ALL THE GREATEST HITS, ALL ON ONE RECORD FOR EVERYONE'S ENJOYMENT.
YUP...AN' WE HAVE A ONE TIME DEAL FER YOU.
I'M A EARS

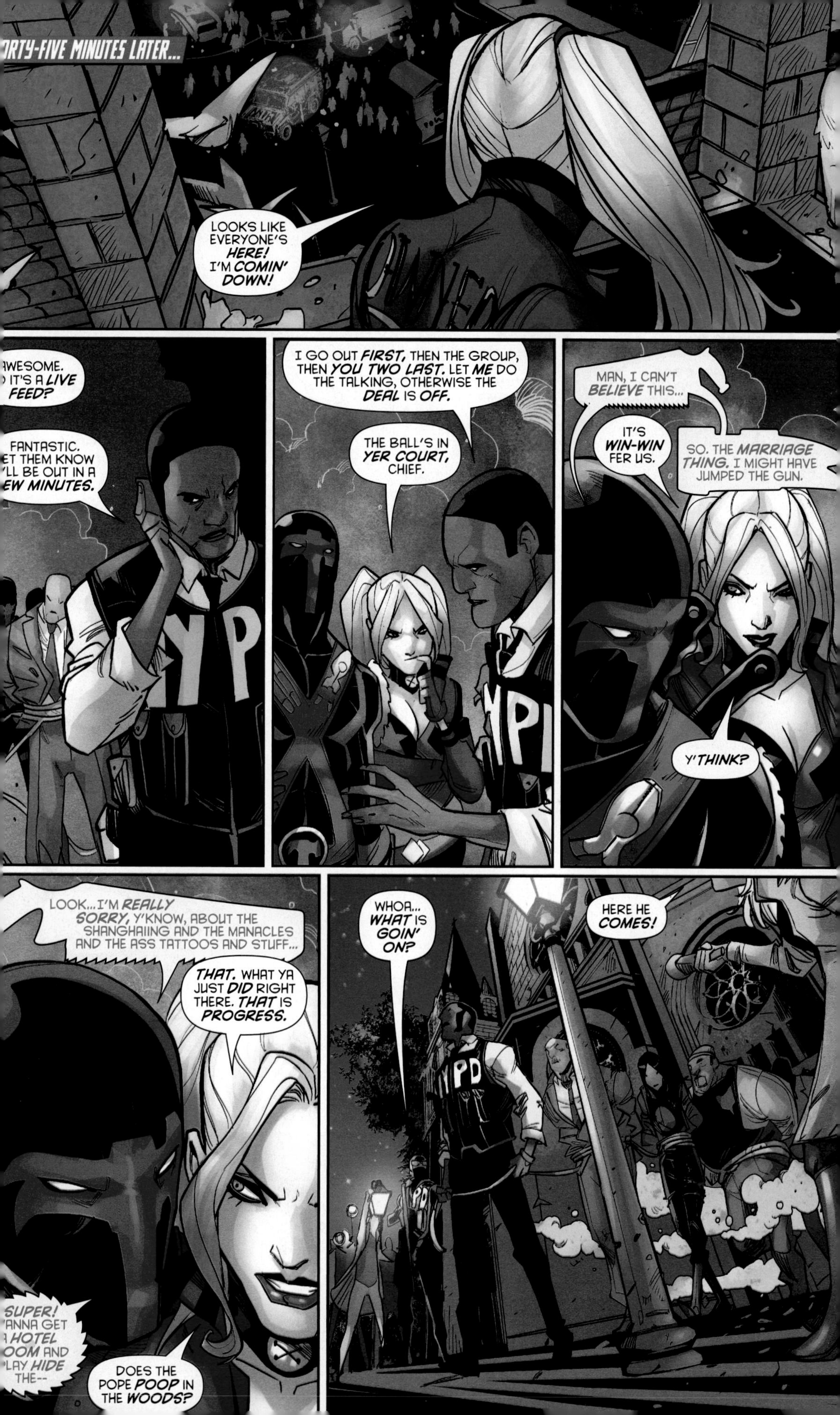

ORTY-FIVE MINUTES LATER...
LOOKS LIKE EVERYONE'S HERE! I'M COMIN' DOWN!
AWESOME. IT'S A LIVE FEED?
FANTASTIC. ET THEM KNOW 'LL BE OUT IN A EW MINUTES.
I GO OUT FIRST, THEN THE GROUP, THEN YOU TWO LAST. LET ME DO THE TALKING, OTHERWISE THE DEAL IS OFF.
THE BALL'S IN YER COURT, CHIEF.
MAN, I CAN'T BELIEVE THIS...
IT'S WIN-WIN FER US.
SO. THE MARRIAGE THING. I MIGHT HAVE JUMPED THE GUN.
Y'THINK?
LOOK...I'M REALLY SORRY, Y'KNOW, ABOUT THE SHANGHAIING AND THE MANACLES AND THE ASS TATTOOS AND STUFF...
THAT. WHAT YA JUST DID RIGHT THERE. THAT IS PROGRESS.
SUPER! ANNA GET A HOTEL OOM AND LAY HIDE THE--
DOES THE POPE POOP IN THE WOODS?
WHOA... WHAT IS GOIN' ON?
HERE HE COMES!

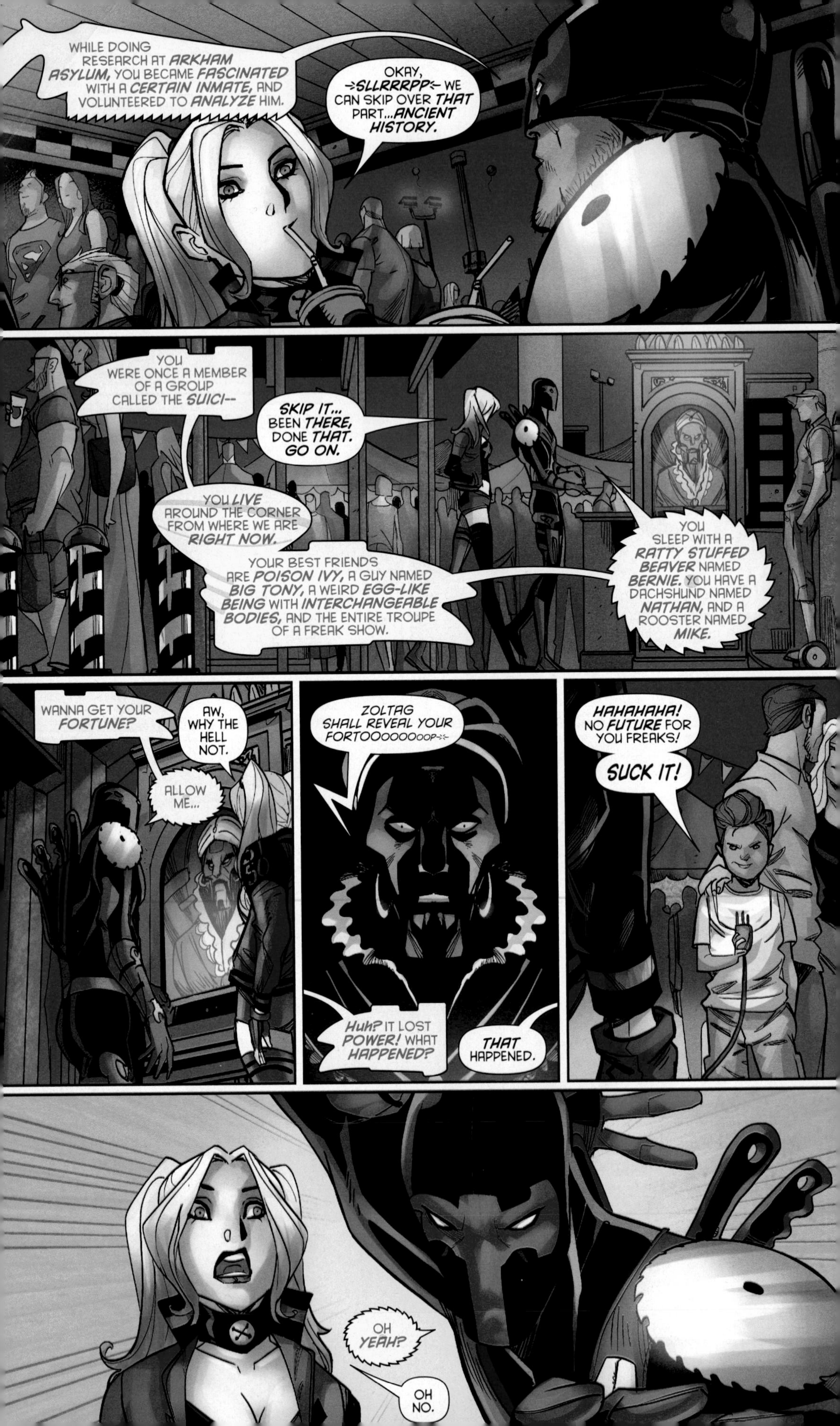
WHILE DOING RESEARCH AT ARKHAM ASYLUM, YOU BECAME FASCINATED WITH A CERTAIN INMATE, AND VOLUNTEERED TO ANALYZE HIM.
OKAY, ⪢SLLRRRPP⪡ WE CAN SKIP OVER THAT PART...ANCIENT HISTORY.
YOU WERE ONCE A MEMBER OF A GROUP CALLED THE SUICI--
SKIP IT... BEEN THERE, DONE THAT. GO ON.
YOU LIVE AROUND THE CORNER FROM WHERE WE ARE RIGHT NOW.
YOUR BEST FRIENDS ARE POISON IVY, A GUY NAMED BIG TONY, A WEIRD EGG-LIKE BEING WITH INTERCHANGEABLE BODIES, AND THE ENTIRE TROUPE OF A FREAK SHOW.
YOU SLEEP WITH A RATTY STUFFED BEAVER NAMED BERNIE. YOU HAVE A DACHSHUND NAMED NATHAN, AND A ROOSTER NAMED MIKE.
WANNA GET YOUR FORTUNE?
AW, WHY THE HELL NOT.
ALLOW ME...
ZOLTAG SHALL REVEAL YOUR FORTOOOOOOOOP⪡
HUH? IT LOST POWER! WHAT HAPPENED?
THAT HAPPENED.
HAHAHAHA! NO FUTURE FOR YOU FREAKS!
SUCK IT!
OH YEAH?
OH NO.

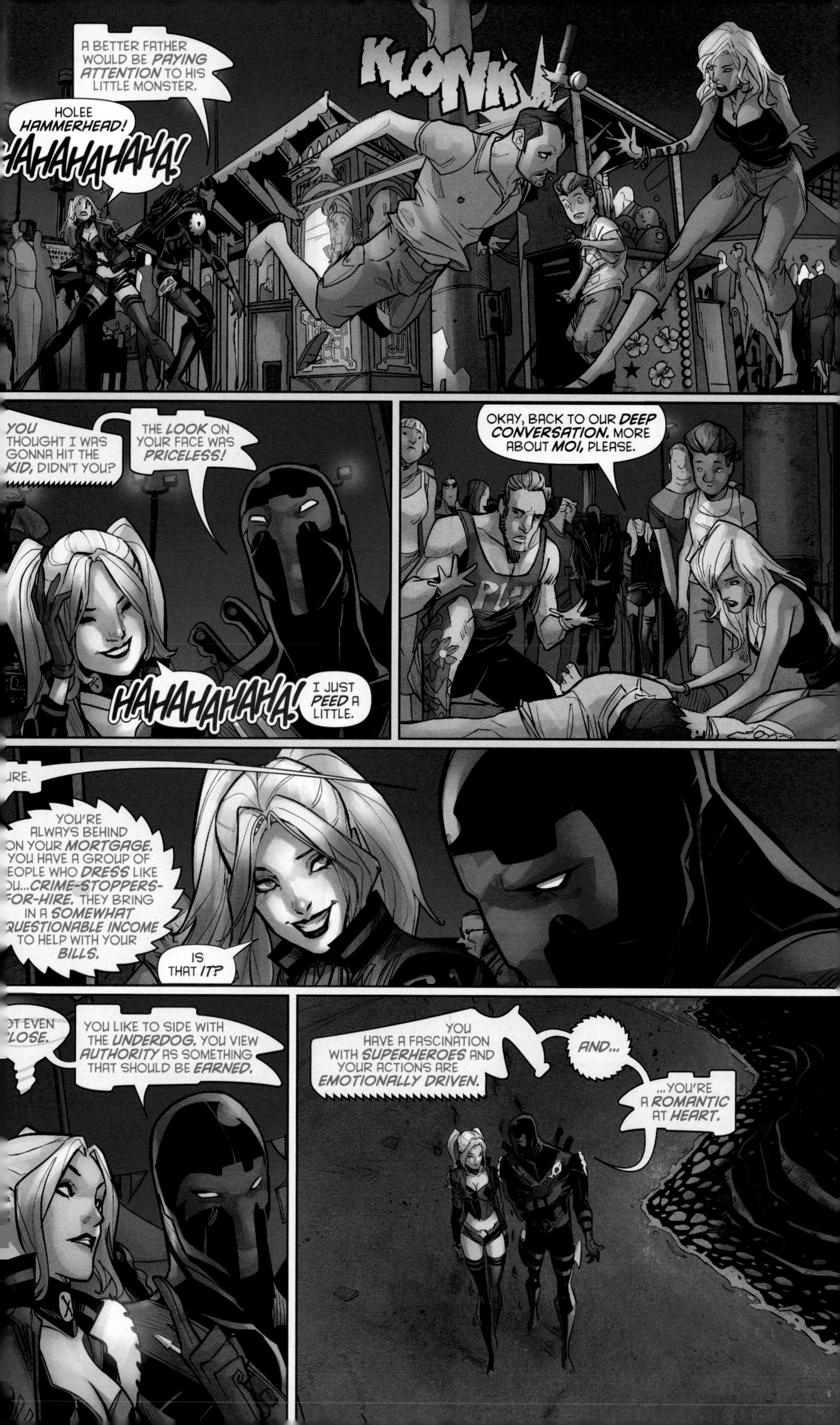
A BETTER FATHER WOULD BE PAYING ATTENTION TO HIS LITTLE MONSTER.
KLONK
HOLEE HAMMERHEAD! HAHAHAHAHA!
YOU THOUGHT I WAS GONNA HIT THE KID, DIDN'T YOU?
THE LOOK ON YOUR FACE WAS PRICELESS!
HAHAHAHAHA!
I JUST PEED A LITTLE.
OKAY, BACK TO OUR DEEP CONVERSATION. MORE ABOUT MOI, PLEASE.
YOU'RE ALWAYS BEHIND ON YOUR MORTGAGE. YOU HAVE A GROUP OF PEOPLE WHO DRESS LIKE YOU...CRIME-STOPPERS-FOR-HIRE. THEY BRING IN A SOMEWHAT QUESTIONABLE INCOME TO HELP WITH YOUR BILLS.
IS THAT IT?
YOU LIKE TO SIDE WITH THE UNDERDOG. YOU VIEW AUTHORITY AS SOMETHING THAT SHOULD BE EARNED.
YOU HAVE A FASCINATION WITH SUPERHEROES AND YOUR ACTIONS ARE EMOTIONALLY DRIVEN.
AND...
...YOU'RE A ROMANTIC AT HEART.

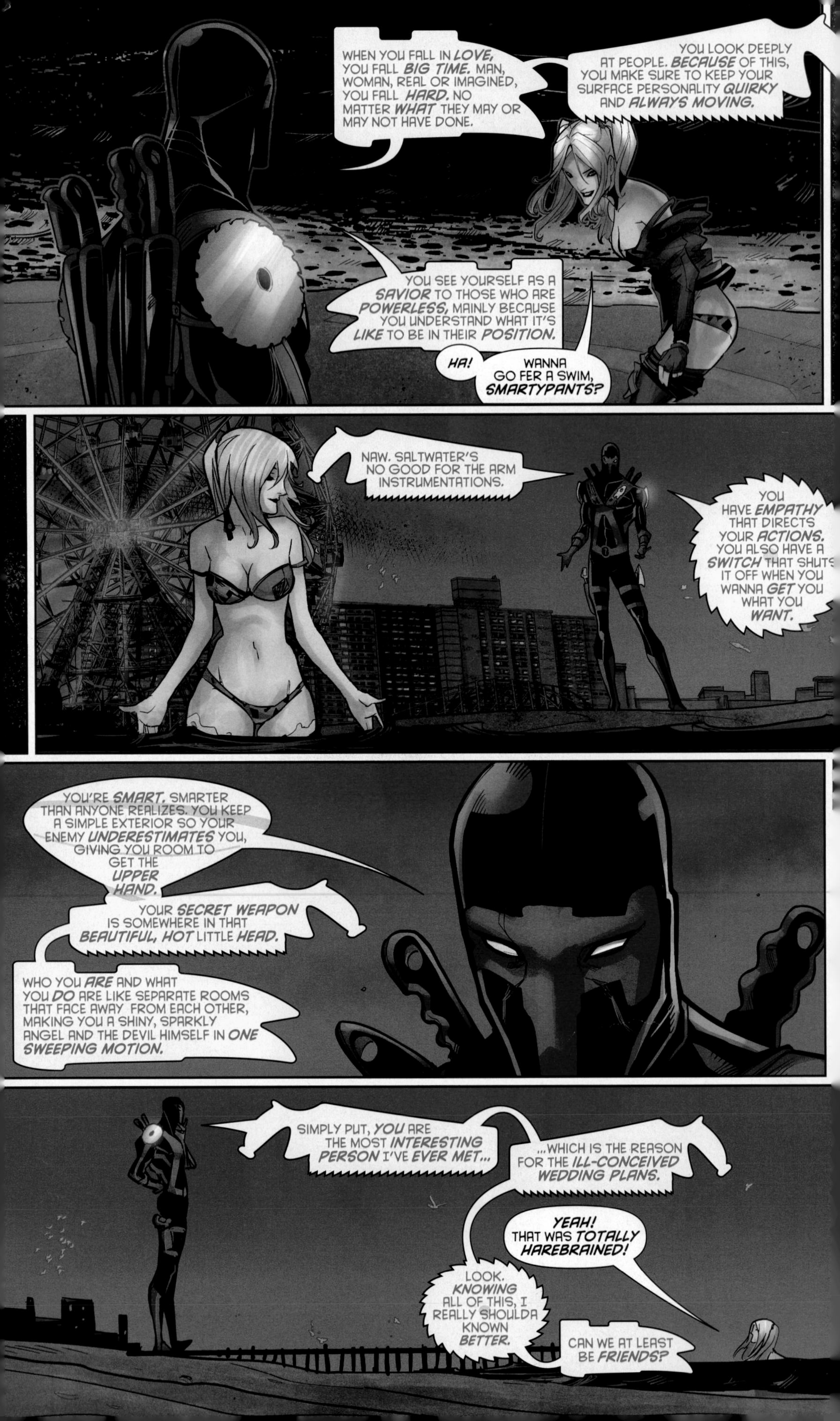
WHEN YOU FALL IN LOVE, YOU FALL BIG TIME. MAN, WOMAN, REAL OR IMAGINED, YOU FALL HARD. NO MATTER WHAT THEY MAY OR MAY NOT HAVE DONE.
YOU LOOK DEEPLY AT PEOPLE. BECAUSE OF THIS, YOU MAKE SURE TO KEEP YOUR SURFACE PERSONALITY QUIRKY AND ALWAYS MOVING.
YOU SEE YOURSELF AS A SAVIOR TO THOSE WHO ARE POWERLESS, MAINLY BECAUSE YOU UNDERSTAND WHAT IT'S LIKE TO BE IN THEIR POSITION.
HA!
WANNA GO FER A SWIM, SMARTYPANTS?
NAW. SALTWATER'S NO GOOD FOR THE ARM INSTRUMENTATIONS.
YOU HAVE EMPATHY THAT DIRECTS YOUR ACTIONS. YOU ALSO HAVE A SWITCH THAT SHUTS IT OFF WHEN YOU WANNA GET YOU WHAT YOU WANT.
YOU'RE SMART. SMARTER THAN ANYONE REALIZES. YOU KEEP A SIMPLE EXTERIOR SO YOUR ENEMY UNDERESTIMATES YOU, GIVING YOU ROOM TO GET THE UPPER HAND.
YOUR SECRET WEAPON IS SOMEWHERE IN THAT BEAUTIFUL, HOT LITTLE HEAD.
WHO YOU ARE AND WHAT YOU DO ARE LIKE SEPARATE ROOMS THAT FACE AWAY FROM EACH OTHER, MAKING YOU A SHINY, SPARKLY ANGEL AND THE DEVIL HIMSELF IN ONE SWEEPING MOTION.
SIMPLY PUT, YOU ARE THE MOST INTERESTING PERSON I'VE EVER MET...
...WHICH IS THE REASON FOR THE ILL-CONCEIVED WEDDING PLANS.
YEAH! THAT WAS TOTALLY HAREBRAINED!
LOOK. KNOWING ALL OF THIS, I REALLY SHOULDA KNOWN BETTER.
CAN WE AT LEAST BE FRIENDS?

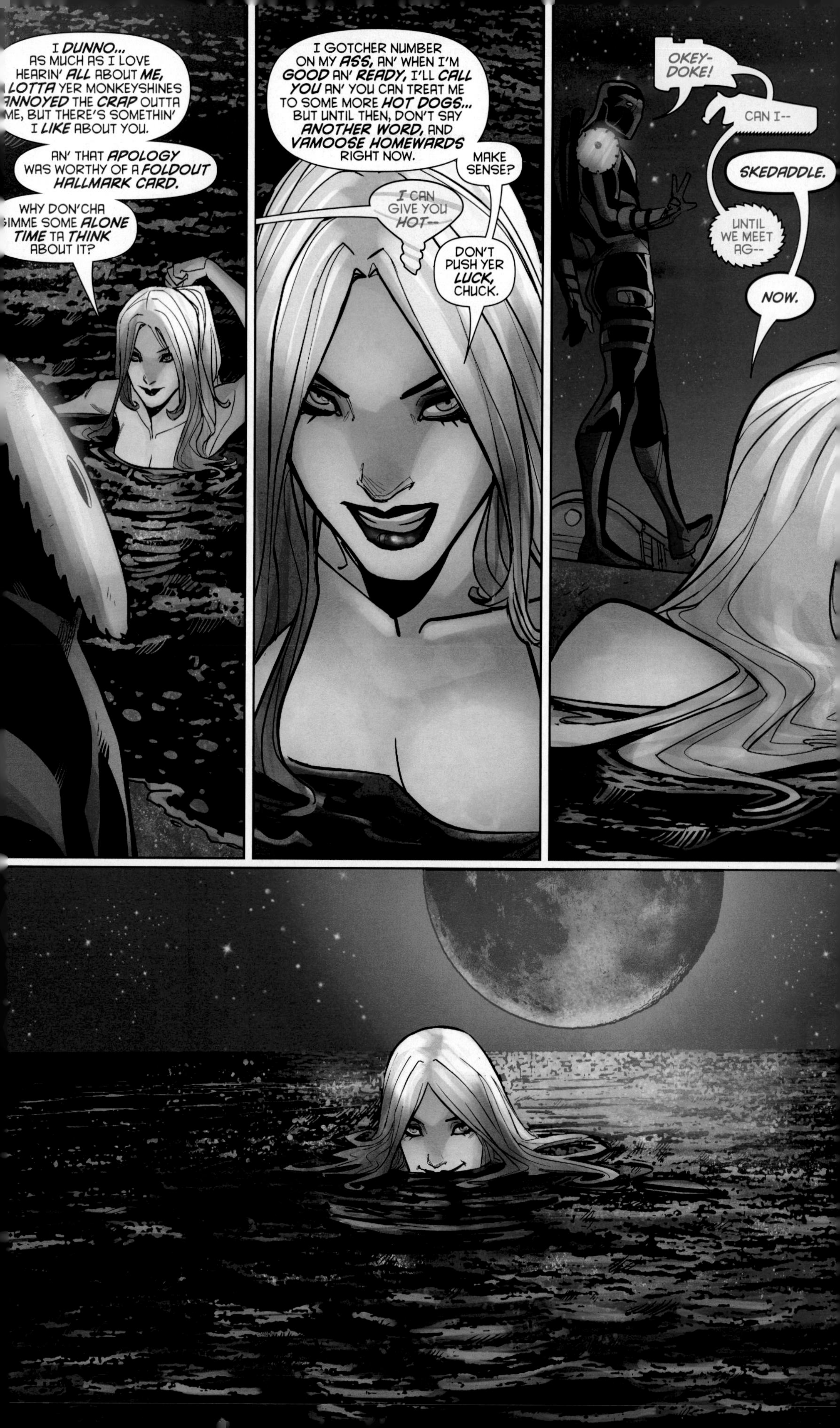
I DUNNO... AS MUCH AS I LOVE HEARIN' ALL ABOUT ME, A LOTTA YER MONKEYSHINES ANNOYED THE CRAP OUTTA ME, BUT THERE'S SOMETHIN' I LIKE ABOUT YOU.
AN' THAT APOLOGY WAS WORTHY OF A FOLDOUT HALLMARK CARD.
WHY DON'CHA GIMME SOME ALONE TIME TA THINK ABOUT IT?
I GOTCHER NUMBER ON MY ASS, AN' WHEN I'M GOOD AN' READY, I'LL CALL YOU AN' YOU CAN TREAT ME TO SOME MORE HOT DOGS... BUT UNTIL THEN, DON'T SAY ANOTHER WORD, AND VAMOOSE HOMEWARDS RIGHT NOW.
MAKE SENSE?
I CAN GIVE YOU HOT--
DON'T PUSH YER LUCK, CHUCK.
OKEY-DOKE!
CAN I--
SKEDADDLE.
UNTIL WE MEET AG--
NOW.

IT'S FER *YOU*, DOMINIC.

NO *KIDDIN'*, EINSTEIN. IT'S *MY* HOUSE. *GIMME* THAT!

EAH? *WHAT?* SKATE CLUB? WHAT THE *HELL* IS--

HARLEY QUINN PUT AN AXE THROUGH HIS HEAD?!

WHAT?! HOW? HE WAS *PROTECTED* IN THERE!

YOU CALL *O'BANNON.* YOU HAVE HIM *TRACK 'ER DOWN* AND *KILL 'ER*, Y'HEAR ME? THAT BALL-THROWING SONUVABITCH *OWES* ME!

HAVE HIM ENLIST HER SERVICES, THEN *TAKE HER OUT.*

SHE'S GONNA *PAY* WITH HER *LIFE!*

SR-LOOSS!

THEY'RE *ALL* GONNA PAY FER *KILLIN'* MY SON!

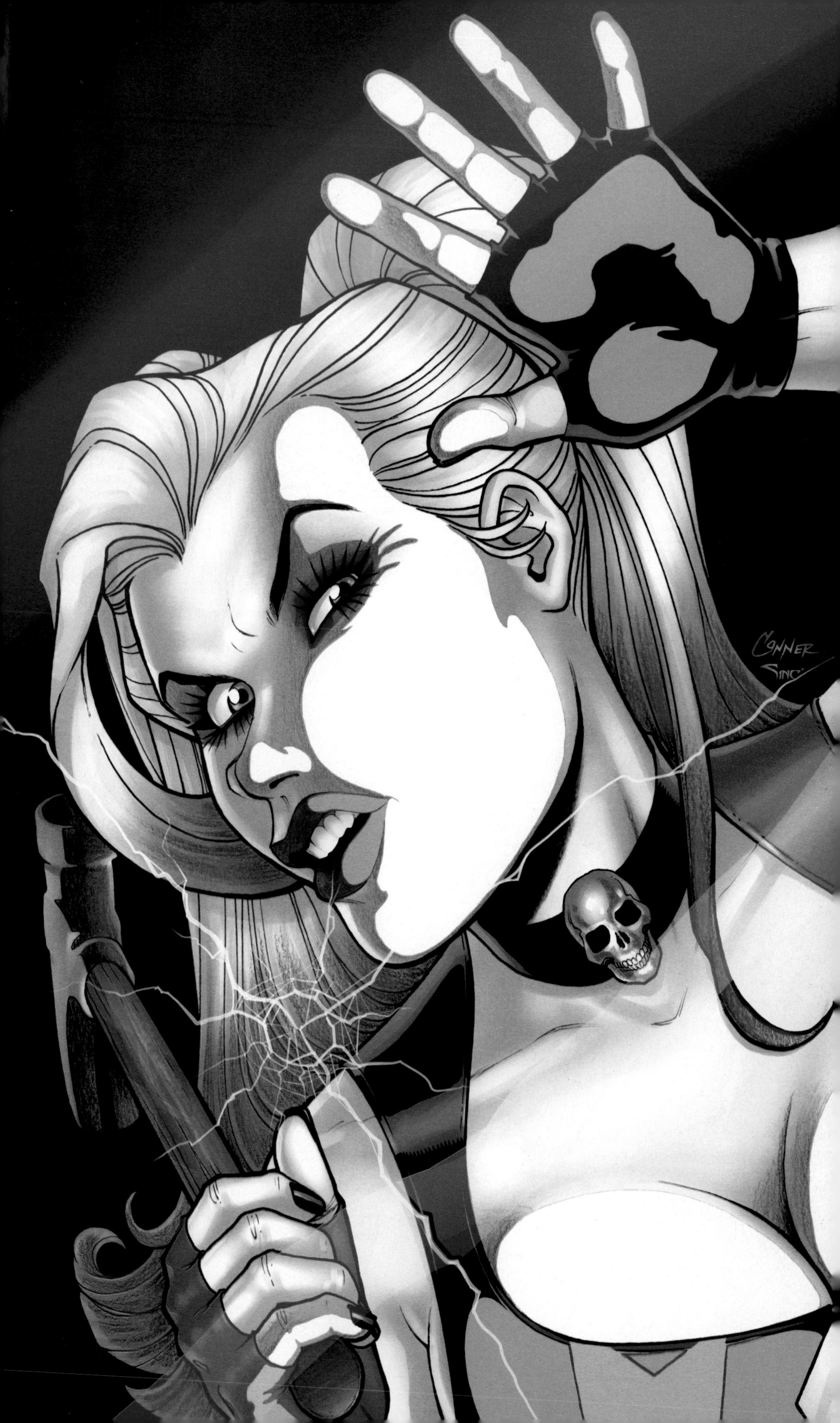
CONNER

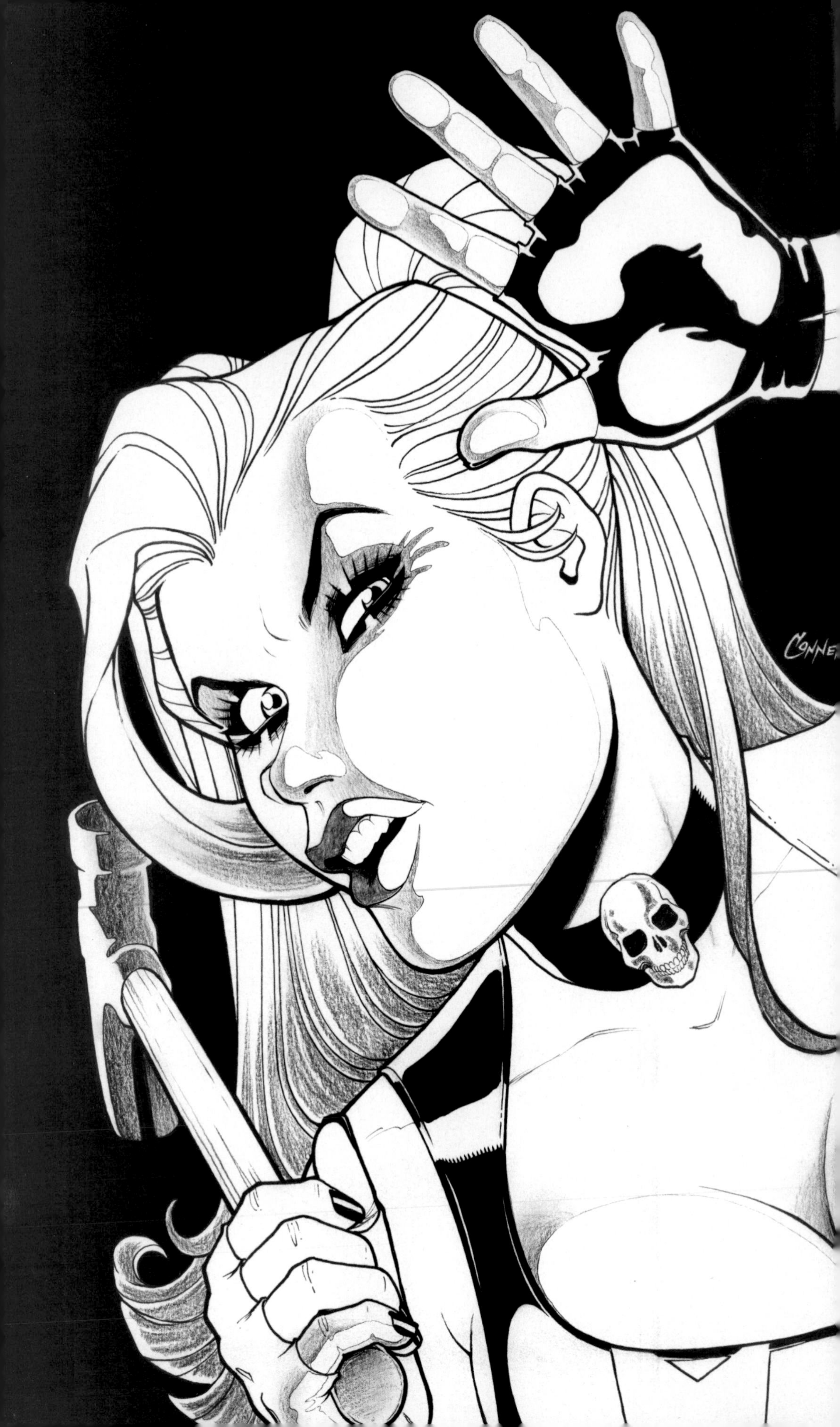

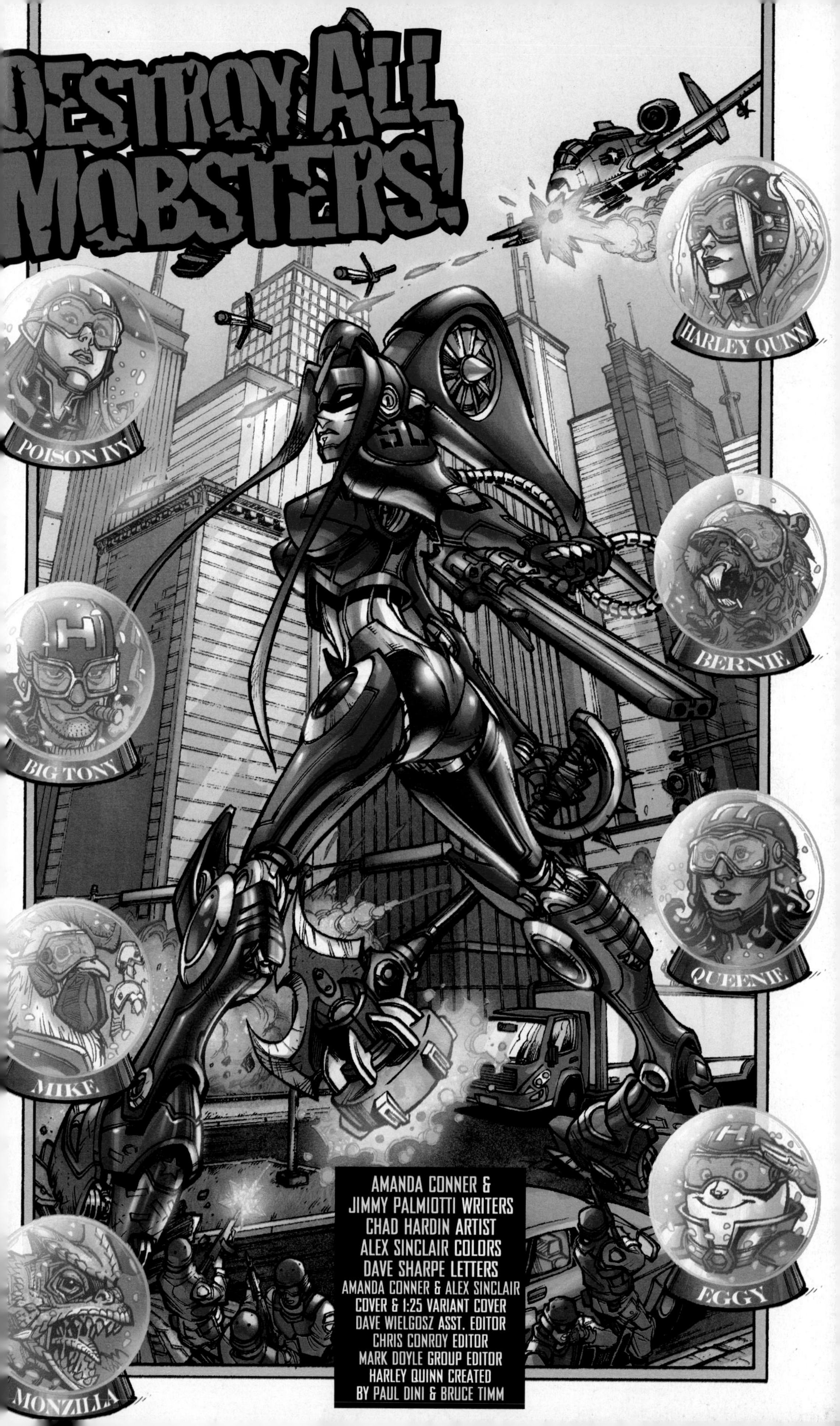
DESTROY ALL MOBSTERS!
HARLEY QUINN
POISON IVY
BERNIE
BIG TONY
QUEENIE
MIKE
EGGY
MONZILLA
AMANDA CONNER & JIMMY PALMIOTTI WRITERS
CHAD HARDIN ARTIST
ALEX SINCLAIR COLORS
DAVE SHARPE LETTERS
AMANDA CONNER & ALEX SINCLAIR COVER & 1:25 VARIANT COVER
DAVE WIELGOSZ ASST. EDITOR
CHRIS CONROY EDITOR
MARK DOYLE GROUP EDITOR
HARLEY QUINN CREATED BY PAUL DINI & BRUCE TIMM

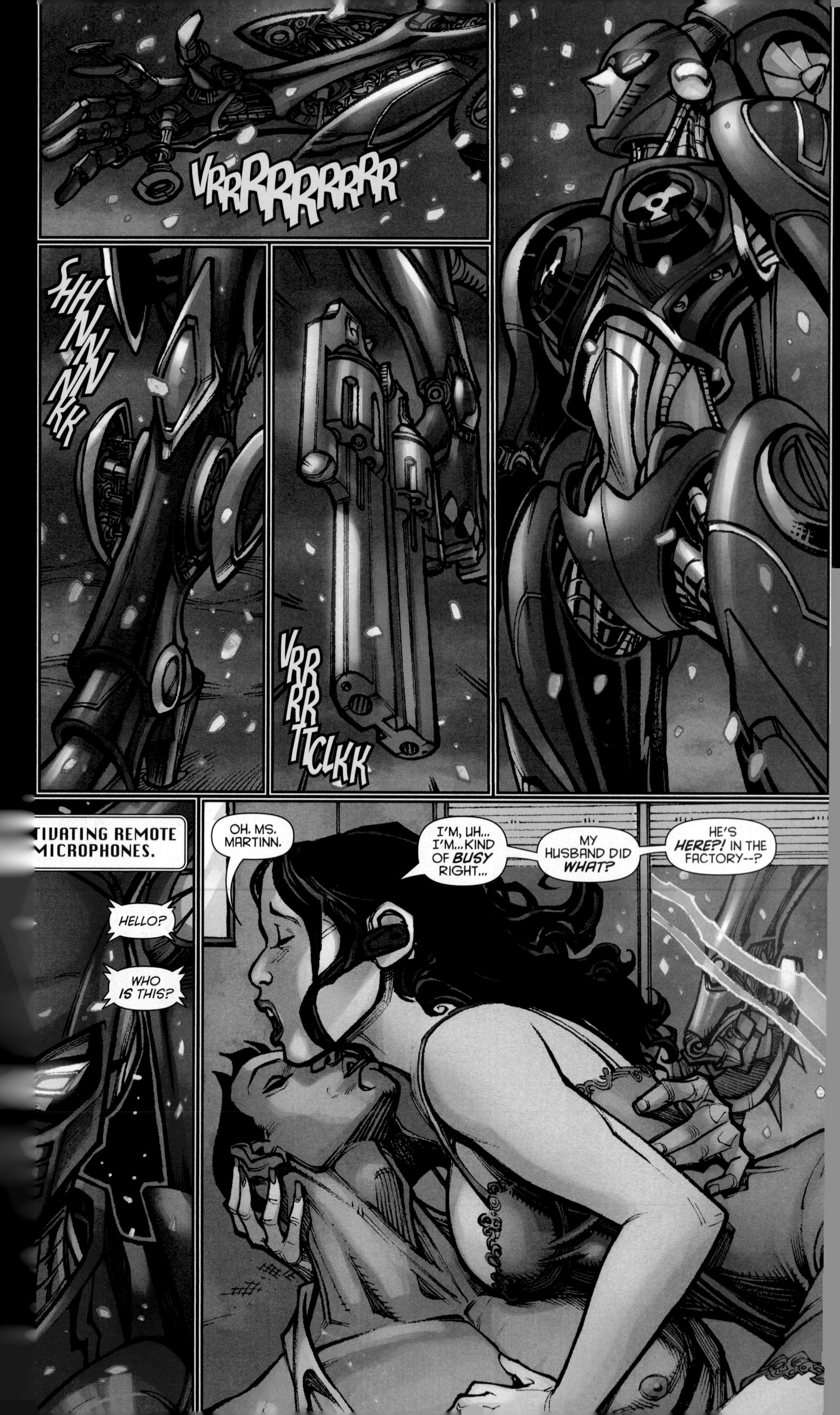

VRRRRRRRRRRR
SHHNNNKK
VRRRRTTCLKK
TIVATING REMOTE MICROPHONES.
HELLO?
WHO IS THIS?
OH. MS. MARTINN.
I'M, UH... I'M...KIND OF BUSY RIGHT...
MY HUSBAND DID WHAT?
HE'S HERE?! IN THE FACTORY--?

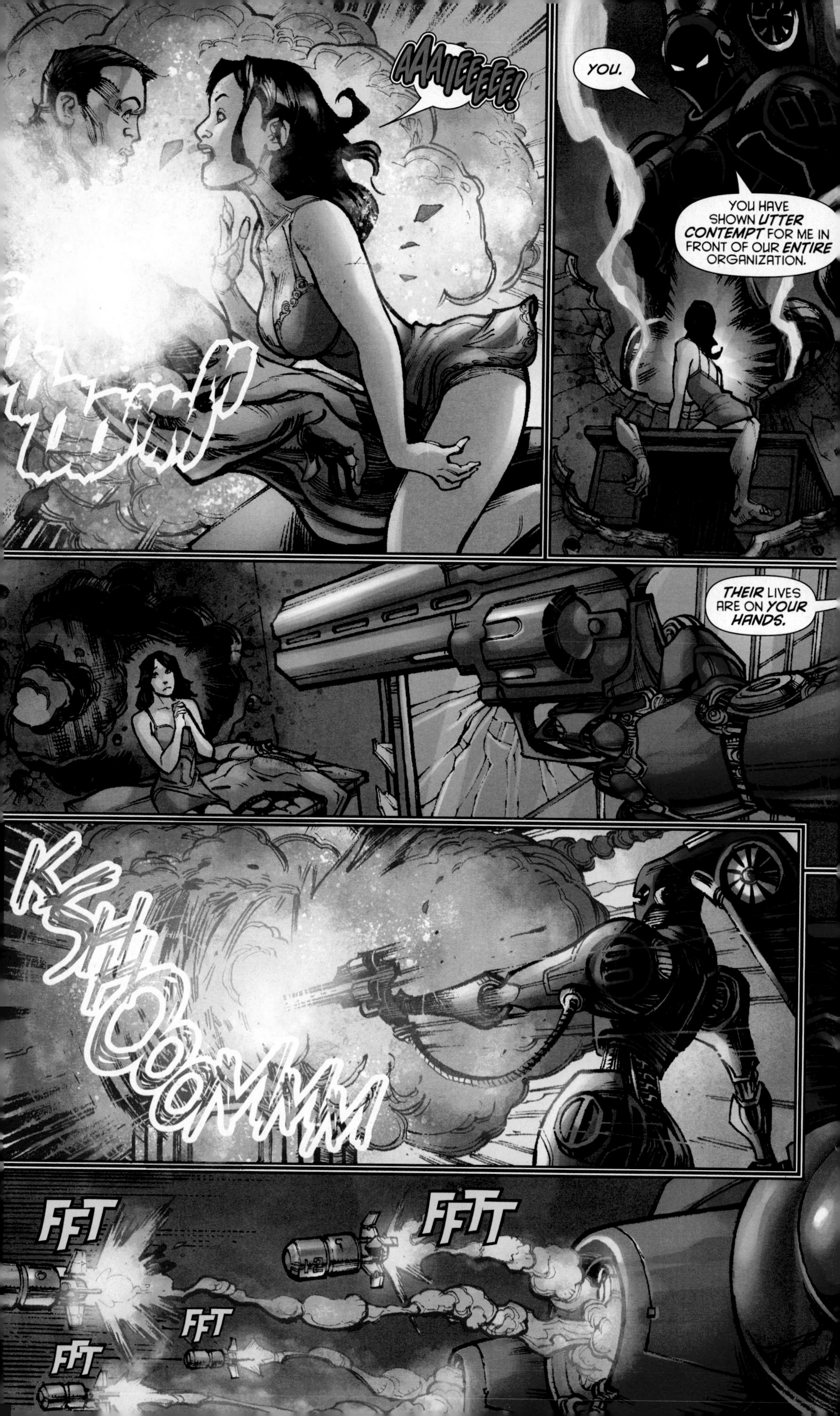
AAAIIEEEEEE!
YOU.
YOU HAVE SHOWN UTTER CONTEMPT FOR ME IN FRONT OF OUR ENTIRE ORGANIZATION.
THEIR LIVES ARE ON YOUR HANDS.
KSHOOOMM
FFT
FFFT
FFT
FFT

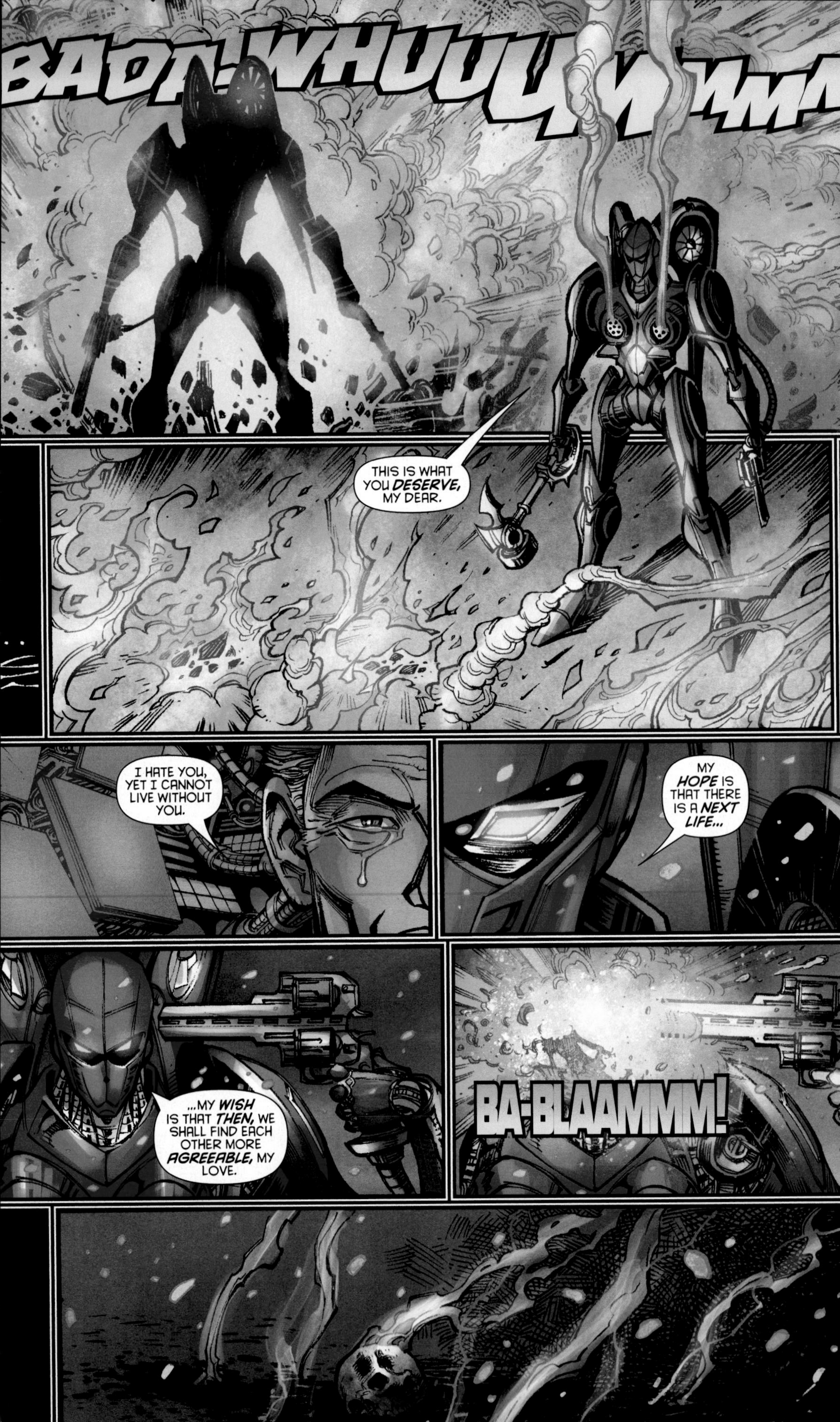
BADA-WHUUUMMMMA
THIS IS WHAT YOU DESERVE, MY DEAR.
I HATE YOU, YET I CANNOT LIVE WITHOUT YOU.
MY HOPE IS THAT THERE IS A NEXT LIFE...
...MY WISH IS THAT THEN, WE SHALL FIND EACH OTHER MORE AGREEABLE, MY LOVE.
BA-BLAAMMMM!

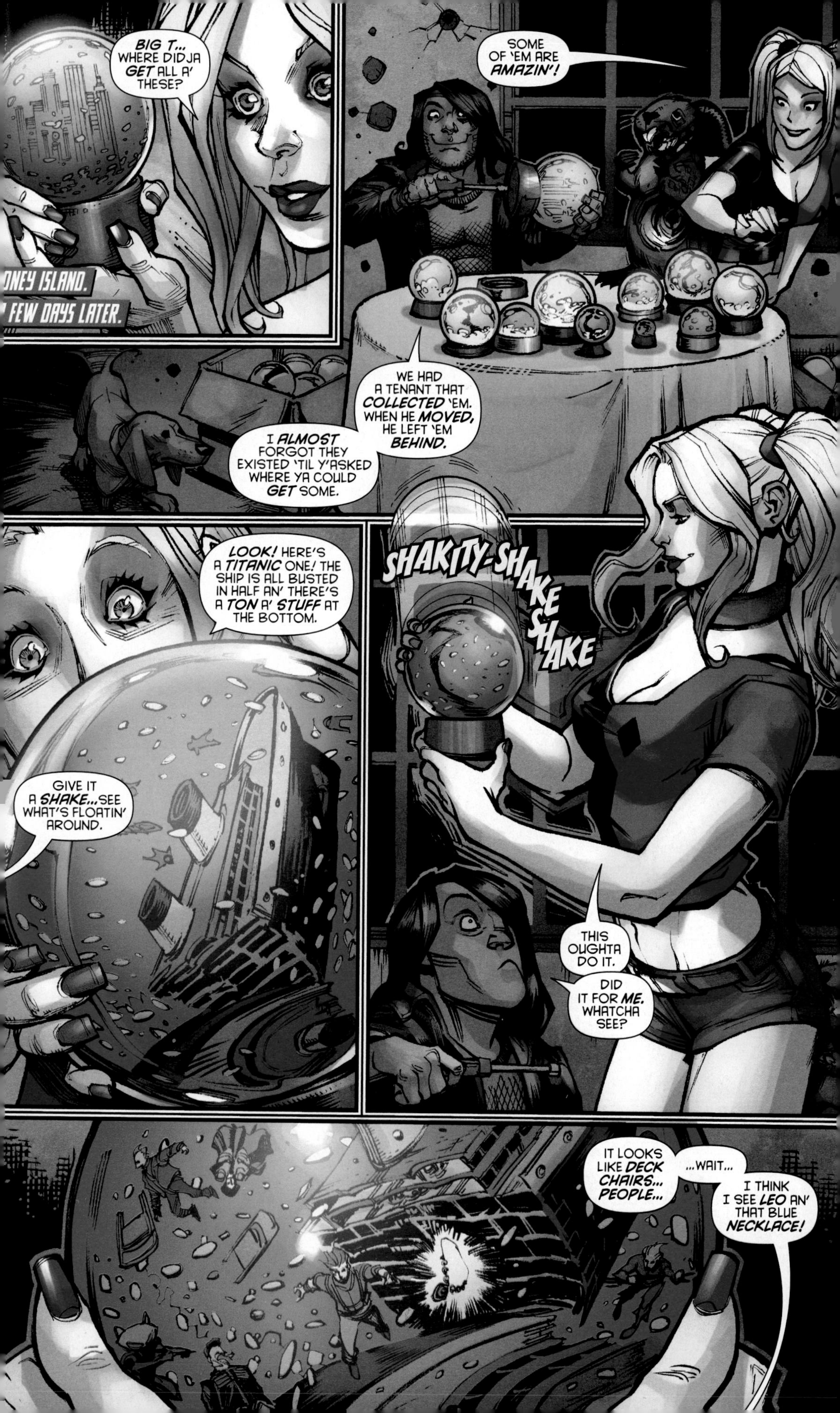
BIG T... WHERE DIDJA GET ALL A' THESE?
ONEY ISLAND.
FEW DAYS LATER.
SOME OF 'EM ARE AMAZIN'!
WE HAD A TENANT THAT COLLECTED 'EM. WHEN HE MOVED, HE LEFT 'EM BEHIND.
I ALMOST FORGOT THEY EXISTED 'TIL Y'ASKED WHERE YA COULD GET SOME.
LOOK! HERE'S A TITANIC ONE! THE SHIP IS ALL BUSTED IN HALF AN' THERE'S A TON A' STUFF AT THE BOTTOM.
GIVE IT A SHAKE...SEE WHAT'S FLOATIN' AROUND.
SHAKITY-SHAKE SHAKE SHAKE
THIS OUGHTA DO IT.
DID IT FOR ME. WHATCHA SEE?
IT LOOKS LIKE DECK CHAIRS... PEOPLE...
...WAIT...
I THINK I SEE LEO AN' THAT BLUE NECKLACE!

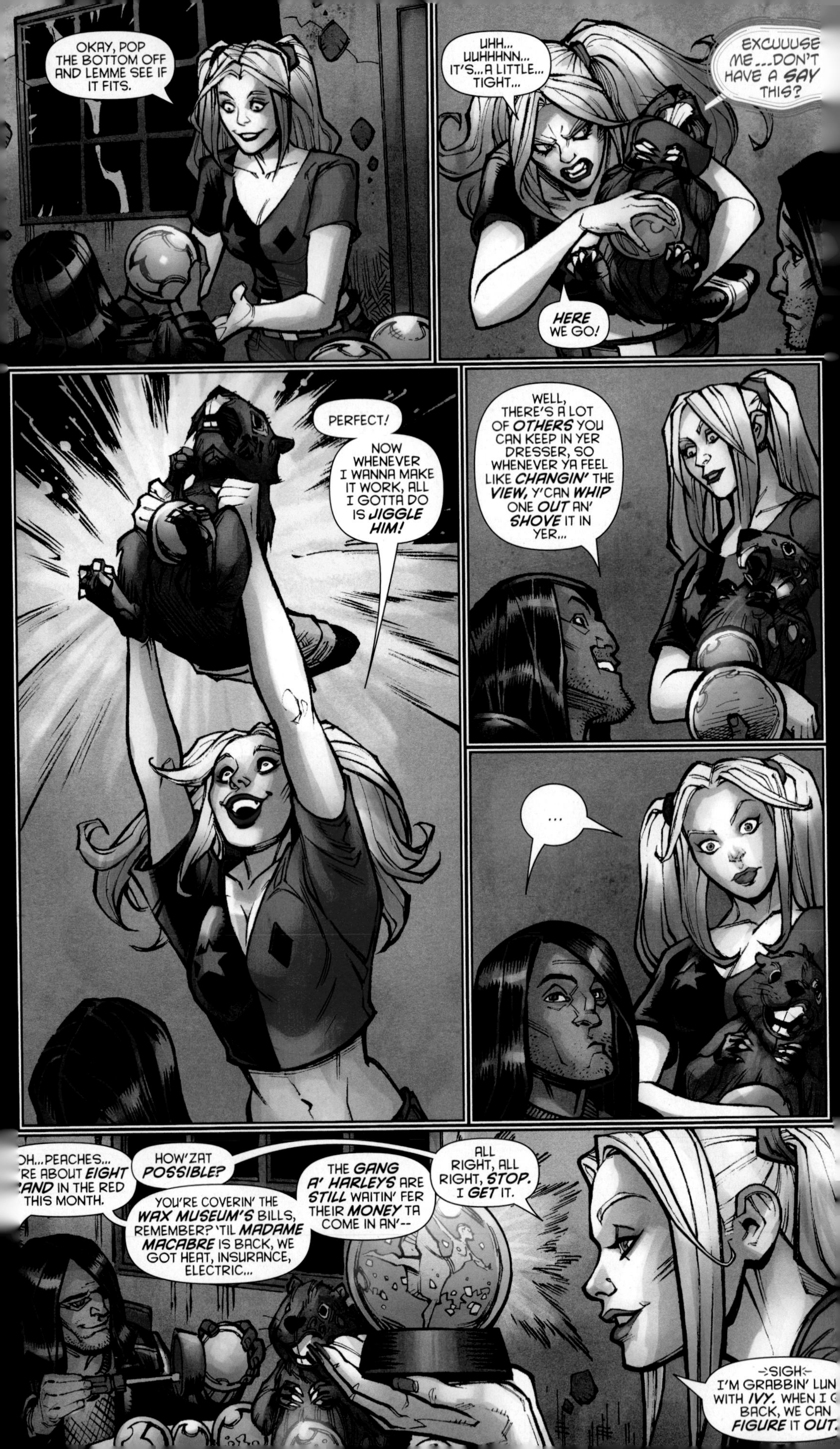
OKAY, POP THE BOTTOM OFF AND LEMME SEE IF IT FITS.
UHH... UUHHHNN... IT'S...A LITTLE... TIGHT...
EXCUUUSE ME ...DON'T HAVE A SAY THIS?
HERE WE GO!
PERFECT!
NOW WHENEVER I WANNA MAKE IT WORK, ALL I GOTTA DO IS JIGGLE HIM!
WELL, THERE'S A LOT OF OTHERS YOU CAN KEEP IN YER DRESSER, SO WHENEVER YA FEEL LIKE CHANGIN' THE VIEW, Y'CAN WHIP ONE OUT AN' SHOVE IT IN YER...
...
...PEACHES... ...RE ABOUT EIGHT ...AND IN THE RED THIS MONTH.
HOW'ZAT POSSIBLE?
YOU'RE COVERIN' THE WAX MUSEUM'S BILLS, REMEMBER? 'TIL MADAME MACABRE IS BACK, WE GOT HEAT, INSURANCE, ELECTRIC...
THE GANG A' HARLEYS ARE STILL WAITIN' FER THEIR MONEY TA COME IN AN'--
ALL RIGHT, ALL RIGHT, STOP. I GET IT.
-SIGH- I'M GRABBIN' LUN... WITH IVY. WHEN I ... BACK, WE CAN FIGURE IT OUT.

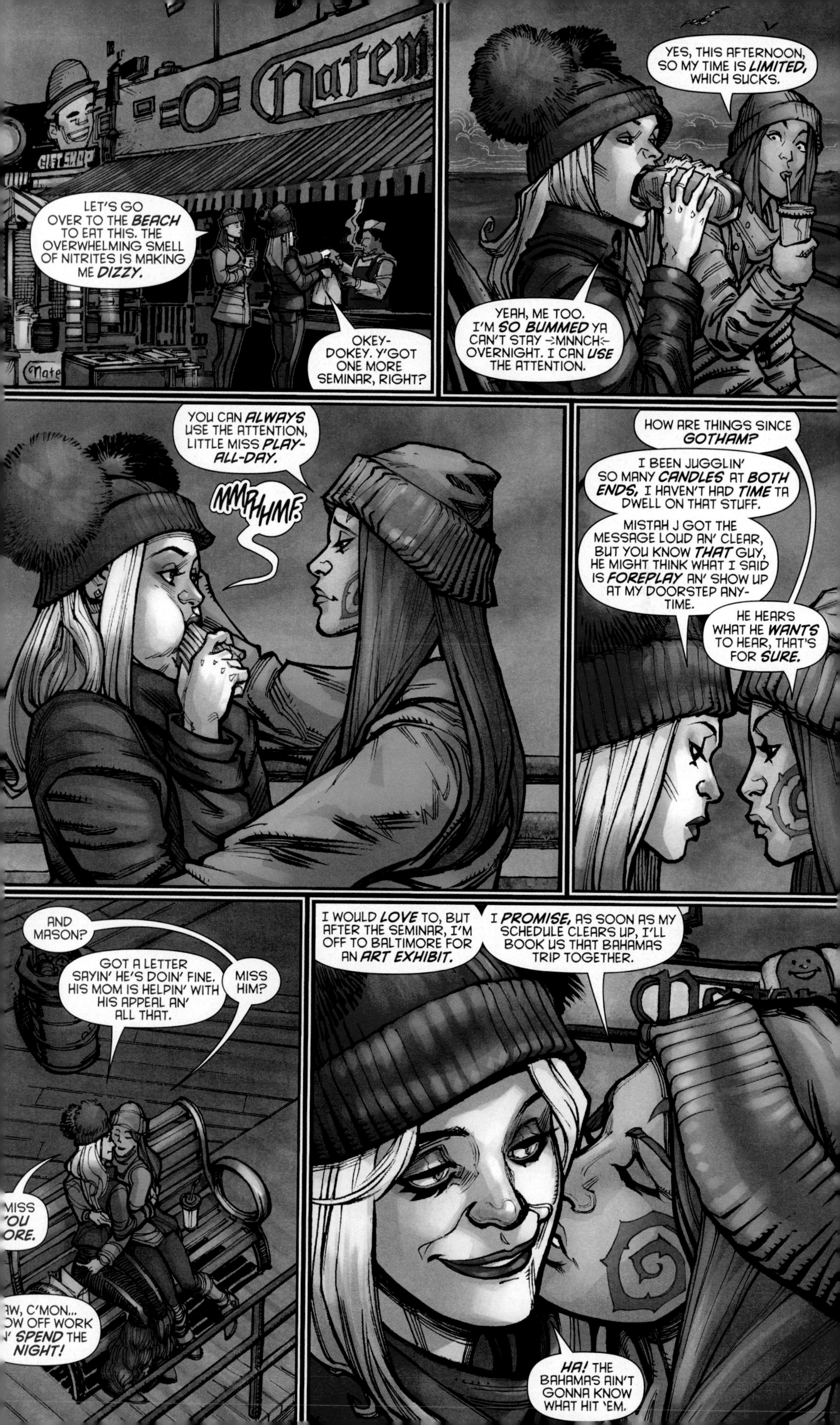

Nate
LET'S GO OVER TO THE BEACH TO EAT THIS. THE OVERWHELMING SMELL OF NITRITES IS MAKING ME DIZZY.
OKEY-DOKEY. Y'GOT ONE MORE SEMINAR, RIGHT?
YES, THIS AFTERNOON, SO MY TIME IS LIMITED, WHICH SUCKS.
YEAH, ME TOO. I'M SO BUMMED YA CAN'T STAY -MNNCH- OVERNIGHT. I CAN USE THE ATTENTION.
YOU CAN ALWAYS USE THE ATTENTION, LITTLE MISS PLAY-ALL-DAY.
MMPHHMF.
HOW ARE THINGS SINCE GOTHAM?
I BEEN JUGGLIN' SO MANY CANDLES AT BOTH ENDS, I HAVEN'T HAD TIME TA DWELL ON THAT STUFF.
MISTAH J GOT THE MESSAGE LOUD AN' CLEAR, BUT YOU KNOW THAT GUY, HE MIGHT THINK WHAT I SAID IS FOREPLAY AN' SHOW UP AT MY DOORSTEP ANY-TIME.
HE HEARS WHAT HE WANTS TO HEAR, THAT'S FOR SURE.
AND MASON?
GOT A LETTER SAYIN' HE'S DOIN' FINE. HIS MOM IS HELPIN' WITH HIS APPEAL AN' ALL THAT.
MISS HIM?
MISS YOU MORE.
AW, C'MON... OW OFF WORK N' SPEND THE NIGHT!
I WOULD LOVE TO, BUT AFTER THE SEMINAR, I'M OFF TO BALTIMORE FOR AN ART EXHIBIT.
I PROMISE, AS SOON AS MY SCHEDULE CLEARS UP, I'LL BOOK US THAT BAHAMAS TRIP TOGETHER.
HA! THE BAHAMAS AIN'T GONNA KNOW WHAT HIT 'EM.

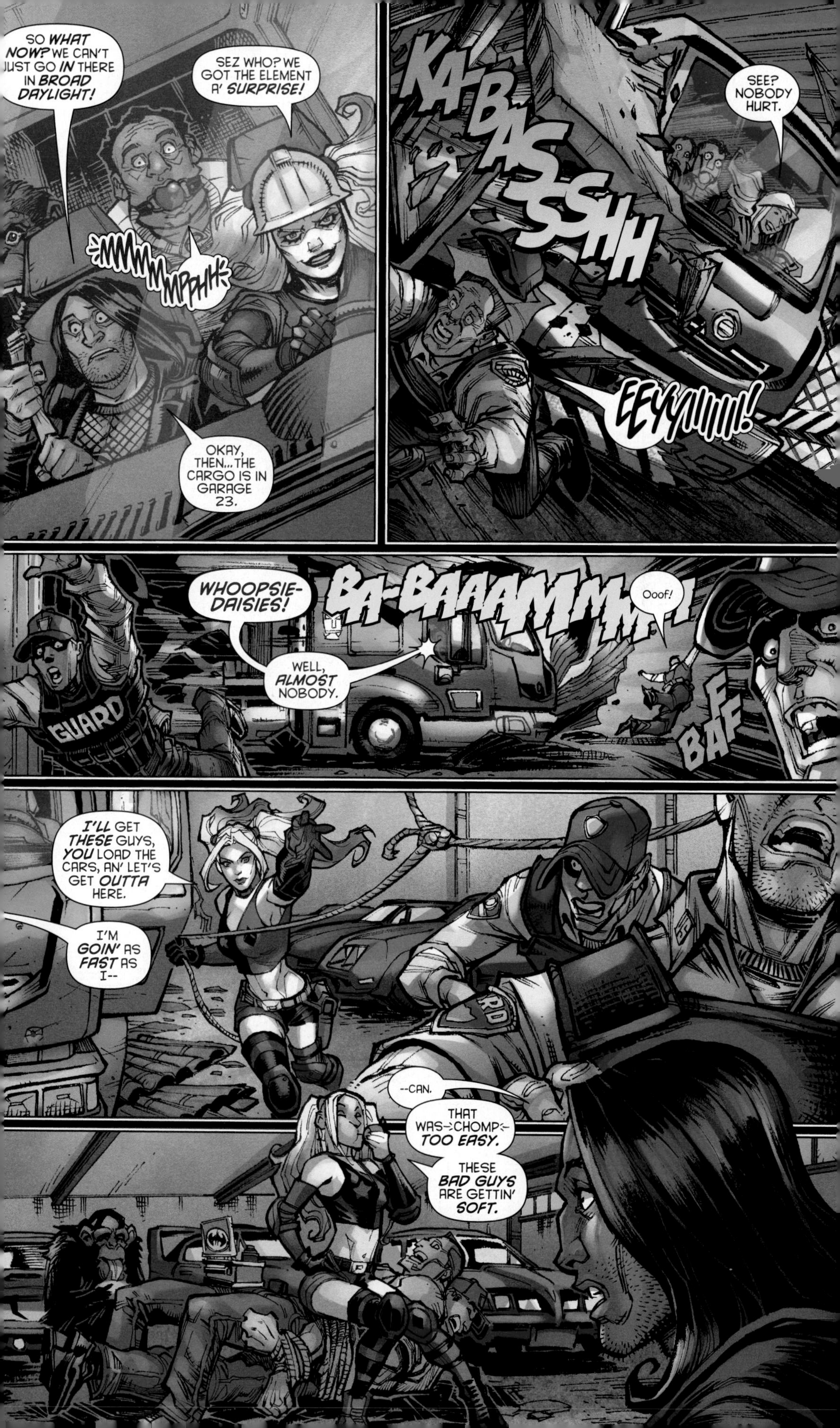
SO WHAT NOW? WE CAN'T JUST GO IN THERE IN BROAD DAYLIGHT!
SEZ WHO? WE GOT THE ELEMENT A' SURPRISE!
MMMMMMMPHH!
OKAY, THEN... THE CARGO IS IN GARAGE 23.
KA-BASSSHH
SEE? NOBODY HURT.
EEYYIIIIIII!
WHOOPSIE-DAISIES!
BA-BAAAMMMM!
Ooof!
WELL, ALMOST NOBODY.
GUARD
BAF
F
I'LL GET THESE GUYS, YOU LOAD THE CARS, AN' LET'S GET OUTTA HERE.
I'M GOIN' AS FAST AS I--
--CAN.
THAT WAS-CHOMP-TOO EASY.
THESE BAD GUYS ARE GETTIN' SOFT.

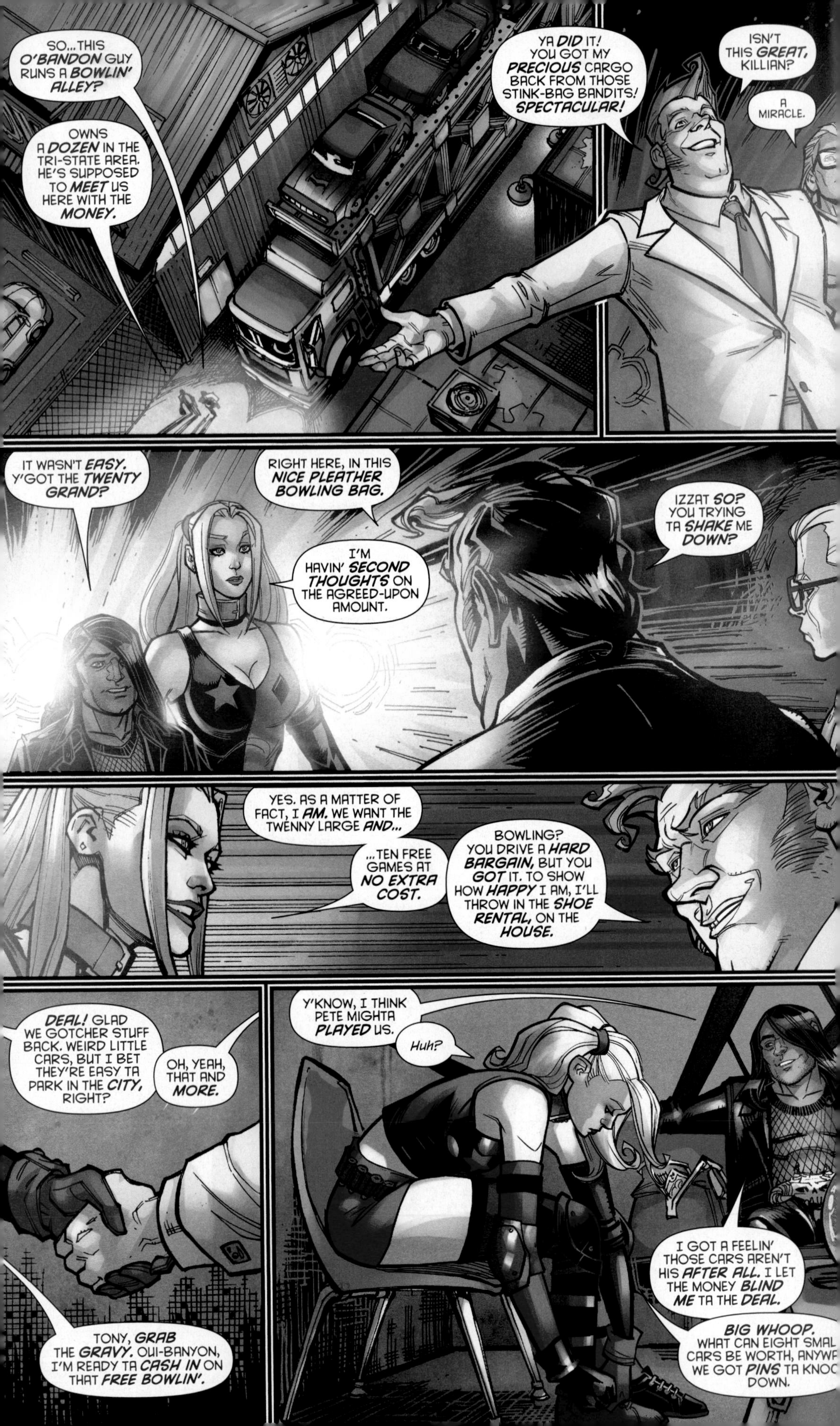
SO... THIS O'BANDON GUY RUNS A BOWLIN' ALLEY?
OWNS A DOZEN IN THE TRI-STATE AREA. HE'S SUPPOSED TO MEET US HERE WITH THE MONEY.
YA DID IT! YOU GOT MY PRECIOUS CARGO BACK FROM THOSE STINK-BAG BANDITS! SPECTACULAR!
ISN'T THIS GREAT, KILLIAN?
A MIRACLE.
IT WASN'T EASY. Y'GOT THE TWENTY GRAND?
RIGHT HERE, IN THIS NICE PLEATHER BOWLING BAG.
I'M HAVIN' SECOND THOUGHTS ON THE AGREED-UPON AMOUNT.
IZZAT SO? YOU TRYING TA SHAKE ME DOWN?
YES. AS A MATTER OF FACT, I AM. WE WANT THE TWENNY LARGE AND...
...TEN FREE GAMES AT NO EXTRA COST.
BOWLING? YOU DRIVE A HARD BARGAIN, BUT YOU GOT IT. TO SHOW HOW HAPPY I AM, I'LL THROW IN THE SHOE RENTAL, ON THE HOUSE.
DEAL! GLAD WE GOTCHER STUFF BACK. WEIRD LITTLE CARS, BUT I BET THEY'RE EASY TA PARK IN THE CITY, RIGHT?
OH, YEAH, THAT AND MORE.
TONY, GRAB THE GRAVY. OUI-BANYON, I'M READY TA CASH IN ON THAT FREE BOWLIN'.
Y'KNOW, I THINK PETE MIGHTA PLAYED US.
Huh?
I GOT A FEELIN' THOSE CARS AREN'T HIS AFTER ALL. I LET THE MONEY BLIND ME TA THE DEAL.
BIG WHOOP. WHAT CAN EIGHT SMAL CARS BE WORTH, ANYWA WE GOT PINS TA KNOC DOWN.

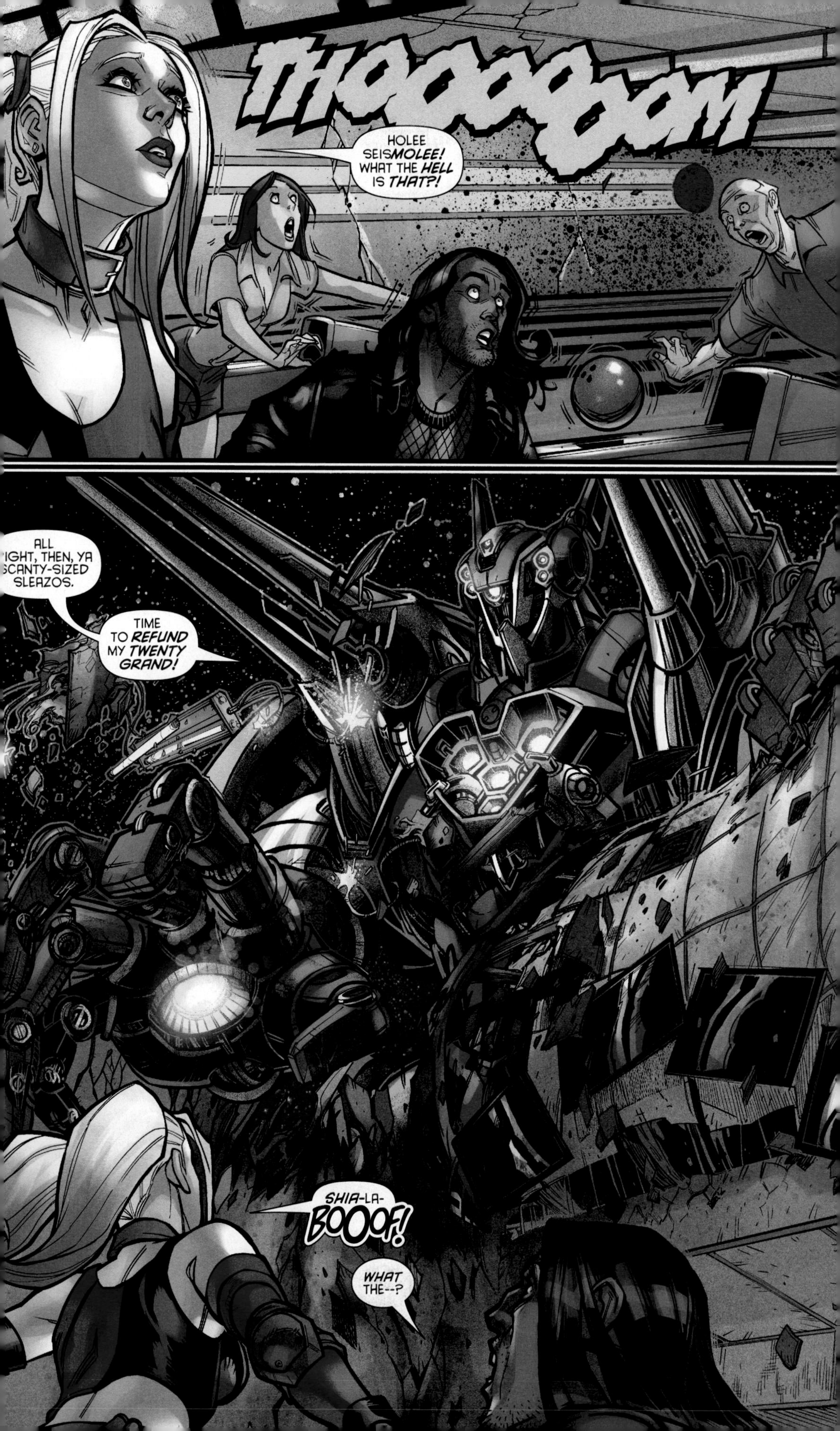
THOOOOOOM
HOLEE SEISMOLEE! WHAT THE HELL IS THAT?!
ALL RIGHT, THEN, YA SCANTY-SIZED SLEAZOS.
TIME TO REFUND MY TWENTY GRAND!
SHIA-LA-BOOOF!
WHAT THE--?

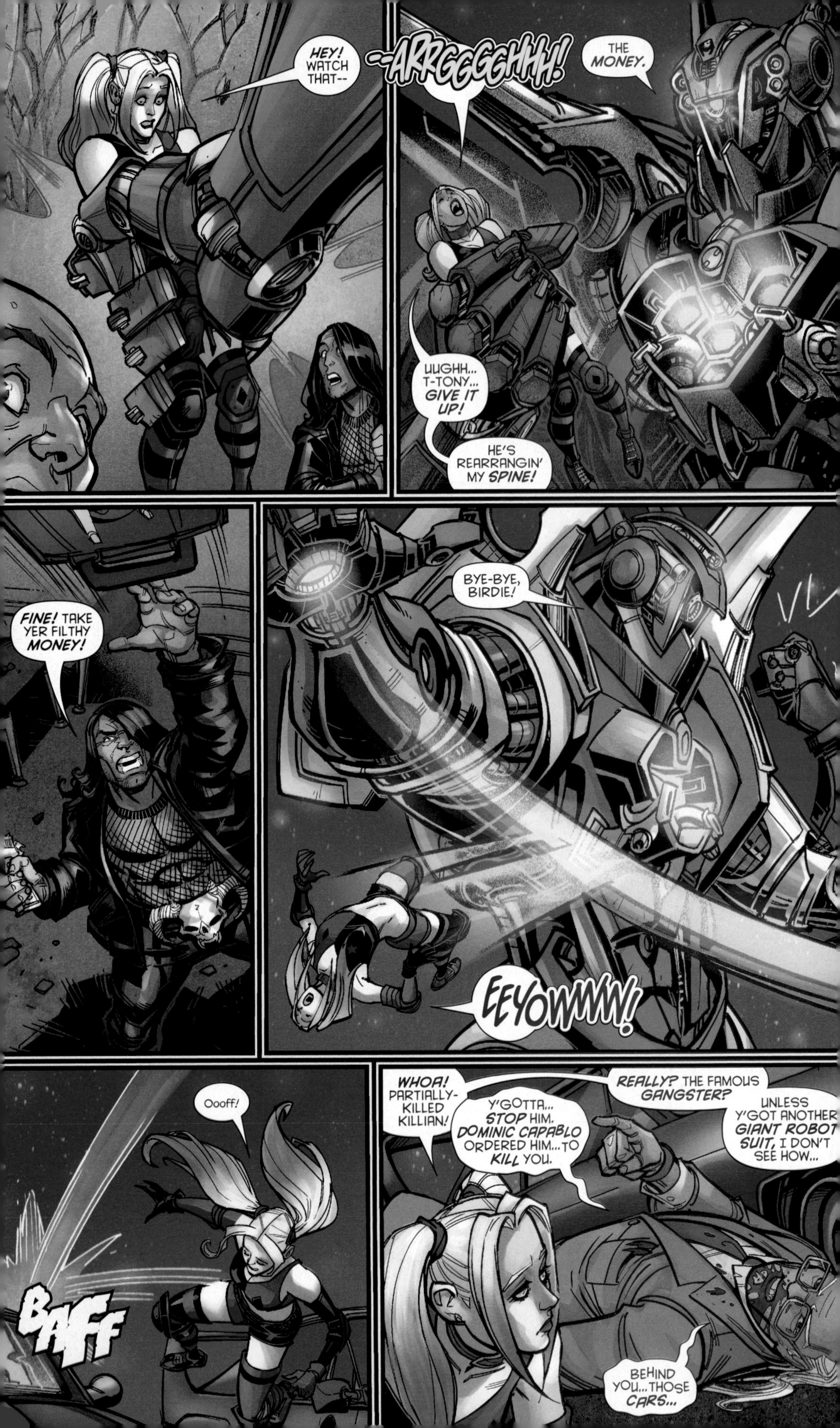
HEY! WATCH THAT--
--ARRRGGGGHHH!
THE MONEY.
UUGHH... T-TONY... GIVE IT UP!
HE'S REARRANGIN' MY SPINE!
FINE! TAKE YER FILTHY MONEY!
BYE-BYE, BIRDIE!
EEYOWWW!
BAFF
Oooff!
WHOA! PARTIALLY-KILLED KILLIAN!
Y'GOTTA... STOP HIM. DOMINIC CAPABLO ORDERED HIM... TO KILL YOU.
REALLY? THE FAMOUS GANGSTER?
UNLESS Y'GOT ANOTHER GIANT ROBOT SUIT, I DON'T SEE HOW...
BEHIND YOU... THOSE CARS...

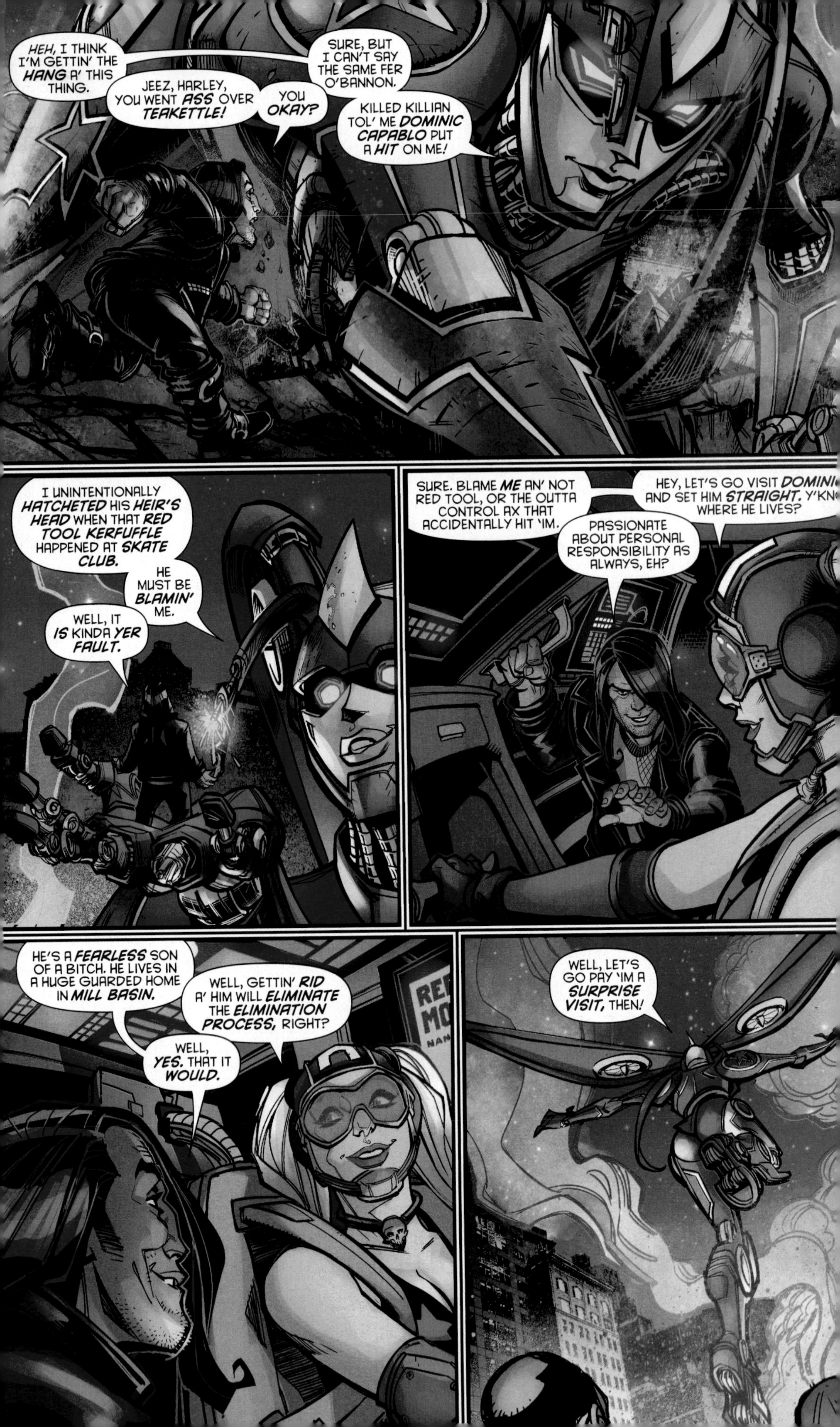

HEH, I THINK I'M GETTIN' THE HANG A' THIS THING.
SURE, BUT I CAN'T SAY THE SAME FER O'BANNON.
JEEZ, HARLEY, YOU WENT ASS OVER TEAKETTLE!
YOU OKAY?
KILLED KILLIAN TOL' ME DOMINIC CAPABLO PUT A HIT ON ME!
I UNINTENTIONALLY HATCHETED HIS HEIR'S HEAD WHEN THAT RED TOOL KERFUFFLE HAPPENED AT SKATE CLUB.
HE MUST BE BLAMIN' ME.
WELL, IT IS KINDA YER FAULT.
SURE. BLAME ME AN' NOT RED TOOL, OR THE OUTTA CONTROL AX THAT ACCIDENTALLY HIT 'IM.
HEY, LET'S GO VISIT DOMINI
AND SET HIM STRAIGHT. Y'KN
WHERE HE LIVES?
PASSIONATE ABOUT PERSONAL RESPONSIBILITY AS ALWAYS, EH?
HE'S A FEARLESS SON OF A BITCH. HE LIVES IN A HUGE GUARDED HOME IN MILL BASIN.
WELL, GETTIN' RID A' HIM WILL ELIMINATE THE ELIMINATION PROCESS, RIGHT?
WELL, YES. THAT IT WOULD.
WELL, LET'S GO PAY 'IM A SURPRISE VISIT, THEN!

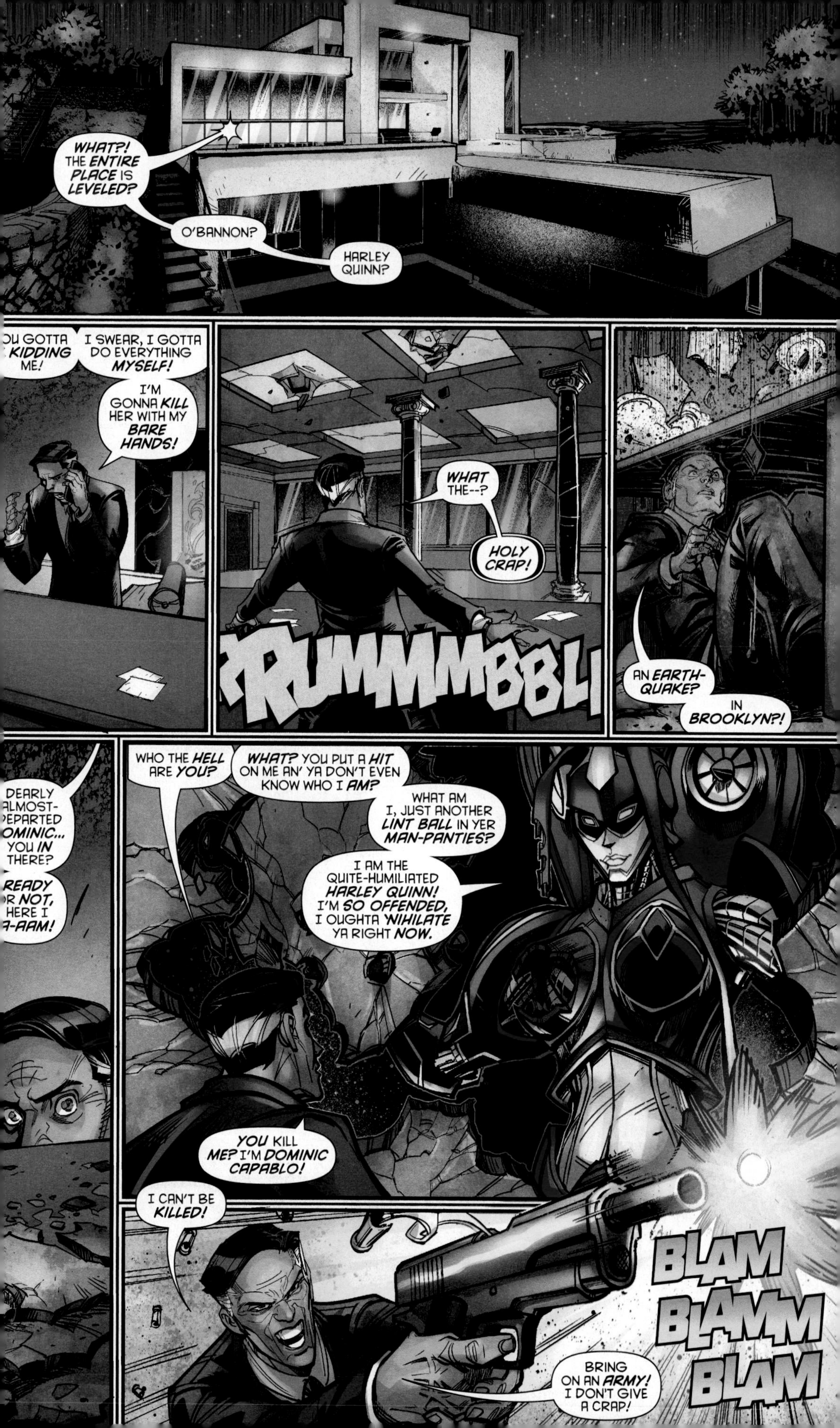
WHAT?! THE ENTIRE PLACE IS LEVELED?
O'BANNON?
HARLEY QUINN?
OU GOTTA KIDDING ME!
I SWEAR, I GOTTA DO EVERYTHING MYSELF!
I'M GONNA KILL HER WITH MY BARE HANDS!
WHAT THE--?
HOLY CRAP!
RUMMMBBL
AN EARTH-QUAKE?
IN BROOKLYN?!
DEARLY ALMOST-EPARTED OMINIC... YOU IN THERE?
READY R NOT, HERE I A-AAM!
WHO THE HELL ARE YOU?
WHAT? YOU PUT A HIT ON ME AN' YA DON'T EVEN KNOW WHO I AM?
WHAT AM I, JUST ANOTHER LINT BALL IN YER MAN-PANTIES?
I AM THE QUITE-HUMILIATED HARLEY QUINN! I'M SO OFFENDED, I OUGHTA 'NIHILATE YA RIGHT NOW.
YOU KILL ME? I'M DOMINIC CAPABLO!
I CAN'T BE KILLED!
BLAM BLAMM BLAM
BRING ON AN ARMY! I DON'T GIVE A CRAP!

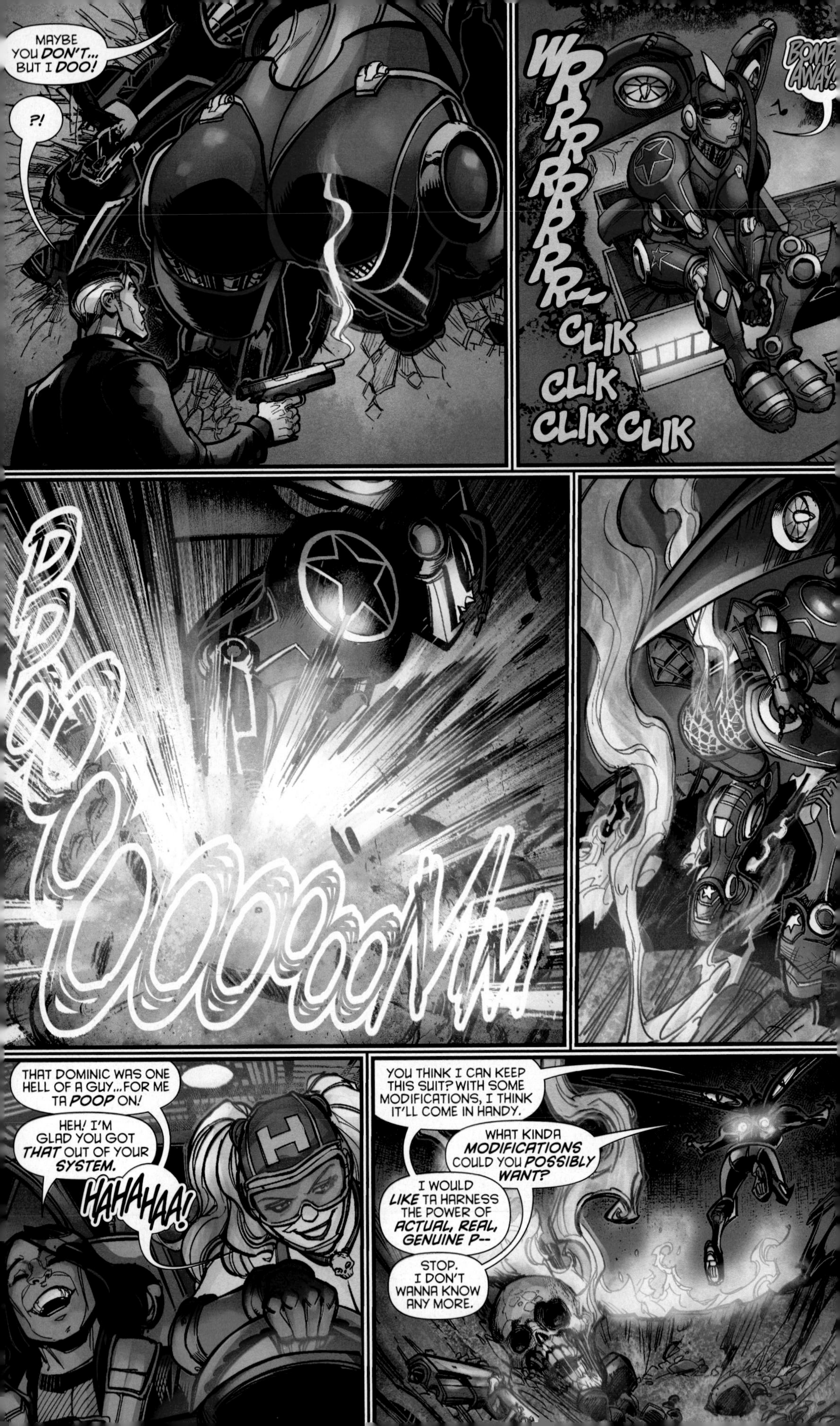
MAYBE YOU DON'T... BUT I DOO!
?!
WRRRRRRRRR--
CLIK CLIK CLIK CLIK
BOMBS AWAY!
DOOOOOOOOOM
THAT DOMINIC WAS ONE HELL OF A GUY...FOR ME TA POOP ON!
HEH! I'M GLAD YOU GOT THAT OUT OF YOUR SYSTEM.
HAHAHAA!
YOU THINK I CAN KEEP THIS SUIT? WITH SOME MODIFICATIONS, I THINK IT'LL COME IN HANDY.
WHAT KINDA MODIFICATIONS COULD YOU POSSIBLY WANT?
I WOULD LIKE TA HARNESS THE POWER OF ACTUAL, REAL, GENUINE P--
STOP. I DON'T WANNA KNOW ANY MORE.

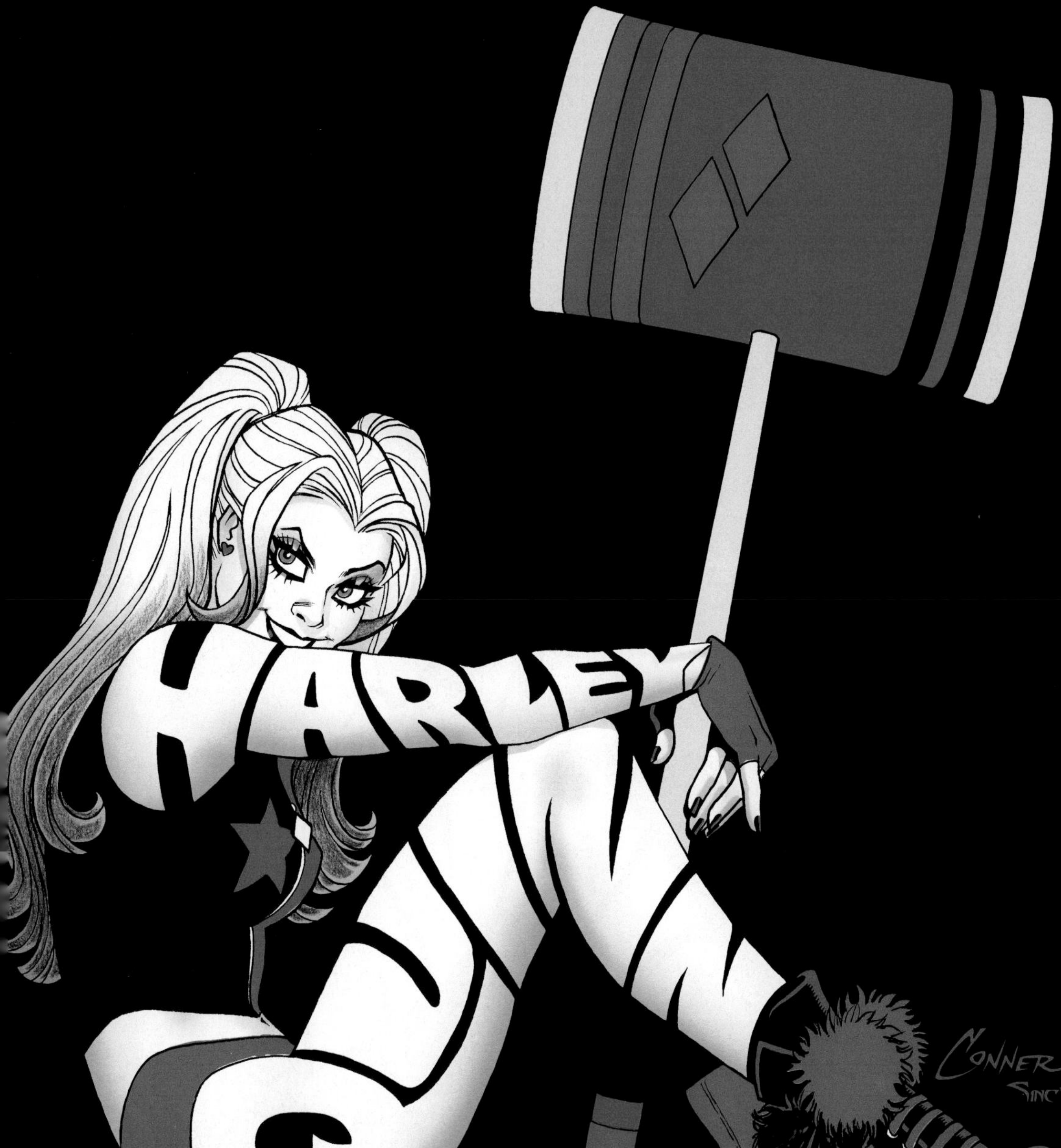
HARLEY
CONNER
SINC

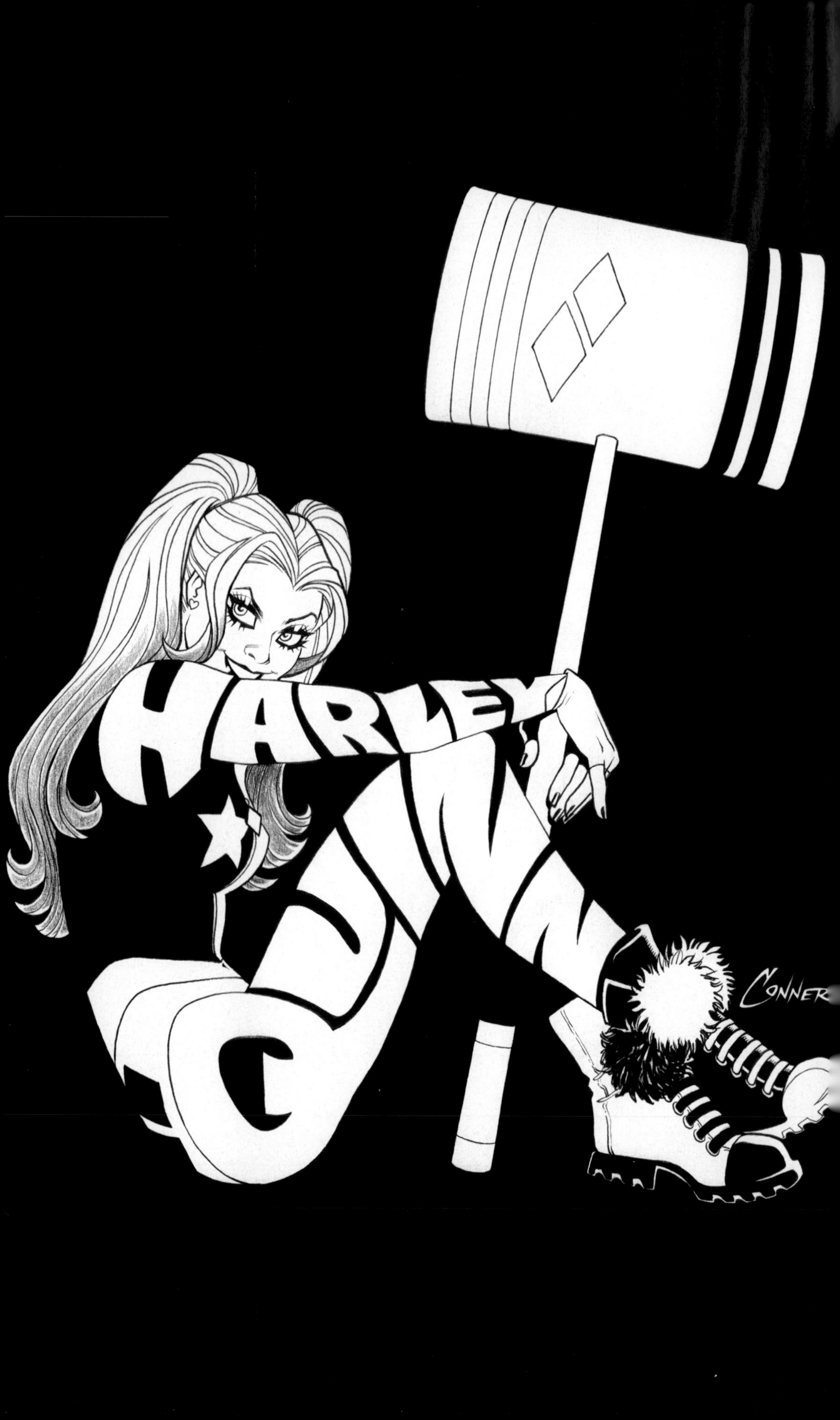
HARLEY
QUINN
CONNER

MAMA TO BE! HERE. TAKE A LOAD OFF.

WOW! THANKS. I REALLY APPRECI--

VWIP

HEY!

OH, IT'S OKAY. I GET OFF AT THE NEXT STOP.

NOT THE POINT.

WHAT THE--? GET OFFA ME!

I WAS GIVING THAT LOVELY EXPECTANT LADY MY SEAT, WHEN YOU BOORISHLY BOOSTED IT INSTEAD. Y'THINK YOUR MOTHER WOULD BE OKAY WITH THAT KINDA BEHAVIOR?

HEY, I GOT HERE FIRST, AND I'M ADOPTED. WHAT MY MOTHER THINKS IS OF NO CONSEQUENCE SINCE SHE HANDED ME OVER TO STRANGERS BEFORE I WAS ABLE TO ADJUST TO THE OUTSIDE WORLD.

NOW GET OFFA ME BEFORE I FLING YOU OFF, YA FLOOZY.

GUESS WHAT? I'M GONNA BE LATE FOR WORK TODAY, BUT I DON'T GIVE A CRAP, 'CAUSE I'M GONNA ATTACH MYSELF TO YOU LIKE A TICK ON A DOG'S ASS 'TIL YOU APOLOGIZE TA ME AN' THAT NICE PREGNANT LADY.

WHAT LADY?

AW, MAN...SHE MUSTA GOTTEN OFF AT HER STOP.

CAN YOU PLEASE GET OFFA ME THEN? YOU MADE YOUR POINT.

HAVE I?

OH, SUUURE. YOU WANTED TO GIVE A KNOCKED-UP HOOCHIE-MAMA MY SEAT, AND I TOOK IT INSTEAD. I WAS SOOO WRONG.

AND BECAUSE OF YOUR HARASSMENT, FROM NOW ON I WILL MAKE SURE TO BE A "BETTER PERSON" AND BE CONSIDERATE TO EVERYONE AROUND ME.

YOUR INTERVENTION HAS SOOO CHANGED MY LIFE. YOU SHOWED ME THAT I CAN BE A POLITE, KIND HUMAN BEING AND THAT MAKING THE WORLD A "BETTER PLACE" STARTS WITH ME.

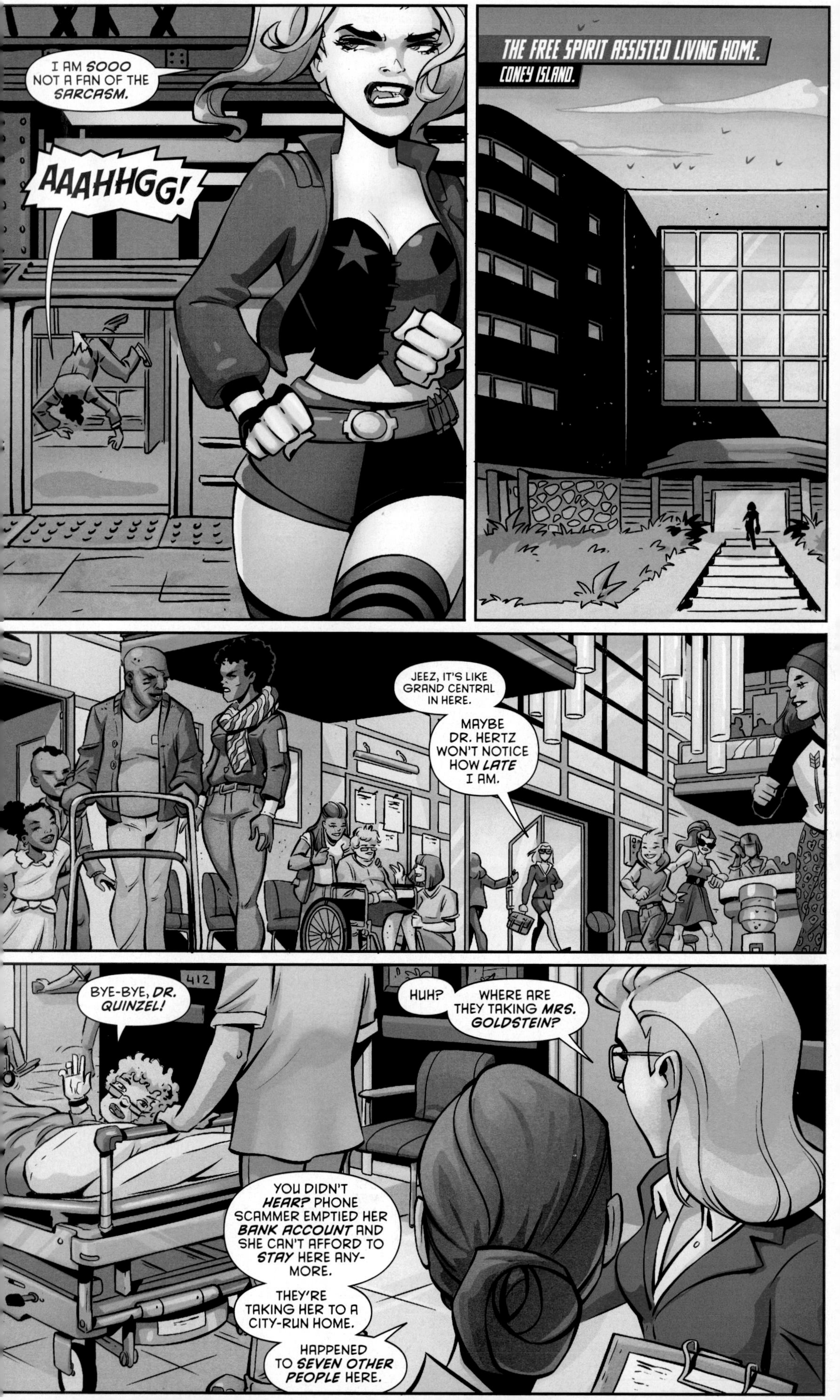

I AM SOOO NOT A FAN OF THE SARCASM.
AAAHHGG!
THE FREE SPIRIT ASSISTED LIVING HOME.
CONEY ISLAND.
JEEZ, IT'S LIKE GRAND CENTRAL IN HERE.
MAYBE DR. HERTZ WON'T NOTICE HOW LATE I AM.
412
BYE-BYE, DR. QUINZEL!
HUH?
WHERE ARE THEY TAKING MRS. GOLDSTEIN?
YOU DIDN'T HEAR? PHONE SCAMMER EMPTIED HER BANK ACCOUNT AND SHE CAN'T AFFORD TO STAY HERE ANY-MORE.
THEY'RE TAKING HER TO A CITY-RUN HOME.
HAPPENED TO SEVEN OTHER PEOPLE HERE.

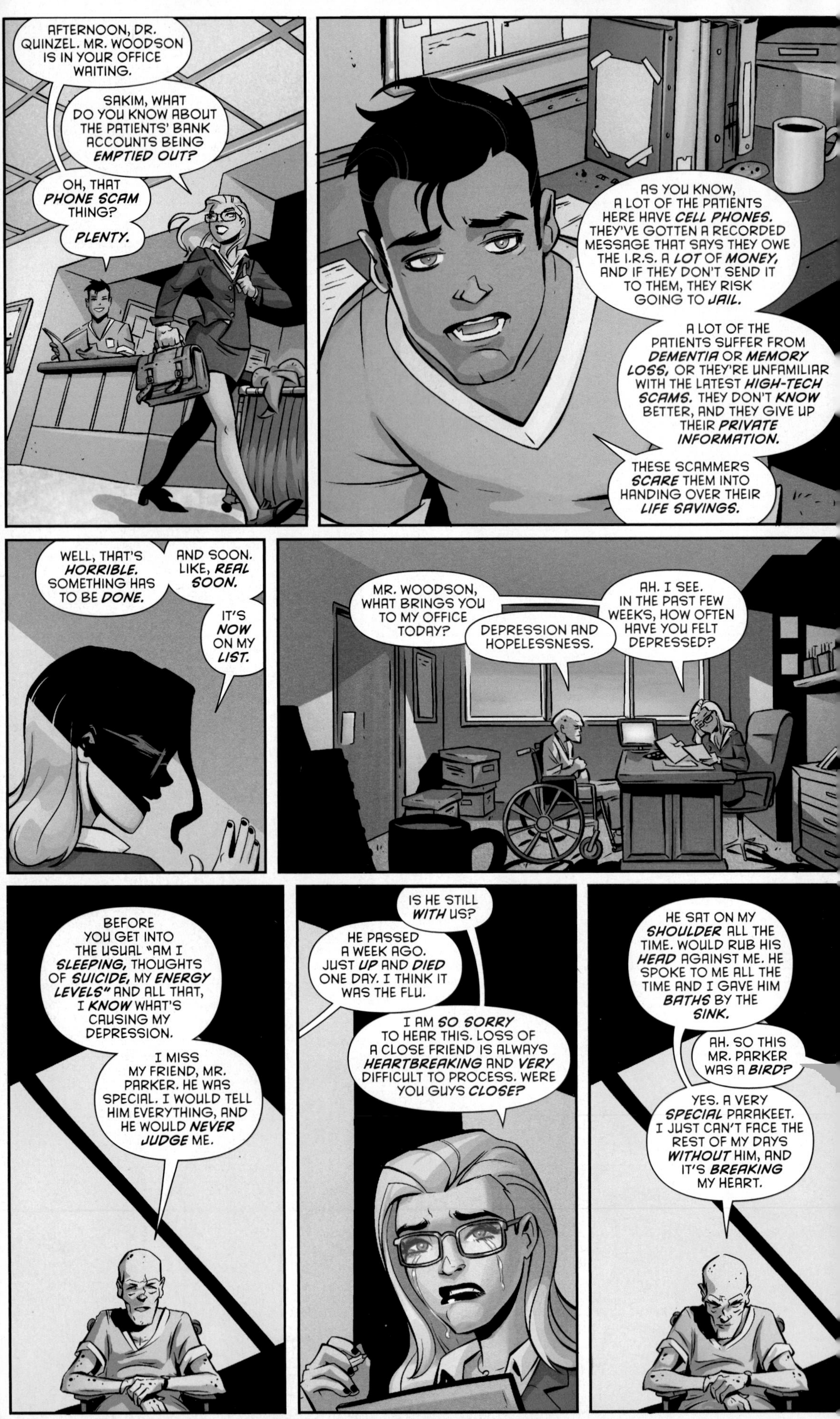
AFTERNOON, DR. QUINZEL. MR. WOODSON IS IN YOUR OFFICE WAITING.
SAKIM, WHAT DO YOU KNOW ABOUT THE PATIENTS' BANK ACCOUNTS BEING EMPTIED OUT?
OH, THAT PHONE SCAM THING?
PLENTY.
AS YOU KNOW, A LOT OF THE PATIENTS HERE HAVE CELL PHONES. THEY'VE GOTTEN A RECORDED MESSAGE THAT SAYS THEY OWE THE I.R.S. A LOT OF MONEY, AND IF THEY DON'T SEND IT TO THEM, THEY RISK GOING TO JAIL.
A LOT OF THE PATIENTS SUFFER FROM DEMENTIA OR MEMORY LOSS, OR THEY'RE UNFAMILIAR WITH THE LATEST HIGH-TECH SCAMS. THEY DON'T KNOW BETTER, AND THEY GIVE UP THEIR PRIVATE INFORMATION.
THESE SCAMMERS SCARE THEM INTO HANDING OVER THEIR LIFE SAVINGS.
WELL, THAT'S HORRIBLE. SOMETHING HAS TO BE DONE.
AND SOON. LIKE, REAL SOON.
IT'S NOW ON MY LIST.
MR. WOODSON, WHAT BRINGS YOU TO MY OFFICE TODAY?
DEPRESSION AND HOPELESSNESS.
AH. I SEE. IN THE PAST FEW WEEKS, HOW OFTEN HAVE YOU FELT DEPRESSED?
BEFORE YOU GET INTO THE USUAL "AM I SLEEPING, THOUGHTS OF SUICIDE, MY ENERGY LEVELS" AND ALL THAT, I KNOW WHAT'S CAUSING MY DEPRESSION.
I MISS MY FRIEND, MR. PARKER. HE WAS SPECIAL. I WOULD TELL HIM EVERYTHING, AND HE WOULD NEVER JUDGE ME.
IS HE STILL WITH US?
HE PASSED A WEEK AGO. JUST UP AND DIED ONE DAY. I THINK IT WAS THE FLU.
I AM SO SORRY TO HEAR THIS. LOSS OF A CLOSE FRIEND IS ALWAYS HEARTBREAKING AND VERY DIFFICULT TO PROCESS. WERE YOU GUYS CLOSE?
HE SAT ON MY SHOULDER ALL THE TIME. WOULD RUB HIS HEAD AGAINST ME. HE SPOKE TO ME ALL THE TIME AND I GAVE HIM BATHS BY THE SINK.
AH. SO THIS MR. PARKER WAS A BIRD?
YES. A VERY SPECIAL PARAKEET. I JUST CAN'T FACE THE REST OF MY DAYS WITHOUT HIM, AND IT'S BREAKING MY HEART.

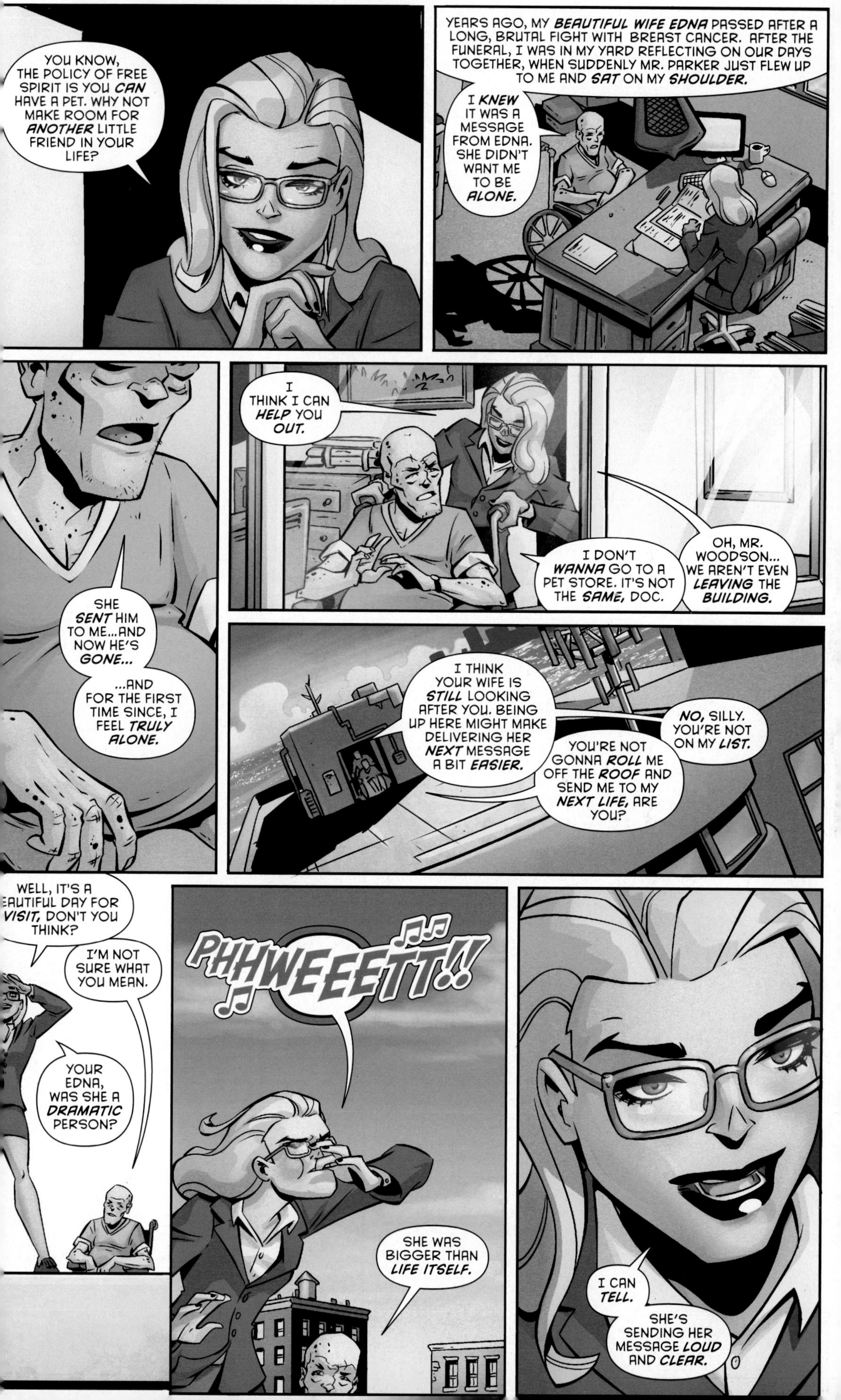
YOU KNOW, THE POLICY OF FREE SPIRIT IS YOU CAN HAVE A PET. WHY NOT MAKE ROOM FOR ANOTHER LITTLE FRIEND IN YOUR LIFE?
YEARS AGO, MY BEAUTIFUL WIFE EDNA PASSED AFTER A LONG, BRUTAL FIGHT WITH BREAST CANCER. AFTER THE FUNERAL, I WAS IN MY YARD REFLECTING ON OUR DAYS TOGETHER, WHEN SUDDENLY MR. PARKER JUST FLEW UP TO ME AND SAT ON MY SHOULDER.
I KNEW IT WAS A MESSAGE FROM EDNA. SHE DIDN'T WANT ME TO BE ALONE.
SHE SENT HIM TO ME...AND NOW HE'S GONE...
...AND FOR THE FIRST TIME SINCE, I FEEL TRULY ALONE.
I THINK I CAN HELP YOU OUT.
I DON'T WANNA GO TO A PET STORE. IT'S NOT THE SAME, DOC.
OH, MR. WOODSON... WE AREN'T EVEN LEAVING THE BUILDING.
I THINK YOUR WIFE IS STILL LOOKING AFTER YOU. BEING UP HERE MIGHT MAKE DELIVERING HER NEXT MESSAGE A BIT EASIER.
YOU'RE NOT GONNA ROLL ME OFF THE ROOF AND SEND ME TO MY NEXT LIFE, ARE YOU?
NO, SILLY. YOU'RE NOT ON MY LIST.
WELL, IT'S A EAUTIFUL DAY FOR VISIT, DON'T YOU THINK?
I'M NOT SURE WHAT YOU MEAN.
YOUR EDNA, WAS SHE A DRAMATIC PERSON?
PHHWEEEETT!!
SHE WAS BIGGER THAN LIFE ITSELF.
I CAN TELL.
SHE'S SENDING HER MESSAGE LOUD AND CLEAR.

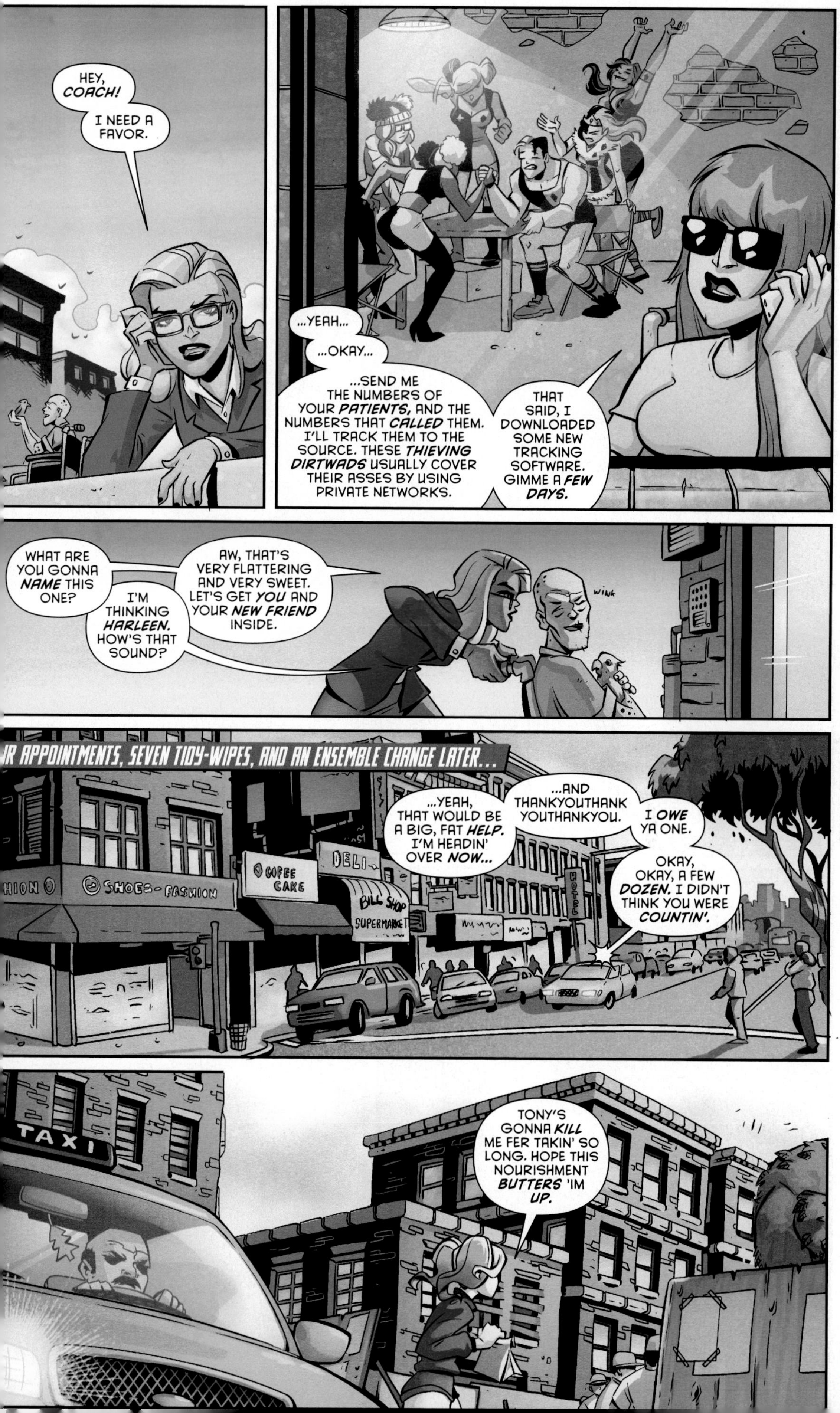
HEY, COACH!
I NEED A FAVOR.
...YEAH...
...OKAY...
...SEND ME THE NUMBERS OF YOUR PATIENTS, AND THE NUMBERS THAT CALLED THEM. I'LL TRACK THEM TO THE SOURCE. THESE THIEVING DIRTWADS USUALLY COVER THEIR ASSES BY USING PRIVATE NETWORKS.
THAT SAID, I DOWNLOADED SOME NEW TRACKING SOFTWARE. GIMME A FEW DAYS.
WHAT ARE YOU GONNA NAME THIS ONE?
I'M THINKING HARLEEN. HOW'S THAT SOUND?
AW, THAT'S VERY FLATTERING AND VERY SWEET. LET'S GET YOU AND YOUR NEW FRIEND INSIDE.
WINK
R APPOINTMENTS, SEVEN TIDY-WIPES, AND AN ENSEMBLE CHANGE LATER...
SHOES-FASHION
COFFEE CAKE
DELI
BILL SHOP
SUPERMARKET
HOTEL
...YEAH, THAT WOULD BE A BIG, FAT HELP. I'M HEADIN' OVER NOW...
...AND THANKYOUTHANKYOUTHANKYOU.
I OWE YA ONE.
OKAY, OKAY, A FEW DOZEN. I DIDN'T THINK YOU WERE COUNTIN'.
TAXI
TONY'S GONNA KILL ME FER TAKIN' SO LONG. HOPE THIS NOURISHMENT BUTTERS 'IM UP.

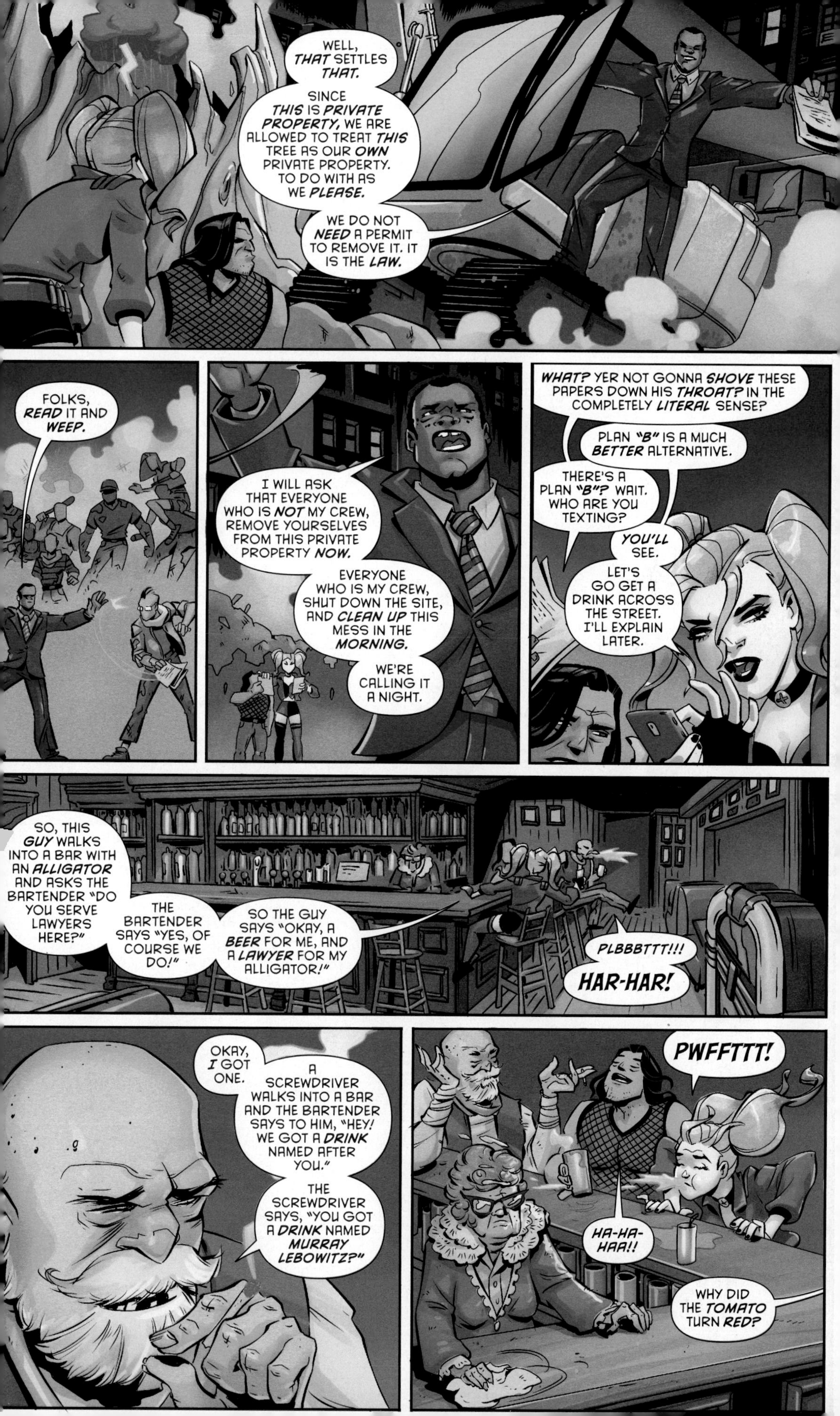
WELL, THAT SETTLES THAT.
SINCE THIS IS PRIVATE PROPERTY, WE ARE ALLOWED TO TREAT THIS TREE AS OUR OWN PRIVATE PROPERTY. TO DO WITH AS WE PLEASE.
WE DO NOT NEED A PERMIT TO REMOVE IT. IT IS THE LAW.
FOLKS, READ IT AND WEEP.
I WILL ASK THAT EVERYONE WHO IS NOT MY CREW, REMOVE YOURSELVES FROM THIS PRIVATE PROPERTY NOW.
EVERYONE WHO IS MY CREW, SHUT DOWN THE SITE, AND CLEAN UP THIS MESS IN THE MORNING.
WE'RE CALLING IT A NIGHT.
WHAT? YER NOT GONNA SHOVE THESE PAPERS DOWN HIS THROAT? IN THE COMPLETELY LITERAL SENSE?
PLAN "B" IS A MUCH BETTER ALTERNATIVE.
THERE'S A PLAN "B"? WAIT. WHO ARE YOU TEXTING?
YOU'LL SEE.
LET'S GO GET A DRINK ACROSS THE STREET. I'LL EXPLAIN LATER.
SO, THIS GUY WALKS INTO A BAR WITH AN ALLIGATOR AND ASKS THE BARTENDER "DO YOU SERVE LAWYERS HERE?"
THE BARTENDER SAYS "YES, OF COURSE WE DO!"
SO THE GUY SAYS "OKAY, A BEER FOR ME, AND A LAWYER FOR MY ALLIGATOR!"
PLBBBTTT!!!
HAR-HAR!
OKAY, I GOT ONE.
A SCREWDRIVER WALKS INTO A BAR AND THE BARTENDER SAYS TO HIM, "HEY! WE GOT A DRINK NAMED AFTER YOU."
THE SCREWDRIVER SAYS, "YOU GOT A DRINK NAMED MURRAY LEBOWITZ?"
PWFFTTT!
HA-HA-HAA!!
WHY DID THE TOMATO TURN RED?

The End.

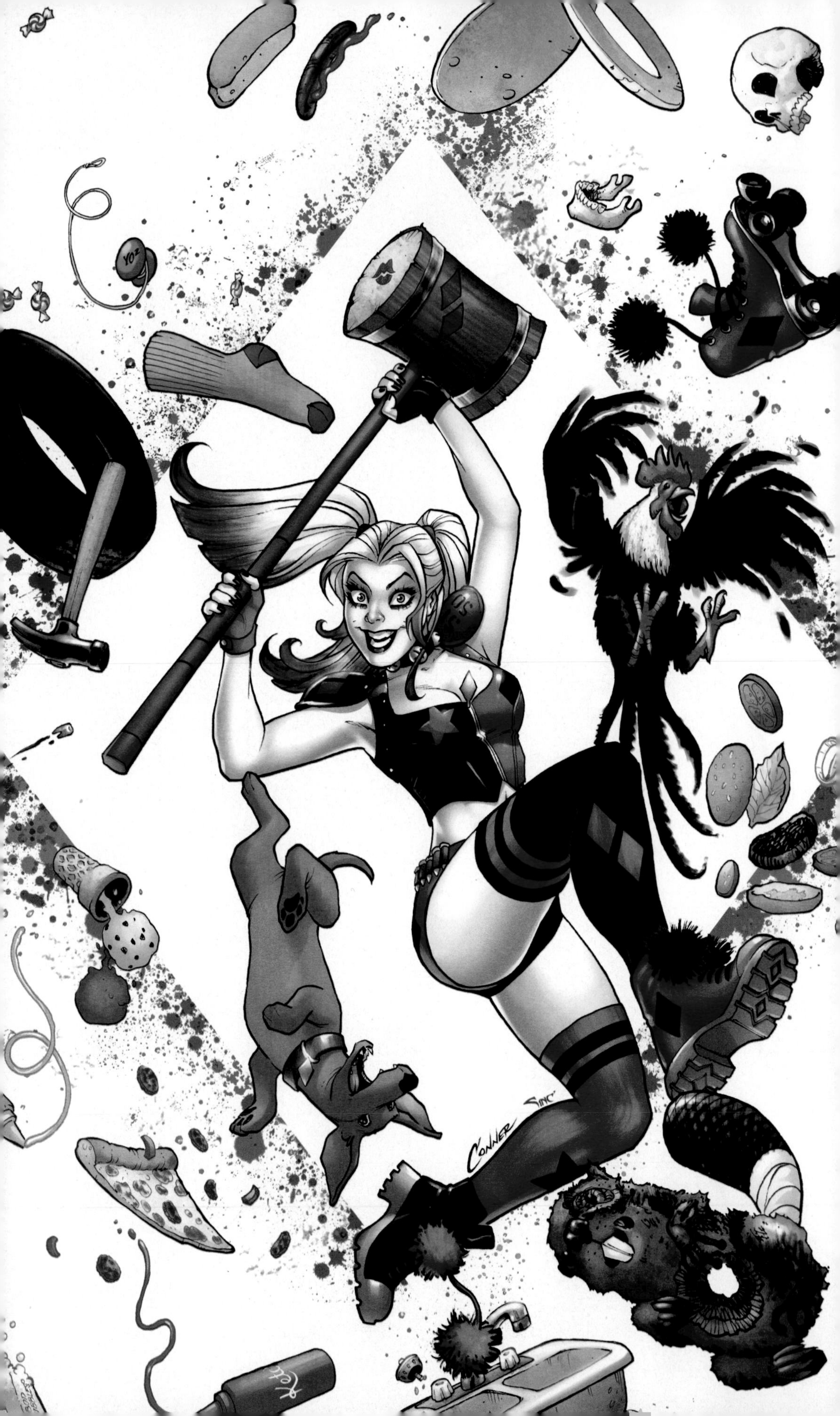
YOZ
CONNER
SINC

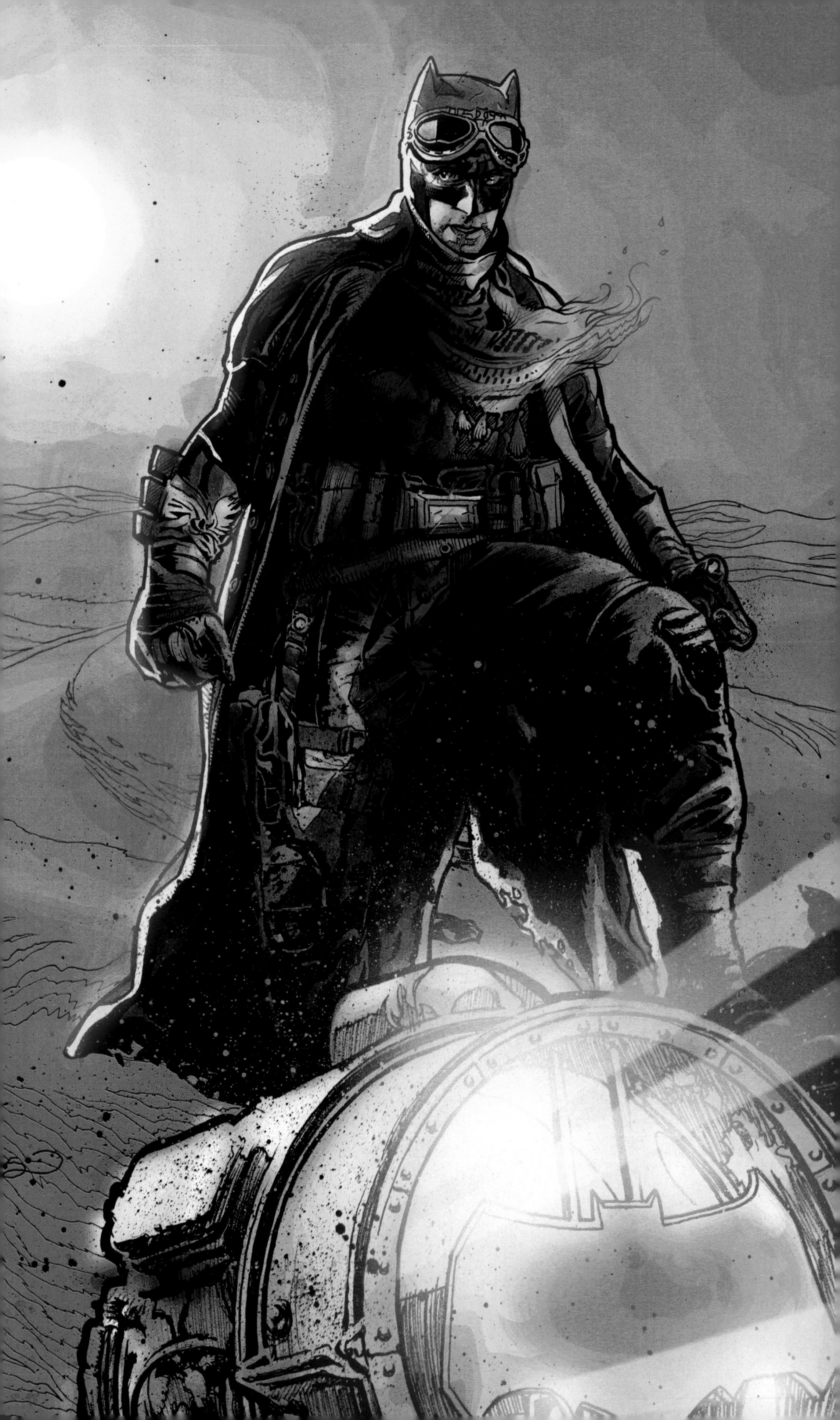

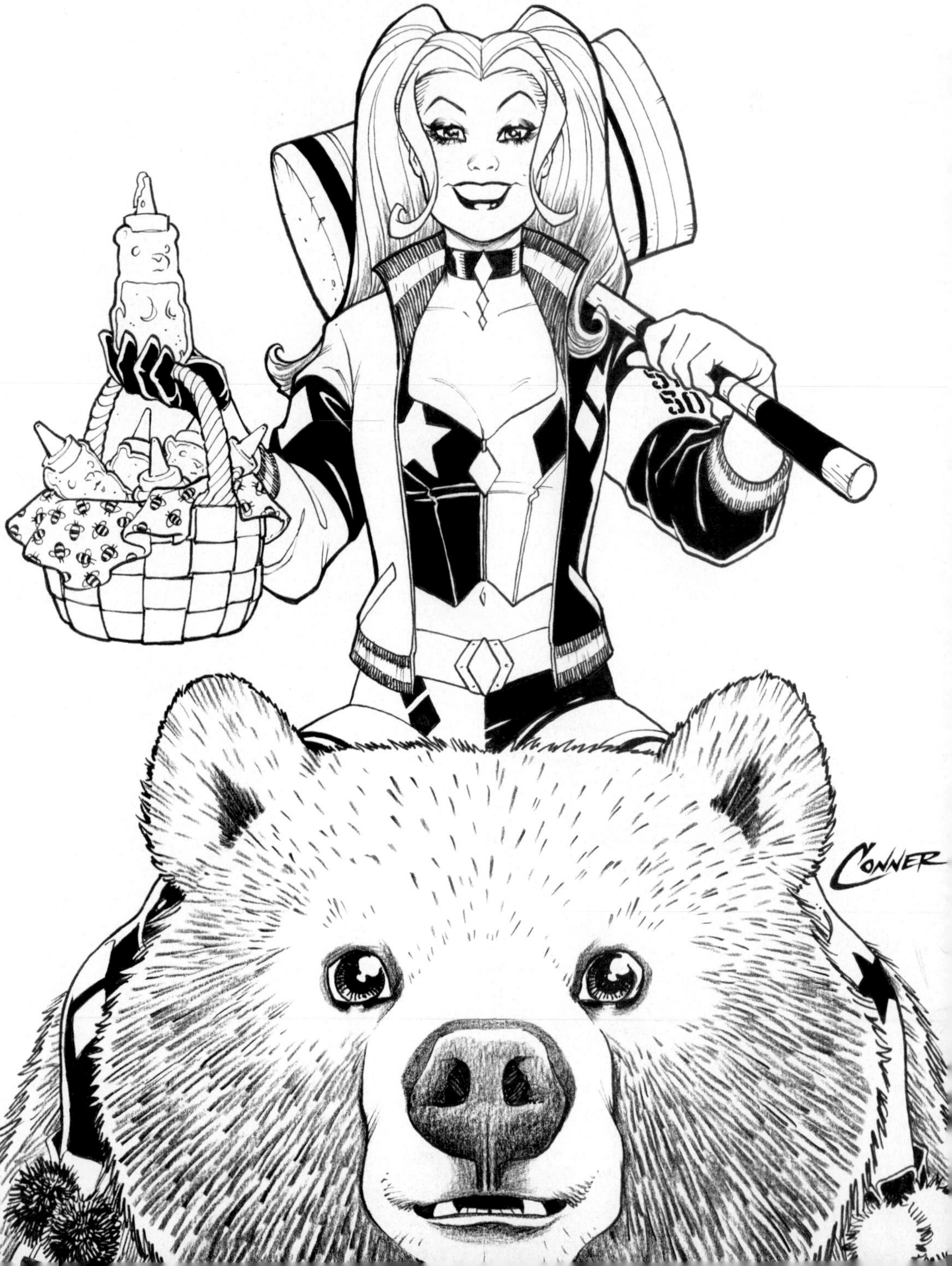
CONNER

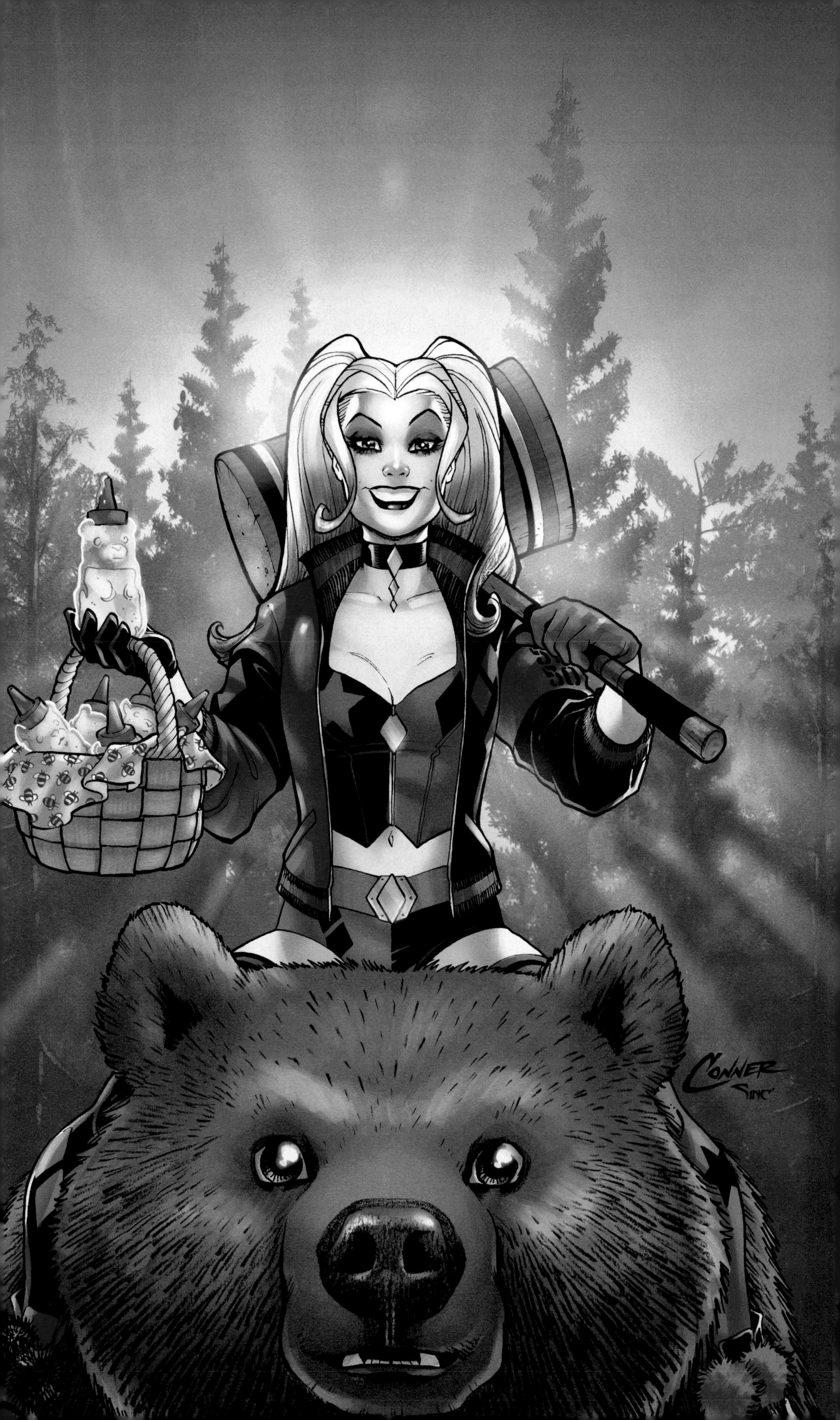
CONNER

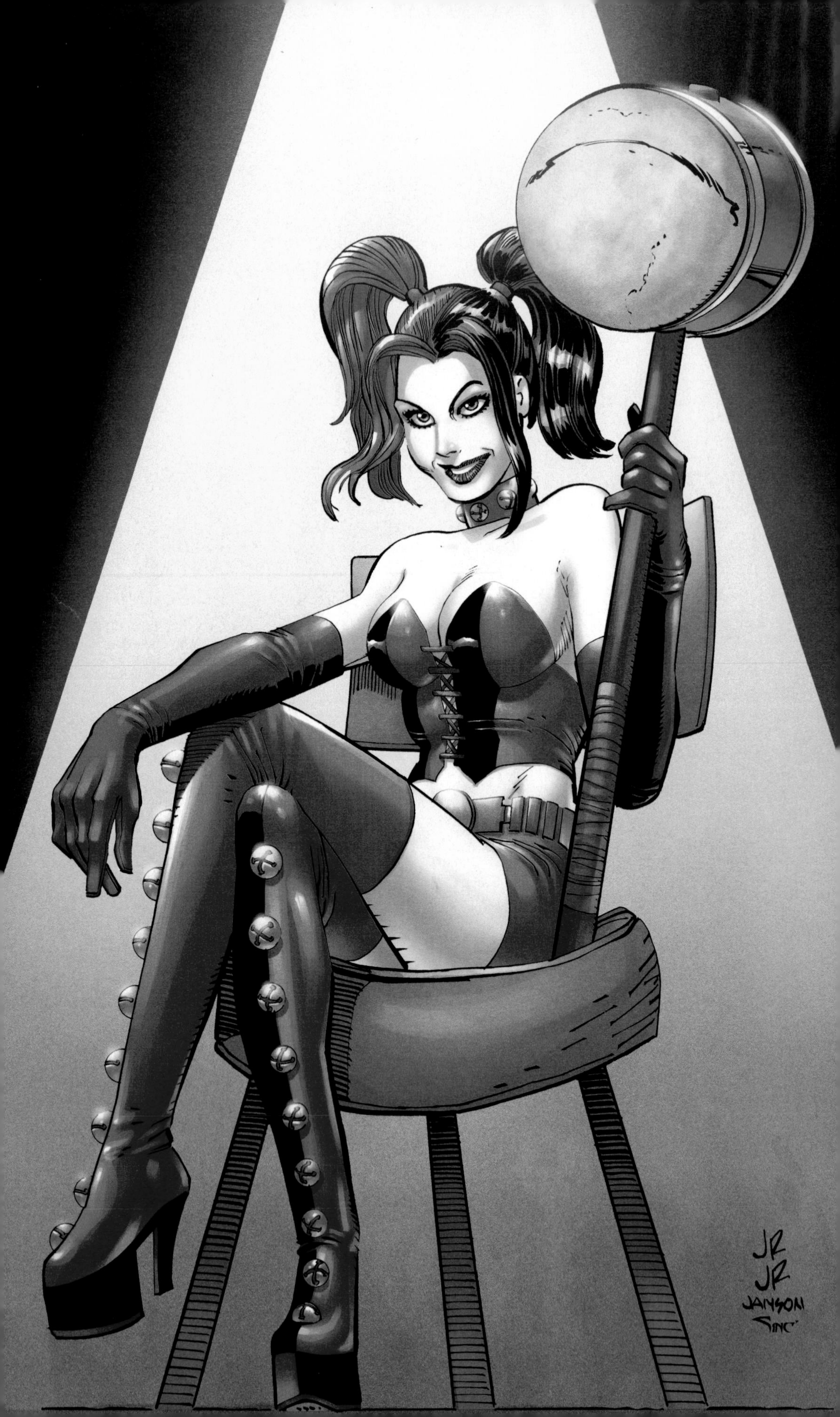

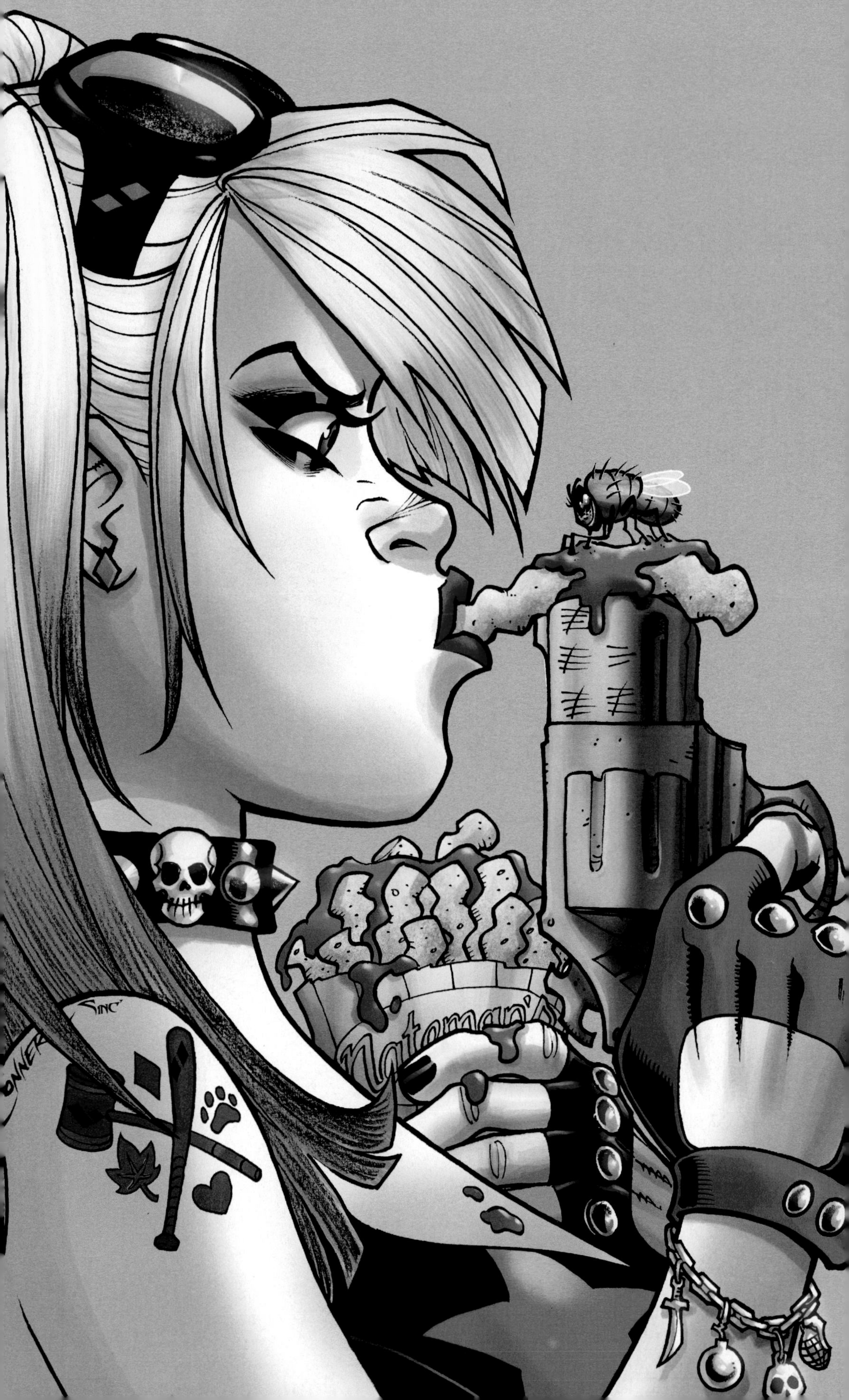
Natoman's

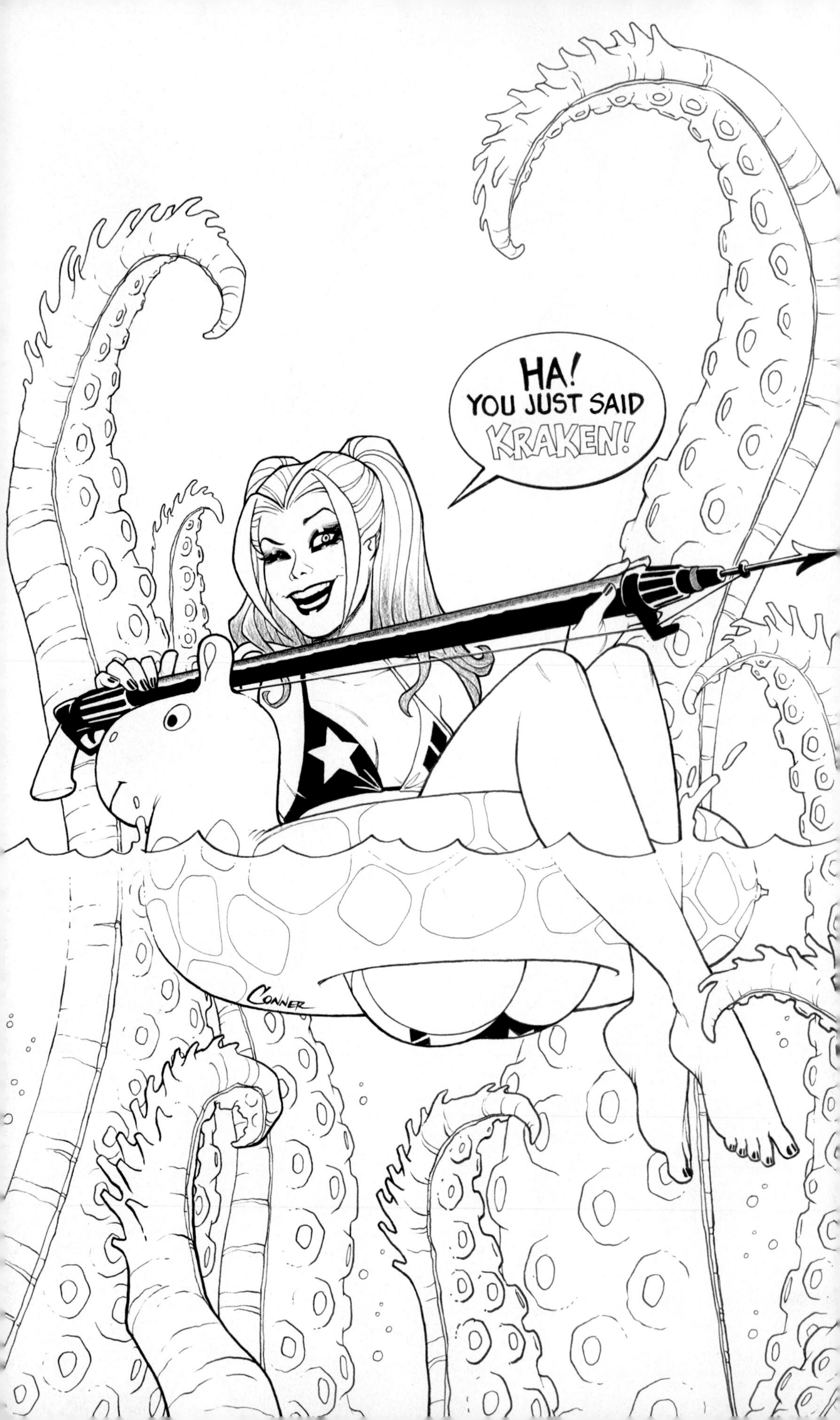
HA! YOU JUST SAID KRAKEN!
CONNER

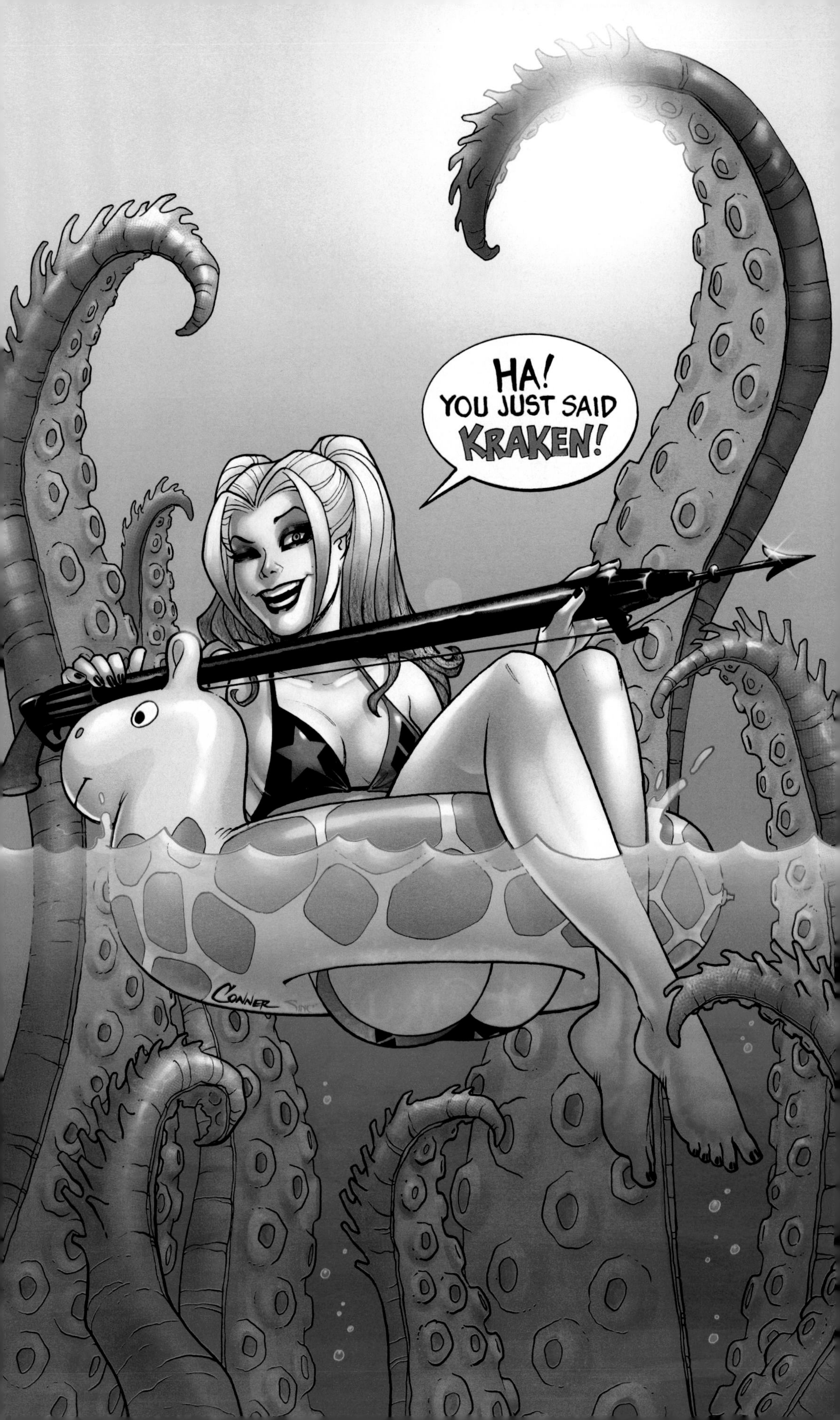
HA! YOU JUST SAID KRAKEN!
CONNER SINC

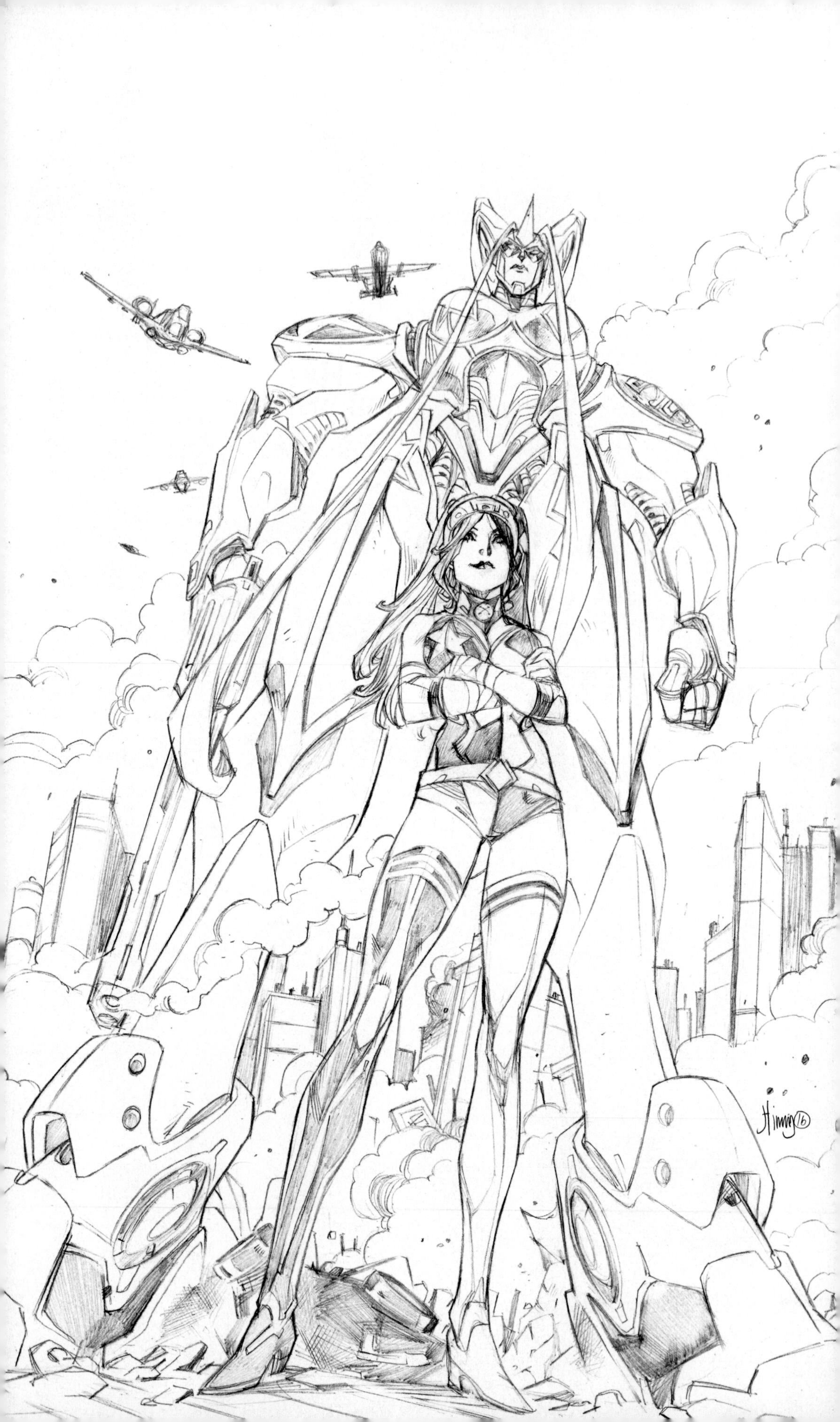

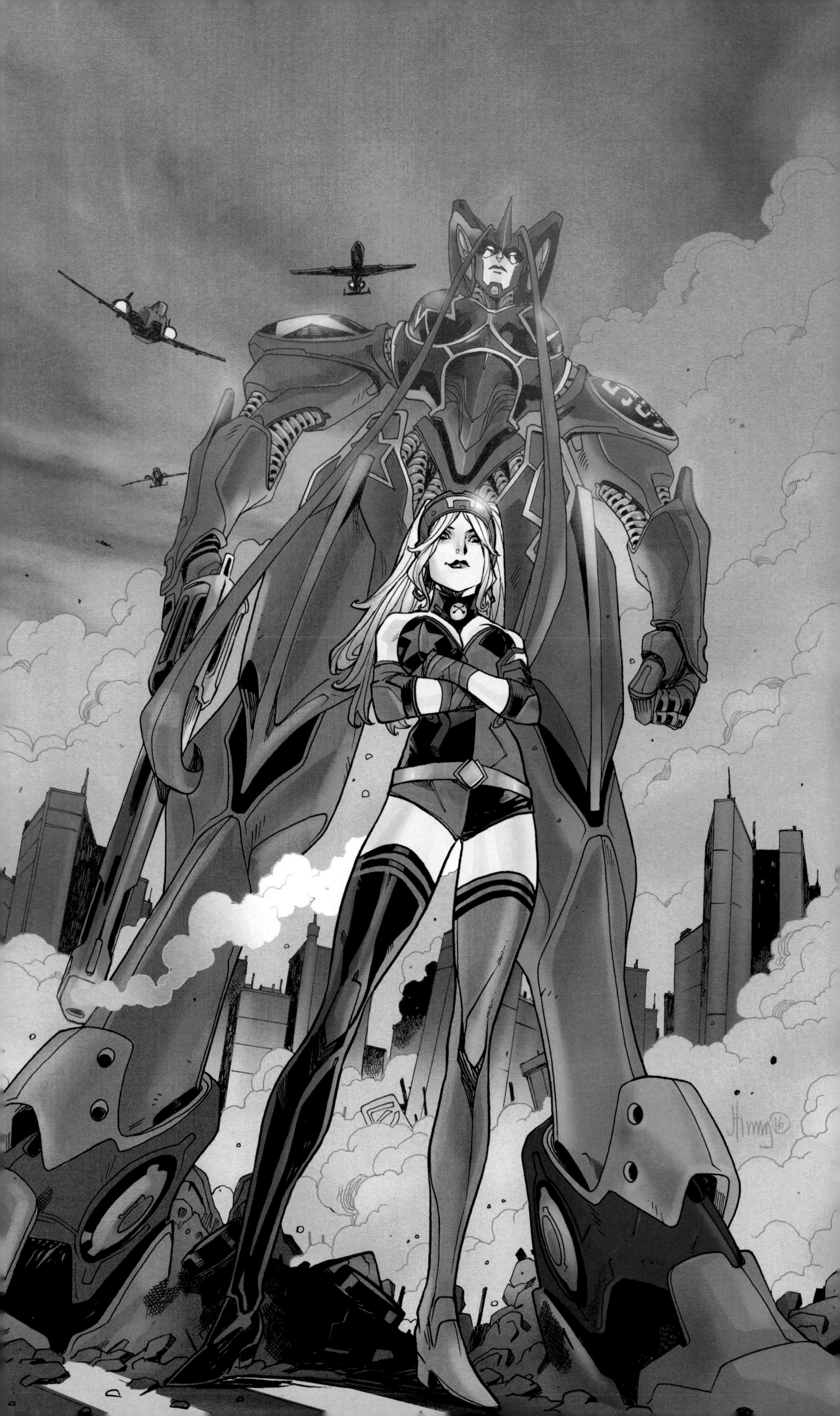

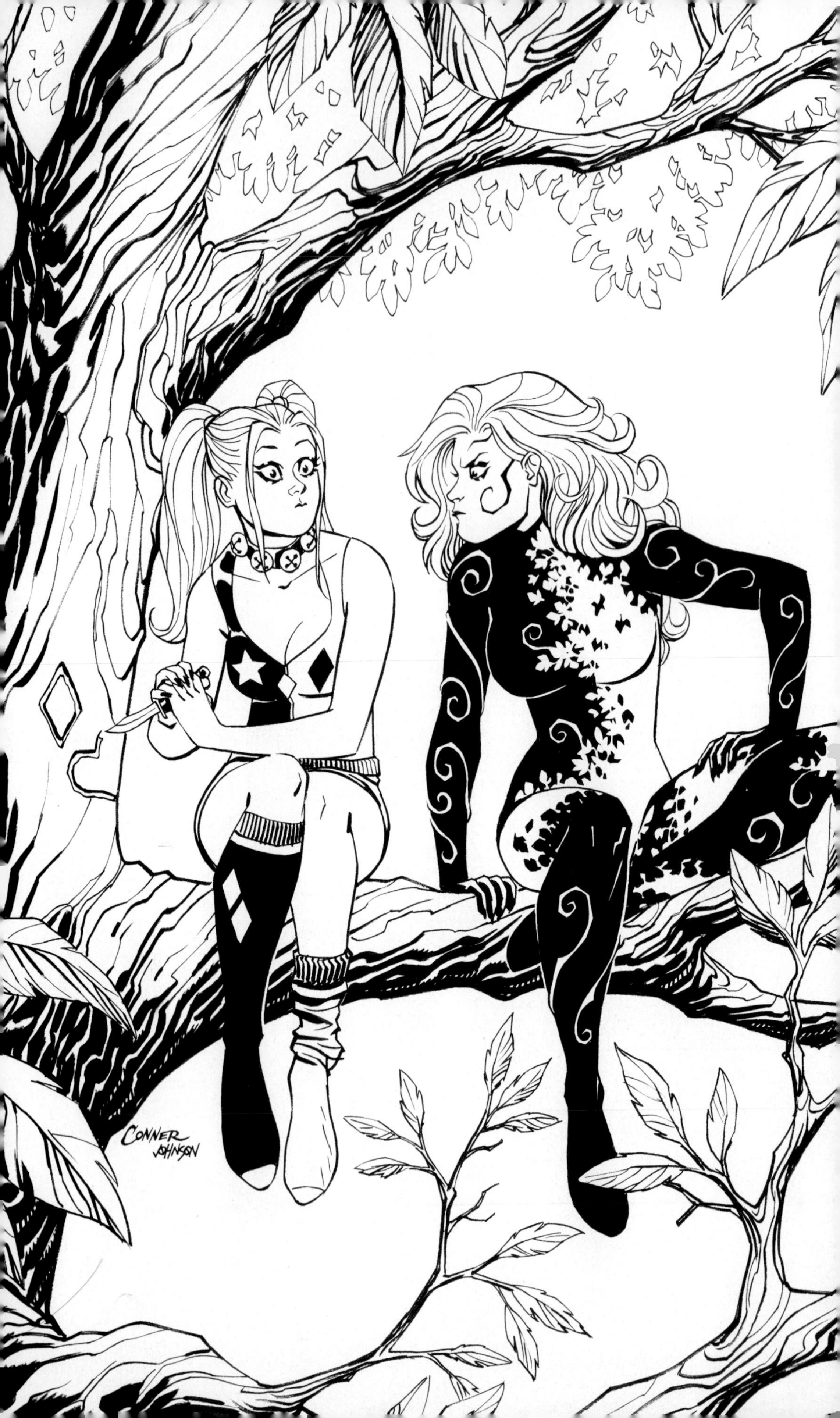
CONNER
JOHNSON

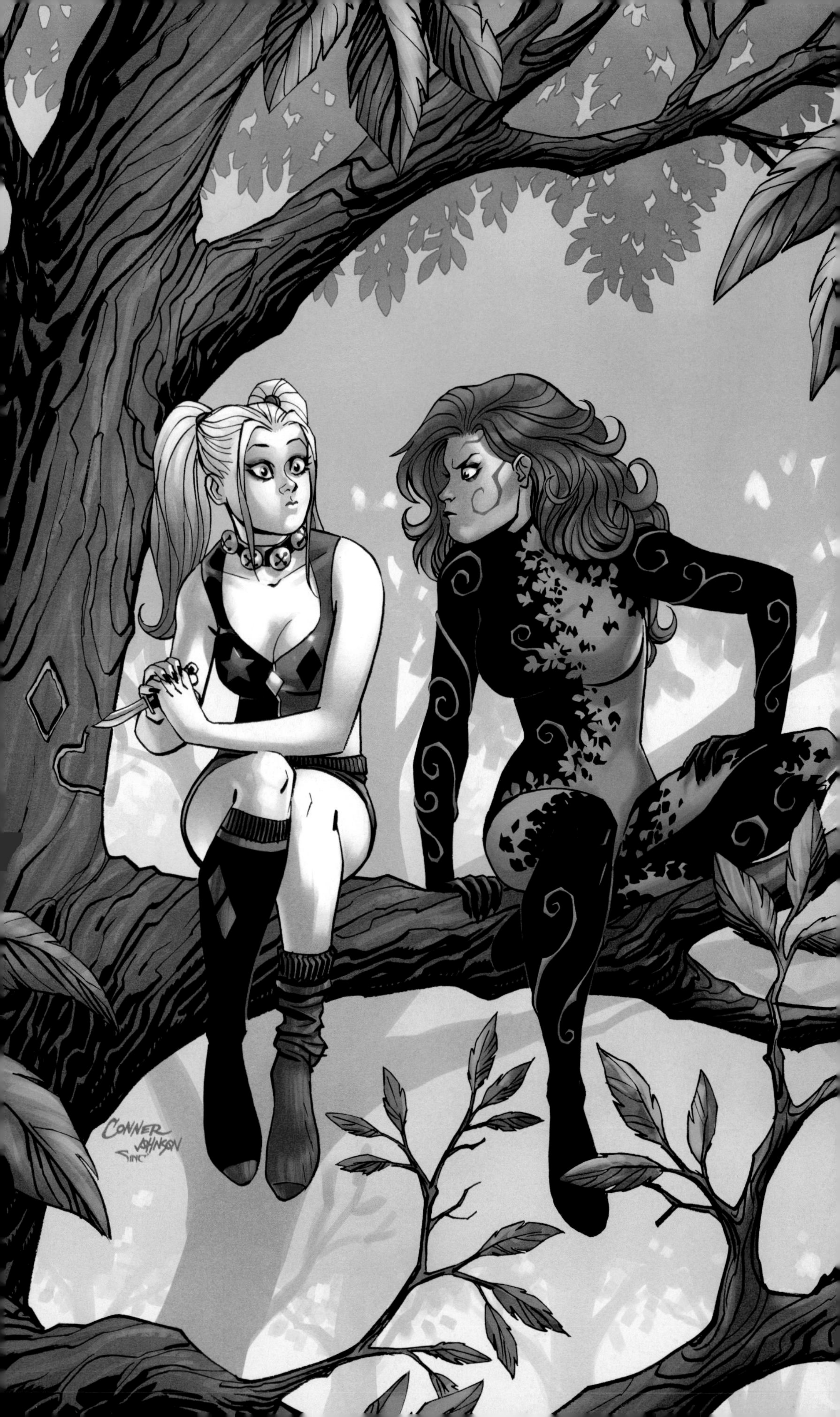
CONNER
JOHNSON
SINC

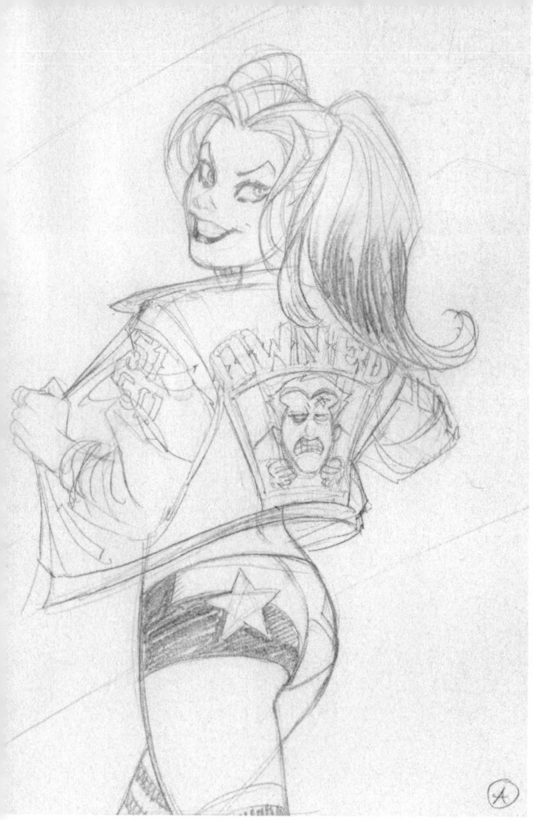
OWNED
A

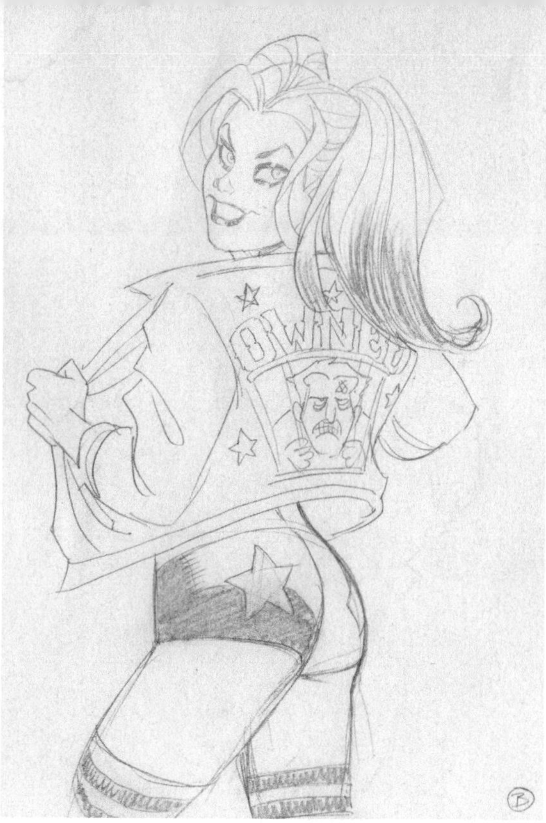
OWNED
B

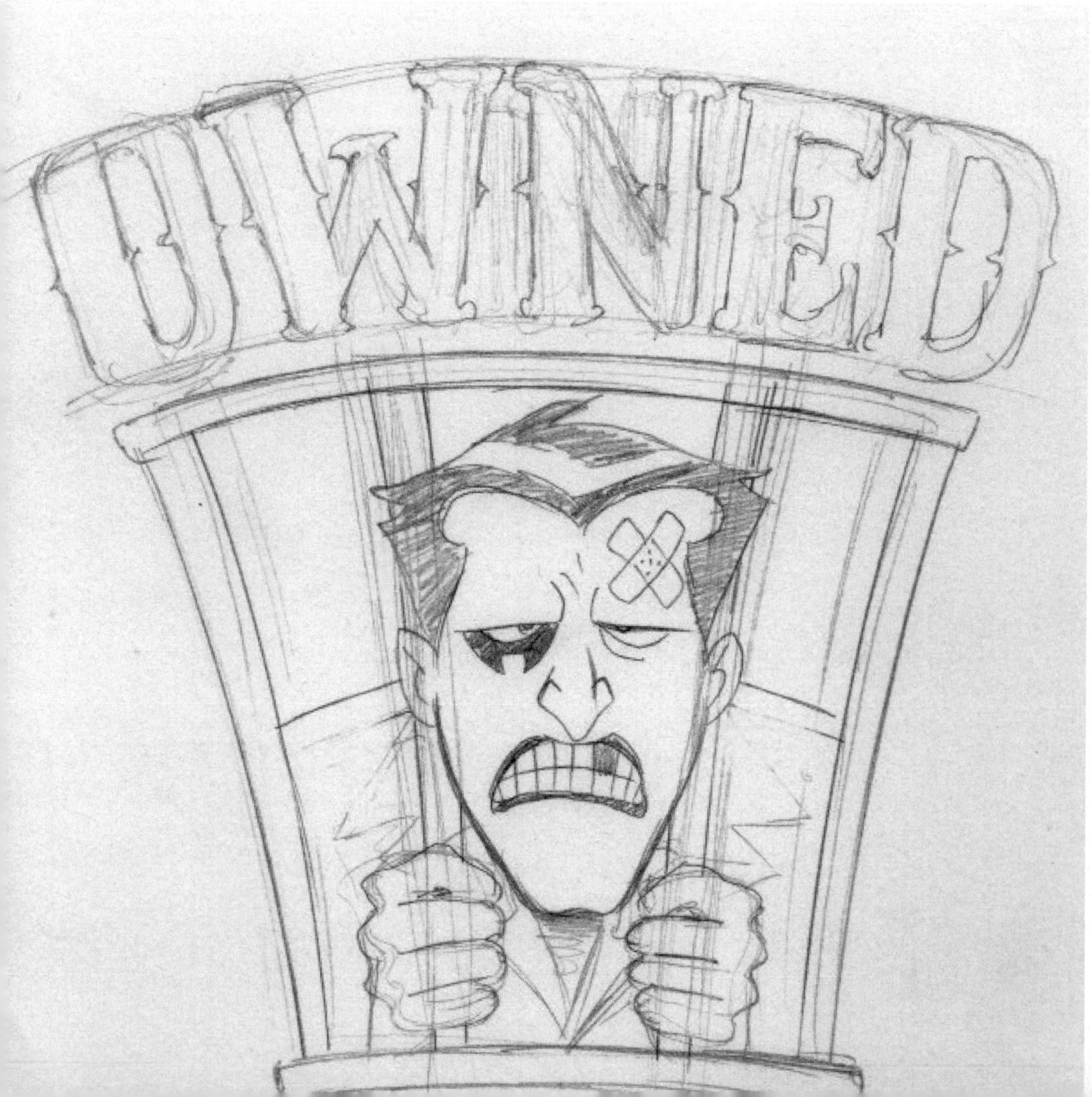
OWNED

Cover sketches for HARLEY QUINN #27, #29, #29 variant and #30 variant

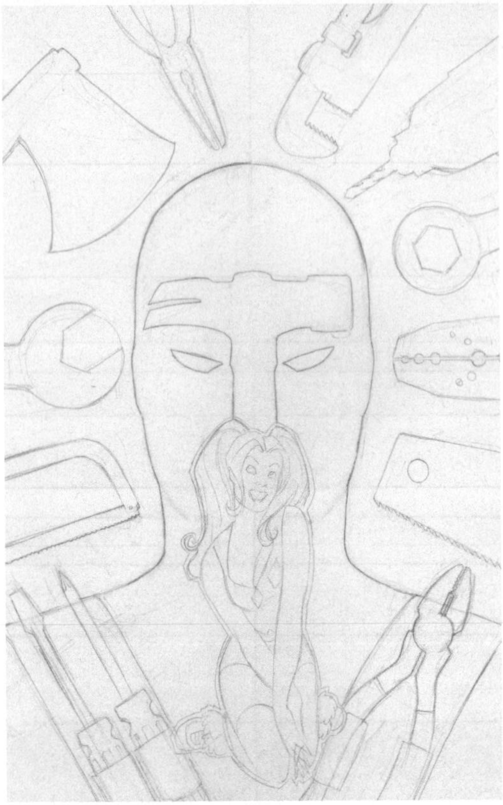

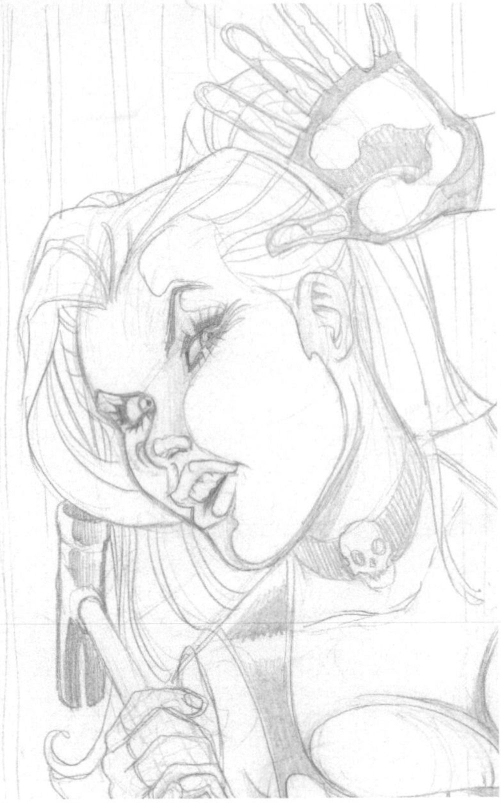

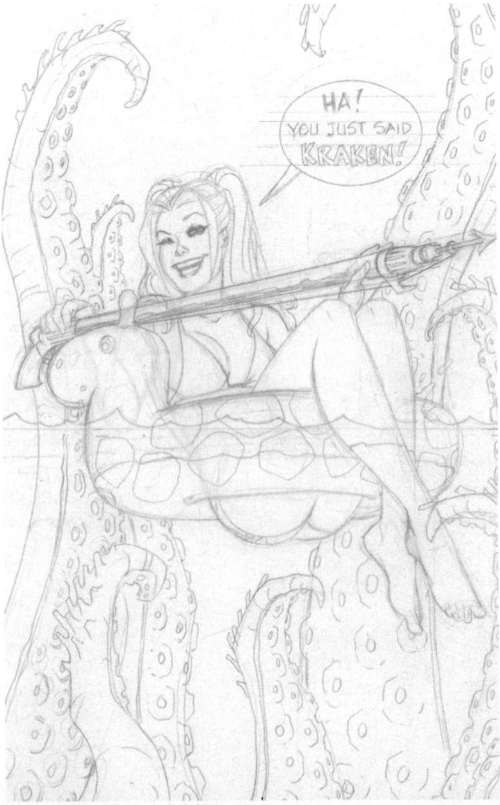
HA! YOU JUST SAID KRAKEN!

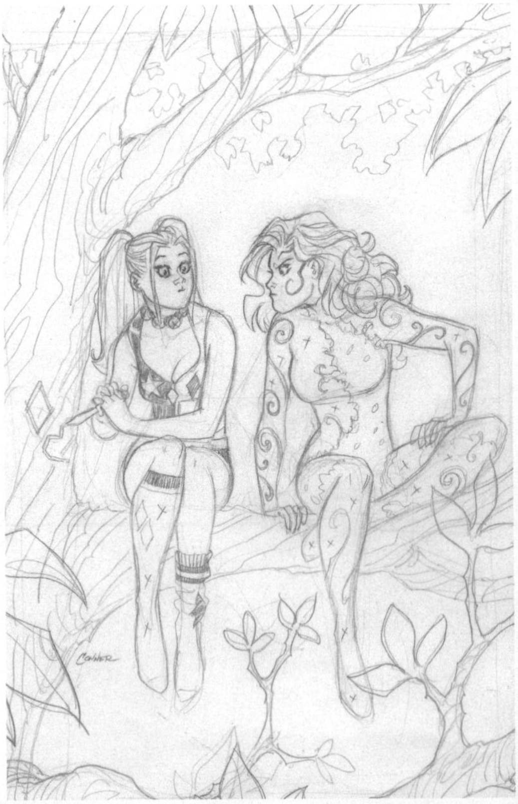
CONNER

Alternate circle version of HARLEY QUINN #28 variant cover

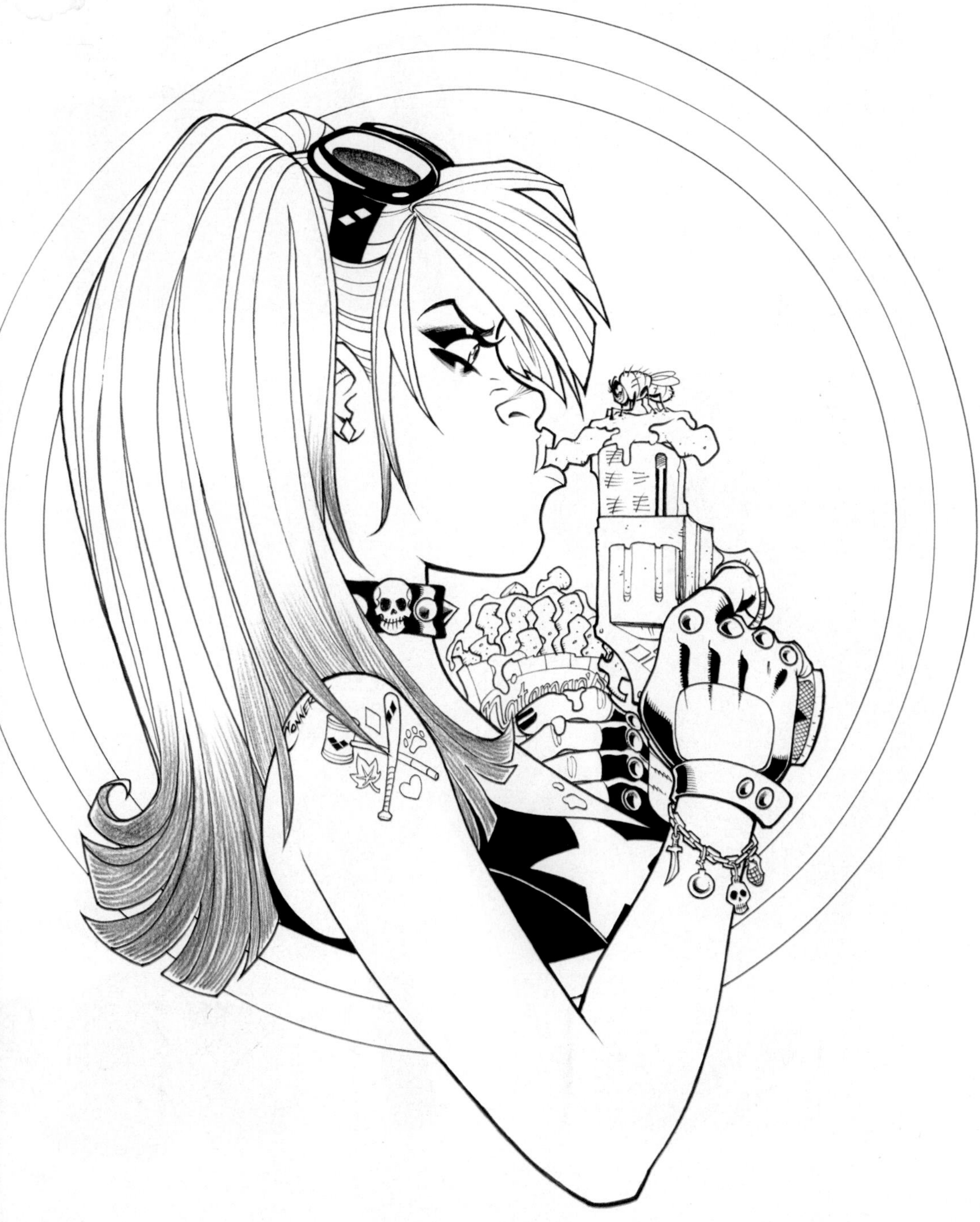

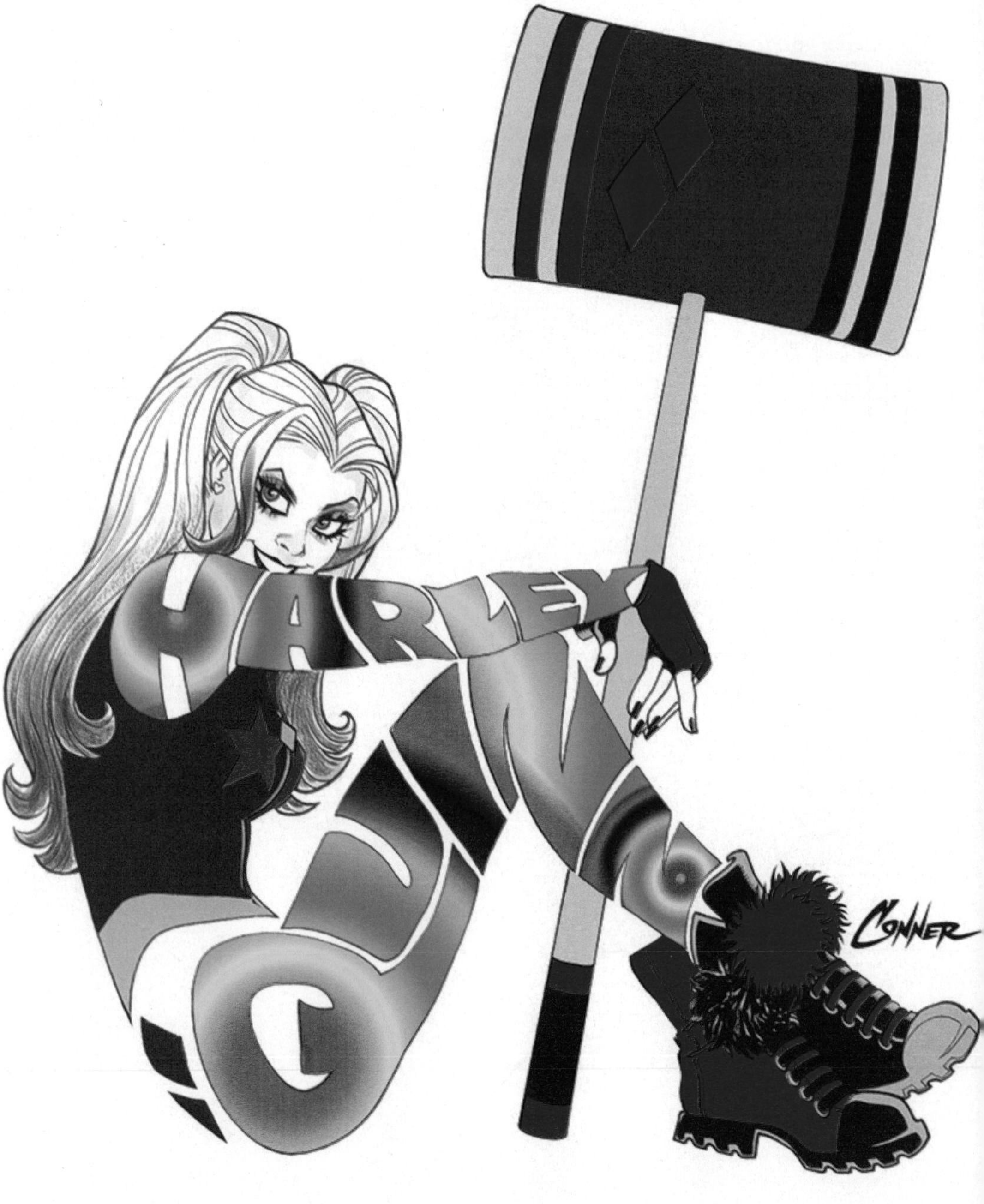
HARLEY
QUINN
CONNER

HARLEY QUINN
VOLUME 1: HOT IN THE CITY

"Chaotic and unabashedly fun."—IGN

"I'm enjoying HARLEY QUINN a great deal;
it's silly, it's funny, it's irreverent."
—COMIC BOOK RESOURCES

HARLEY QUINN
VOLUME 1: PRELUDES AND KNOCK-KNOCK JOKES

HARLEY QUINN VOL. 2:
NIGHT AND DAY

with KARL KESEL,
TERRY DODSON,
and PETE WOODS

HARLEY QUINN VOL. 3:
WELCOME TO METROPOLIS

with KARL KESEL,
TERRY DODSON and
CRAIG ROUSSEAU

HARLEY QUINN VOL. 4:
VENGEANCE UNLIMITED

with A.J. LIEBERMAN
and MIKE HUDDLESTON

PRELUDES AND
KNOCK-KNOCK
JOKES

Karl Kesel
Terry Dodson
Rachel Dodson